美国语文

—★ 带着历史去旅行 ★—

5

[美] 埃德温 · 埃尔德曼◎主编
钱志慧　等◎译

苏州新闻出版集团
古吴轩出版社

图书在版编目（CIP）数据

美国语文．带着历史去旅行 /（美）埃德温·埃尔德曼主编；钱志慧等译．-- 苏州：古吴轩出版社，2016.12（2024.9重印）
ISBN 978-7-5546-0804-3

Ⅰ．①美… Ⅱ．①埃… ②钱… Ⅲ．①英语课－小学－美国－教材 Ⅳ．①G624.311

中国版本图书馆CIP数据核字(2016)第268941号

责任编辑： 蒋丽华
见习编辑： 薛　芳
策　　划： 党霄羽
封面设计： 沈加坤

书　　名： 美国语文——带着历史去旅行
主　　编：［美］埃德温·埃尔德曼
译　　者： 钱志慧　等
出版发行： 苏州新闻出版集团
古吴轩出版社
地址：苏州市八达街118号苏州新闻大厦30F
电话：0512-65233679　　　邮编：215123

出 版 人： 王乐飞
印　　刷： 天津旭非印刷有限公司
开　　本： 690mm × 980mm　1/16
印　　张： 18.25
版　　次： 2016年12月第1版
印　　次： 2024年9月第2次印刷
书　　号： ISBN 978-7-5546-0804-3
定　　价： 49.80元

如有印装质量问题，请与印刷厂联系。022-22520876

推荐序一

李江月

（伊利诺斯大学PHD，湖北省高考作文满分获得者）

我在美国留学的时候，不仅要承担繁重的学习任务，还要传道授业，帮自己的导师们带本科新生。那时候我就经常想，要是有一套全新的教材，难度适中，学生和教师都能在书中获得营养，让来自中国的学生既能学习原汁原味的地道的美式英语，又能对自己所学的专业有所帮助，还能和各个领域的大咖们谈笑风生，打破很多美国人觉得中国人就是书呆子的刻板印象，那该多好啊！

这部千呼万唤始出来的《美国语文》丛书，解决了大家英语学习和教学的需求。每一篇课文都有精美的翻译，译文都做到了信达雅，读起来让人感觉如沐春风，甚至有时候让人感动，让学习英语这个看上去很繁重很枯燥的历程充满了惊喜。

众所周知，英语是不断变化的语言，也许需要每个学习者终身不断地学习。本套书的英文原版，是由常青藤名校校长精编精选，汇集了许多名家的经典之作，所以我们每一位读者，不仅是学生，还包括老师和家长，都能在这样美妙的阅读中感受到自己的进步，得到切切实实的满足感。这些美丽的体验，是市面上一般读物难以给予我们的。

相比很多所谓“高屋建瓴”的语言学著作，这部丛书经历了实践的考验，是一部非常亲民和接地气的青少年读物，也是家长和老师很好的帮手。

很多时候，因为应试教育的需求，同学们不得不死记硬背许多文学大家的作品，但是他们并不理解这些作品。于是，虽然短期内成绩提高了，却在成年后丧失了对文学的爱好和学习的欲望。不论在中国还是美国，总能看到这样令人遗憾的现象。对此，我们觉得很可惜，学习文学本来应该是一种乐趣，而不应该是一种负担。我们希望孩子们开心地学，家长们愉快地陪伴他们学习，老师们欣喜地发现孩子们的进步，而不是扼杀他们的兴趣，阻碍他们进一步追求知识的脚步。

我们知道，很多文学大师虽然不是专门的儿童作家，但是他们并不是没有给孩子写过作品。本套书的一大亮点就是集结了很多大家笔下从未被翻译成汉语的遗珠之作——在各领域专门为孩子创作的作品。通过阅读本套书，孩子们能在书中了解到许多新奇的知识，坐在家里就环游世界，也为未来的学习打下扎实的基础。

本书主编埃德温·埃尔德曼先生，用他的智慧和孜孜不倦的努力，代替了我们在文山书海的盲目搜寻，就像我们的另一双眼睛，带我们遨游浩瀚的书海，获取人类文明的精华。

一言以蔽之，这套丛书是我用过的最好的美国语文学习、教学的教材，既可以用来自学，也可以用到课堂上。特此，我将这部丛书诚挚推荐给大家。让我们一起在《美国语文》的海洋里自由地冲浪吧！

推荐序二

曹海元

（MIT PHD）

迄今为止，阅读一直是我最大的爱好，而在现今残存的记忆里，我最早读到可以真正称得上书的，正是父亲给我的那套页面泛黄的《上下五千年》。我在脑海里至今仍旧清晰地记得那套书的封面，茕茕孑立的烽火台，赭红的城楼，残阳如血。华夏五千年那时而诡谲绵密时而波澜壮阔的历史也随着作者娓娓道来的小故事，奔涌到我充满好奇的内心，溅起了一片片波澜。虽然以我当时的阅历和见识无法理解许多深奥的名词和藏在历史故事背后深刻的道理，但是那套书唤起了我内心对于知识的渴望。阅读让我得以坐上时光机，身临其境般在华夏文明的浩瀚长河中自由穿梭，在我的心中种下了星星之火。正是这些星星点点的火种，照亮了我内心通往知识殿堂的道路，让阅读成了我生命中最大的乐趣，从而造就了我今天这副模样。

《上下五千年》那套书在我如今看来，也许简陋不堪，只是一些历史小故事汇编，但在当年那个懵懂少年看来却已然是通往圣杯的指路明灯。如今这套《美国语文》无论从文章的文学艺术性、选材的宽泛多样性来说，还是从编排的科学合理性上来看，都要遥遥领先。阅读这套书的少年从中可以先领略中世纪灿若星河的文艺复兴，再遇见近现代疾风怒涛般的工业革命；可以先认识一生锋芒毕露最后却功亏一篑的拿破仑，再偶遇始终沉默寡言却在危难之际挽大厦于将倾的华盛顿。从弗吉尼亚的崎岖山岭到欧亚大陆的广袤平原，短短千言却包罗万象、荟萃乾坤，包含了世界历史、地理、博物、人物、传奇、诗歌等领域的精华。

在我看来，如果说《上下五千年》只是星星点点的火苗，那么这套《美国语文》则是那光芒四射的火炬。我想读者尤其是那些处于学习阶段的青少年，必然可以像当年的我那样，从这套书中找到点燃自己心中火种的火焰，照亮通往圣杯的道路。

最后，用我最爱的诗歌《伊萨卡岛》中的一句话来结尾——“当你启程，前往伊萨卡岛时，愿你的道路漫长，充满奇迹，充满发现。”这也是我对所有有幸读到这套丛书的读者的祝福。我想说的就这么多了，希望我无知和浅薄的序言不会让这套书的光芒逊色。

Preface

The Fifth Reader in the Series "Classics, Old and New", is given to the schools in the belief that it will commend itself to teachers and pupils by reason of its literary quality, its careful grading, and its illustration of the principle of unity in variety. Great care has been taken in the choice of material to have all the sections complete literary units of thought and style. These vary in length——and while some are very short, they are by no means the least valuable. Realizing that the love of reading depends, with most boys and girls, upon the amount of interest awakened, the lessons have been chosen with a view to interest the pupil, and through his interest to cultivate his taste and to put him in the way of knowing and appreciating good literature.

Any reading book compiled for pupils may be rated as to its excellence according to three standards: technical arrangement, literary quality, and moral purpose. Under technical arrangement is understood the proper grading of lessons, the orderly presentation of new words to be mastered, and such helps in the mechanism of reading as will call out the power of the pupil to help himself. The literary quality and the moral purpose cannot be so easily outlined. In quiet ways a perception of their meaning should grow into the youth's heart and mind. Love of country, pride of home, scorn of a lie, sympathy for the weak, love of wild life, courage to dare, and devotion to duty are some of the lessons taught in this book in myth and fable, in song and story, and in the record of human deeds told by men and women who could write with freshness and charm.

To teach a child to love to read is to give him an education. And although it is foolish to attempt to lay down formal rules for doing this great thing, there are a few principles that a teacher may well hold in mind. The child must know what the story or the poem is all about. This involves, of course, a knowledge of the separate words that stand for the ideas, and I believe a wise use of a few minutes of recitation would consist in questioning the class as to thought and words, and in causing pupils to reveal what their minds hold of the matter before them. All this should be done after the pupil has read the selection to himself and before oral reading begins.

Let many of the poems be learned by heart, and not merely by rote. There is in true poetry a power to linger in the memory, to become a part of life and to reappear after long years, fresh and helpful.

In addition to the acknowledgments made in the biographies, my thanks are due to the following publishers for cordial permission to use copyrighted material: to Messrs. Houghton, Mifflin and Company, for "Ascent of Mt. Mitchell," by Charles D. Warner, from his "On Horseback in Virginia"; for "Dickens," by James T. Fields, from his "Yesterdays with Authors"; for "Elms and Other Trees," by Oliver Wendell Holmes, from his "Autocrat of the Breakfast Table"; and for "Choosing a Class of People to be Exterminated," from the prose of Edward Rowland Sill; to Messrs. Little, Brown and Company, for the extract from "The Man Without a Country," by Edward Everett Hale; and to the Whitaker and Ray Company, for "The Defense of the Alamo," by Joaquin Miller. I am indebted also to Mr. William O. Partridge for permission to use the reproduction of his statue of Pocahontas.

译文

前言

本套书的第五册已经推向校园，它文字优美，篇目分类细致，插图丰富协调，相信会受到师生的喜爱。我们在文章的选材上倾注了大量的心血，以便展现各种文学类型的思想与风格。这些文章长短不一——虽然有些文章非常短小精悍，但这并不代表它没有价值。考虑到大多数孩子的阅读热情取决于兴趣的唤醒程度，因此这些文章的甄选标准是激起学生的兴趣，并以此培养他的品味，带他走上感知与欣赏优美文学的道路。

任何一本为学生编写的读物都可以依据三个标准来判别其是否优秀：专业的课程安排、文字质量以及道德导向。专业的课程安排，可以让我们理解的分类方式有多么恰当，明白需要掌握的新词是如何有序地展示，而阅读过程中诸如此类的帮助会激发学生的自学能力。文字质量与道德导向则是潜移默化的。对这两者的理解，应当以“润物细无声”的方式植根于孩子们的内心与思想。对祖国的热爱，对家乡的骄傲，对谎言的轻蔑，对弱者的同情，对野生动物的喜爱，对挑战的勇气，对责任的担当，这些正是这本书有所教益的内容，并以神话、寓言、诗歌、故事以及人物故事的形式展现。那些讲述人物故事的男女作者，笔下散发着鲜活迷人的气息。

教会一个孩子热爱阅读就是使他受到教育。尽管为这一伟业而试图制定拘泥的规则愚不可及，但仍有一些原则是一个教师需要时刻牢记的。孩子们必须懂得一篇故事或是一首诗歌在讲述什么。当然，他们也要懂得表达这些内容的不同单词的意思，而且我相信每次课前利用几分钟进行复习，检查学生们对思想内容和词汇的掌握情况，督促他们表达对眼前事物的想法，是极为有效的方法。所有这些都必须在学生默读之后、朗诵之前进行。

要让孩子们用心感知这多如繁星的诗歌，而不仅仅是死记硬背。在真正的诗歌艺术中，有一种力量会在记忆中长久萦绕，并转化为生命的一部分，待数年之后涌上心头，依旧鲜活而有助益。

除了作者简介中提及的出版商以外，我们还要感谢以下这些热情提供版权许可的出版商：霍顿·米夫林出版公司，提供了选自查尔斯·杜德利·沃纳《在弗吉尼亚州的山岭上》的《登米歇尔峰》一文、选自詹姆斯·托马斯·菲尔兹《与作家共度的昨日》的《狄更斯》一文、选自奥利弗·温德尔·霍姆斯《早餐桌上的独裁者》的《榆树与其他树》一文以及爱德华·罗兰·希尔的散文《选择消灭一类人》；小布朗出版公司，提供了爱德华·埃弗雷特·黑尔《没有国家的人》节选；惠特克和雷出版公司，提供了杰奎因·米勒的《阿拉莫防卫战》。另外，我还要感谢威廉·奥德威·帕特里奇先生对其雕塑作品《宝嘉康蒂》的版权许可。

目　录

Chapter 1

Historical Figure | 历史人物

预习

invulnerable /ɪnˈvʌlnərəbl/ 不会受伤害的

nicety /ˈnaɪsəti/ 精确

organ /ˈɔːrgən/ 媒介

plenitude /ˈplenɪtuːd/ 丰富

policy /ˈpɑːləsi/ 政策

reverse /rɪˈvɜːrs/ 相反的

Napoleon Bonaparte

Napoleon understood his business. Here was a man that in each moment and emergency knew what to do next. It is an immense comfort and refreshment to the spirits, not only of kings, but of citizens. Few men have any next; they live from hand to mouth, without plan, and are ever at the end of their line, and, after each action, wait for an impulse from abroad.

Napoleon had been the first man of the world, if his ends had been purely public. As he is, he inspires confidence and vigor by the extraordinary unity of his action. He is firm, sure, self-denying, self-postponing, sacrificing everything to his aim,——money, troops, generals, and his own safety also; not misled, like common adventurers, by the splendor of his own means. "Incidents ought not to govern policy," he said, "but policy incidents." "To be hurried away by every event, is to have no political system at all."

His victories were only so many doors, and he never for a moment lost sight of his way onward in the dazzle and uproar of the present circumstance. He knew what to do, and he flew to his mark. He would shorten a straight line to come at his object. Horrible anecdotes may, no doubt, be collected from his history, of the price at which he bought his successes, but he must not, therefore, be set down as cruel, but only as one who knew no impediment to his will: not blood-thirsty, not cruel; but woe to what thing or person stood in his way!

"Sire, General Clarke cannot combine with General Junot for the dreadful fire of the Austrian battery.""Let him carry the battery.""Sire, every regiment that approaches the heavy artillery is sacrificed. Sire, what orders?""Forward! Forward!"

In the plenitude of his resources every obstacle seemed to vanish. "There shall be no Alps," he said; and he built his perfect roads, climbing by graded galleries their steepest precipices, until Italy was as open to Paris as any town in France. Having decided what was to be done, he did that with might and main. He put out all his strength. He risked everything and spared nothing,——neither ammunition, nor money, nor troops, nor generals, nor himself. If fighting be the best mode of adjusting national differences, certainly Bonaparte was right in making it thorough.

He fought sixty battles. He had never enough. Each victory was a new weapon."My power would fall, were I not to support it by new achievements. Conquest has made me what I am, and conquest must maintain me." His vigor was guarded and tempered by the coldest prudence and punctuality. A thunderbolt in the attack, he was found invulnerable in his intrenchments. His every attack was never the inspiration of courage, but the result of calculation. His idea of the best defence consisted in being always the attacking party. "My ambition," he said, "was great, but was of a cold nature."

Everything depended upon the nicety of his combinations;the stars were not more punctual than his arithmetic. His personal attention descended to the smallest particulars. "At Montebello, I ordered Kellerman to attack with eight hundred horses; and with these he separated the six thousand Hungarian grenadiers before the very eyes of the Austrian cavalry. This cavalry was half a league off, and required a quarter of an hour to arrive at the field of action. I have observed that it is always these quarters of an hour that decide the fate of a battle."

Before he fought a battle Bonaparte thought little about what he should do in case of success, but a great deal about what he should do in case of a reverse of fortune. The same prudence and good sense marked all his behavior. His instructions to his secretary at the palace are worth remembering: "During the night, enter my chamber as seldom as possible. Do not awake me when you have any good news to communicate; with that there is no haste; but when you bring bad news, rouse me instantly, for then there is not a moment to be lost." His achievement of business was immense, and enlarges the known powers of man. There have been many working kings, from Ulysses to William of Orange, but none who accomplished a tithe of this man's performance.

Those who had to deal with him found that he was not to be imposed upon, but could cipher as well as another man. When the expenses of the empress, of his household, of his palaces, had accumulated great debts, Napoleon examined the bills of the creditors himself, defeated overcharges and errors, and reduced the claims by considerable sums.

His grand weapon, namely, the millions whom he directed, he owed to the representative character which clothed him. He interests us as he stands for France and for Europe; and he exists as captain and king only as far as the Revolution or the interests of the industrious masses found an organ and a leader in him.

In the social interests he knew the meaning and value of labor, and threw himself naturally on that side. The principal works that have survived him are his magnificent roads. He filled his troops with his spirit, and a sort of freedom and companionship grew up between him and them, which the forms of his court never permitted between the officers and himself. They performed under his eye that which no others could do. The best document of his relation to his troops is the order of the day on the morning of the battle of Austerlitz, in which Napoleon promises his troops that he will keep his person out of reach of fire. This declaration, which is the reverse of that ordinarily made by generals on the eve of battle, sufficiently explains the devotion of the army to their leader.

(Ralph Waldo Emerson)

译文

拿破仑·波拿巴

拿破仑知道该如何行动，他就是这样一个男人，时时刻刻都很清楚下一步该如何行动，即使遇到紧急情况，也能从容应对。拿破仑的这种性格不仅能给一般市民，而且也能给国王带来极大的慰藉和鼓舞。很少有人能像他那样规划未来，大多数人脑子里想到什么，就去做什么，毫无计划性可言，把事情拖到最后一刻才做，而且十分被动，每完成一步就要等到别人催促，才去做下一步。

如果拿破仑的目的是为了人民大众，他原可以成为世界上第一流的人物，可他并不是这样的人。像他这样，行为始终如一，就能够振奋人心，激发人民的力量。在实现目标的过程中，拿破仑既坚定又自信，但他也会不断自省，不惜牺牲小我，牺牲一切，无论是金钱，还是士兵和将领，甚至是自己的生命。但是，不同于一般的投机家，他拥有自己独到的见解。“事态的发展不能决定政策，”他说，“而是政策决定事态的发展。”“要是让政策随每个特定事件而改变，那政治体系就不复存在了。”

在走向成功的过程中，拿破仑不曾有过一丝松懈，面对当前兵荒马乱的局面，他始终对未来保持清醒的头脑，做好计划，缩短与目标的距离，再飞速地实现目标。当然，在拿破仑的一生中，不乏骇人听闻之事。那些是他成功的代价，但是并不能就此认为他是嗜杀成性的人、残酷的人，他只是眼里容不下一粒沙子。阻碍他前进的人或事，他都会毫不留情地予以扫除。

“陛下，奥地利炮兵火力凶猛，克拉克将军无法和朱诺将军会合。”“让他干掉这些炮兵。”“陛下，接近敌军炮口的兵团全都牺牲了，请指示。”“前进！前进！”

拿破仑足智多谋，眼里没有克服不了的困难。他说：“阿尔卑斯山也要给我让路。”于是，在悬崖峭壁上，他修建了许多完美的公路，最后从法国去意大利就像去任何别的法国城市一样轻而易举。一旦决定要做什么事，拿破仑就会不遗余力，全力以赴，为此赌上一切，不管是他的武器、他的金钱，还是他的士兵、将领，甚至是自己的安危。如果说，战争是解决国家间分歧最好的方式，那么拿破仑当然要在战术上精益求精。

在拿破仑的一生当中，他总共打过六十场仗，然而他还觉得远远不够。每一次的成功都让他的武力更加强大。“如果我不能取得新的胜利，我的势力就会衰退。征战造就了我，也支撑着我。”拿破仑行事高度严谨，十分守时，而他的力量正来源于此。在一次炮火攻击中，拿破仑藏身于壕沟里，安然无恙。他的每次进攻并不是一时的冲动，而是深思熟虑的结果。他认为，进攻就是最好的防守。“我有远大志向，”他说，“但冷酷无情。”

所有的一切都在拿破仑的精密筹划下进行，他的神机妙算胜过天体运算，他不放过任何一个小细节。“在蒙特贝洛的时候，我命令凯勒曼率领八百骑兵进攻，他用这些人马在奥地利骑兵队的眼皮底下冲散了六千匈牙利步兵。这个骑兵队离作战区域半里格远，并且要一刻钟的时间才能抵达。经过观察，我发现这些一刻钟正是决定战争成败的关键。”

在上战场之前，拿破仑很少思考战胜后的事情，而是把大部分的精力用于思考战败后该做些什么。无论在什么时候，他都谨慎行事，保持敏锐的洞察力。宫中的大臣必须牢记拿破仑的指示：“在夜里，尽量别进我的房间。有好消息要通报时，不要吵醒我，因为没必要弄得这么仓促；但有坏消息时，要立刻叫醒我，因为这时必须争分夺秒。”拿破仑处理事务的能力很强，已经超出了人们已知的限度。历史上有很多勤奋的国王，从尤利西斯到威廉三世，他们都不是拿破仑的对手。

接触过拿破仑的人都说，他决不会被欺骗，总能识破别人的诡计。当他的皇后，在家用和宫殿上的开销负债严重时，他就会亲自检查债务账单，废除索价过高的账单及错误的账单，减少了大笔债务款项。

拿破仑之所以能拥有强大的武力——他所统领的百万大军，是他身上独特的品质使然。拿破仑既代表法国，又代表欧洲，这一点很吸引我们。只要法国大革命或者是工人的利益决定了他既是领袖，又是国家的一部分，他就是唯一的领袖和君王。

在社会利益方面，拿破仑深知劳动人民的意义和价值，于是他自然而然地偏向这个阶层。拿破仑身后留下的重要工程，莫过于那些宽阔的道路。拿破仑用他的精神鼓舞士兵们，于是在他和士兵之间形成了一种自由的气氛和伙伴关系，这种上下级关系无人能比。拿破仑与士兵的关系用一个例子就能很好地诠释：在出征奥斯特利茨战场的清晨，拿破仑向士兵们保证，他本人不会加入战斗，这样的誓言和一般的将军在出征前夜所说的大有不同，而这样的与众不同也充分说明了士兵们对拿破仑有多么忠诚。

（拉尔夫 · 沃尔多 · 爱默生）

A Letter to the President of Congress

Washington at Trenton
Headquarters, Morristown
December 27, 1776.

To the President of Congress:

SIR: I have the pleasure of congratulating you upon the success of an enterprise which I had formed against a detachment of the enemy lying in Trenton, and which was executed yesterday morning.

The evening of the twenty-fifth I ordered the troops intended for this service to parade back of McKonkey's ferry, that they might begin to pass as soon as it grew dark, imagining that we should be able to throw them all over, with the necessary artillery, by twelve o'clock and that we might easily arrive at Trenton by five in the morning, the distance being about nine miles. But the quantity of ice made that night impeded the passage of the boats so much that it was three o'clock before the artillery could all be got over and near four before the troops took up their line of march.

This made me despair of surprising the town, as I well knew that we could not reach it before the day was fairly broke, but as I was certain there was no making a retreat without being discovered, and harassed on repassing the river, I determined to push on at all events.

I formed my detachment into two divisions, one to march by the lower or river road, the other by the upper or Pennington road. As the divisions had nearly the same distance to march, I ordered each of them immediately, upon forcing the outguards, to push directly into the town, that they might charge the enemy before they had time to form.

The upper division arrived at the enemy's advanced post exactly at eight o'clock, and in three minutes after I found from the fire on the lower road that that division had also got up. The out guards made but small opposition; though, for their numbers, they behaved very well, keeping up a constant retreating fire from behind houses. We presently saw their mainbody formed, but from their motions, they seemed undetermined how to act.

Being hard-pressed by our troops, who had already got possession of their artillery, they attempted to file off by a road on their right leading to Princeton. But, perceiving their intention, I threw a body of troops in their way, which immediately checked them. Finding from our disposition that they were surrounded, and that they must inevitably be cut to pieces if they made any further resistance, they agreed to lay down their arms.

The number that submitted in this manner was twenty-three officers and eight hundred and eighty-six men. Colonel Rahl, the commanding officer, and seven others were found wounded in the town. I do not know exactly how many they had killed; but I fancy not above twenty or thirty, as they never made any regular stand. Our loss is very trifling indeed,——only two officers, and one or two privates wounded.

I find that the detachment consisted of the three Hessian regiments of Lanspach, Kniphausen, and Rahl, amounting to about fifteen hundred men, and a troop of British light horse; but immediately upon the beginning of the attack, all those who were not killed or taken pushed directly down toward Bordentown. These would have likewise fallen into our hands could my plan have been completely carried into execution.

General Ewing was to have crossed before day at Trenton ferry and taken possession of the bridge leading out of the town; but the quantity of ice was so great that though he did everything in his power to effect it, he could not get over.

This difficulty also hindered General Cadwalader from crossing with the Pennsylvania militia from Bristol. He got part of his foot soldiers over; but finding it impossible to embark his artillery, he was obliged to desist.

I am fully confident that could the troops under General Ewing and Cadwalader have passed the river, I should have been able, with their assistance, to drive the enemy from all their posts below Trenton. But the numbers I had with me being inferior to them below me, and a strong battalion of light infantry being at Princeton above me, I thought it most prudent to return the same evening with the prisoners and the artillery we had taken. We found no stores of any consequence in the town.

In justice to the officers and men, I must add that their behavior upon this occasion reflects the highest honor upon them. The difficulty of passing the river in a very severe night, and their march through a violent storm of snow and hail did not in the least abate their ardor; but when they came to the charge, each seemed to vie with the other in pressing forward; and were I to give a preference to any particular corps, I should do great injustice to the others.

Colonel Baylor, my first aide-camp, will have the honor of delivering this to you; and from him you may be made acquainted with many other particulars. His spirited behavior upon every occasion requires me to recommend him to your particular notice.

I have the honor to be, etc.

G. W.

(George Washington)

译文

致大陆议会主席的一封信

致大陆议会主席：

阁下：我很高兴地向您报喜，我之前制定的对付特伦顿敌军小分队的计划成功了。这一计划是昨天早晨执行的。

二十五日晚，为执行这一计划，我命令部队撤回至麦克康基渡口，这样他们就能在天黑前尽快渡河。我原本设想在必要的火炮助攻下，他们能在十二点钟前过河。这样我们就能轻松地在清晨五点抵达大约一万五千米外的特伦顿。但那天晚上河里的大量冰块严重阻碍了渡船的航程，结果直到三点钟炮兵部队才全部渡过河流，直到四点钟整个部队才准备就绪。

我清楚地知道我们无法在天色大亮之前到达特伦顿，这让我对突袭这个城市失去了信心。但我同时也很确定，我们不可能不被敌军发现而撤退，也不可能在再次渡河时不被敌军袭击，所以我决定无论如何都要继续进军。

我把队伍分成两支，一支从较低的沿河公路进攻，另外一支从较高的潘宁顿路进攻。由于两支队伍进攻路程几乎相同，我命令他们在夺取前哨阵地后立刻直接向城里进军。这样在敌军有时间集结之前，他们还有可能发起进攻。

高路小队在八点整抵达了敌人的前方岗哨。不到三分钟，我从低处公路上的射击声中发现这路小队也已经就位。敌人的前哨勉强反抗了一下，由于他们人数多，也有几分威力。他们一边撤退，一边从房屋后方连续不断地射击。很快，我们就看到他们的主力部队集结起来，但从举动上看，他们似乎不确定该如何行动。

由于我们夺取了他们的大炮，迫于巨大的压力，他们试图从右边一条通往普林斯顿的路列队离开。但我察觉了他们的意图，在沿路布下兵力，切断了他们的退路。从我们的部署中，他们发现自己陷入了包围，如果继续抵抗的话不可避免地会溃不成军，因此同意举手投降。

投降的有二十三名军官和八百八十六名士兵，我们还在城里发现了受伤的指挥官拉尔上校和其他七名军官。我不确定战士们到底击毙了多少人，但我猜不会超过二三十人，因为他们并没有做什么正式的抵抗。我们的伤亡人数确实非常微不足道——只损失了两名军官，另有一两名士兵受伤。

我发现敌军的这支分队由三个黑森雇佣兵兵团和一支英国轻骑兵部队组成，大约总共有一千五百人。黑森兵团分别是兰斯帕克兵团、克尼普豪森兵团和拉尔兵团。但在进攻一开始的时候，他们所有没有被杀或是被抓的人，就都直接向博登敦推进。要是这些人也同样落入我们手里的话，我的计划才称得上是完全实现。

尤因将军按计划应于天亮之前在特伦顿渡口过河，并占领通往城外的大桥。但是河里结了大量的浮冰，虽然他用尽一切办法想要达成目标，结果却是徒劳。

这个难关同样也阻碍了和宾夕法尼亚民兵一起从布里斯托尔渡河的卡德瓦拉德将军。他设法让部分步兵过了河，但却发现不可能把大炮弄上船。他不得不停止行军。

如果尤因将军和卡德瓦拉德将军的部队渡河成功，我非常确信我能在他们的帮助下驱逐所有驻守在特伦顿的敌军。但和他们相比，我的兵力处于下风。在普林斯顿有一整营的轻步兵让我感到压力不小。于是，我认为最慎重的做法是带着我们的大炮和俘虏们在当天晚上撤军而返。重要的是，我们在城里没有找到任何补给。

为了公平起见，我必须要补充一点，那就是官兵们在这次行动中的表现反映出他们极强的荣誉感。在一个严寒的夜晚渡河，在凶猛的冰雪风暴中行军，这些艰难困苦丝毫没有减弱他们的激情。当他们开始冲锋的时候，看起来人人奋勇争先，敢于向前。如果我对任何一支个别兵团表示偏爱的话，对其他兵团都是严重的不公正。

我的首席副官贝勒上校将有幸将这封信送给您，从他那里您也许能了解到许多其他细节。出于他在每一次战役中的英勇表现，我有必要将他推荐给您，以获得您的青睐。

深感荣幸！

乔治·华盛顿

于莫里斯顿司令部

1776年12月27日

（乔治·华盛顿）

Thomas Jefferson, the "Pen of the Revolution"

I

On the day when Patrick Henry made his great speech against the Stamp Act, a number of students from William and Mary College were standing at the door listening. Among these was a young man of twenty-two, who drank in every word. When he was afterward asked about the debate, he said it was "most bloody". He was unknown at the time, but he was destined to become as famous as Henry himself; for the name of this youth was Thomas Jefferson.

He was the son of a wealthy farmer in Albemarle County, Virginia, and was born in the month of April, 1743. As was then the fashion, he was sent to William and Mary College at Williamsburg, and here for a part of his time he studied very hard. While not thus engaged he was visiting young ladies, and from all accounts he was very much liked by them. He was tall and not very graceful, and had sandy hair; but he was full of wit and fun and fond of dancing and other amusements. There is no reason to believe that he neglected his studies for the society of young ladies, but he certainly had his share of the fun and frolic around him. He tells us so himself. He had a friend named John Page, who was afterward Governor of Virginia, and wrote him a number of letters, which were published. In these he gave an account of his daily doings, and it is amusing to read them. In one, he describes a night which he spent at an old country house, where the rain leaked upon his watch, and the rats ate up his pocket-book; and in another he speaks of "dancing with Belinda in the 'Apollo'", and tells his friend how happy he felt while doing so.

The "Apollo" was a large room in the old Raleigh Tavern at Williamsburg, and became famous afterward, like Faneuil Hall in Boston, as the place of meeting of the patriots. At that early day, however, it was used only as a ball-room, and the "Belinda" the young man speaks of was a young lady with whom he had fallen in love. His letters are full of her; and it is amusing to find a person, who afterward became the grave President of the United States breaking forth into exclamation sat the delight he felt in dancing with her. They were never married, and young Jefferson either was, or pretended to be, very disconsolate. He meant to rig out a boat, he said, and sail to Europe, and remain absent two years; but this was probably a jest, and he turned his attention elsewhere.

Soon afterward he left college and began the practice of law, and it was not till he was nearly thirty that he was married. On this occasion an interesting little scene occurred; and as it gives us a good idea of his light-hearted disposition. I will relate it.

His bride was a beautiful young widow of Charles City County, named Mrs. Skelton. She was about twenty-three, and lived at a place called "The Forest"; and, as she was very wealthy, she had a number of admirers. Of these she preferred Mr. Thomas Jefferson, and in January, 1772, they were married at "The Forest". It was an old Virginia party, with crowds of friends and relatives, huge roaring fires, and music and dancing, which was kept up throughout the night. On the next morning the bride and groom set out in their carriage, drawn by four horses, for the mountains, where Jefferson lived, and then their troubles began.

It was the depth of winter, and a snow-storm began to fall. They stopped at "Blenheim" the residence of Colonel Carter, not far from the end of their journey; but as the family were not at home, they determined to push on and reach "Monticello", the name of Jefferson's place, before night. They therefore continued their way, but it proved a terrible undertaking. The snow was falling steadily, and the mountain roads were full of drifts, through which they could scarcely force their way. The horses plunged and snorted, and the coach rolled from side to side, and it seemed probable that they would be compelled to spend the night in the fields or forests, without fire or food. It must have tried the young lady's courage, but she laughed and kept up her good spirits, and at last the coach plunged through and ascended the winding road to "Monticello".

The sight before them was dreary enough. The hill was covered with snow, and not a light or a fire was to be seen. But this did not affect the young married couple. Jefferson opened a small pavilion, and led his bride in. He then kindled a fire, and brought out a bottle of wine and some biscuits from behind the books on the shelves, and they supped, and laughed, and sang, and were as gay as if they had been two children enjoying a frolic.

This is one of the small incidents which I set out with the intention of relating. They are not very important in themselves, but they afford us an idea of the persons who figured in them, and that is precisely what we wish to obtain. Jefferson's good-humor on this occasion shows one trait in his character which many persons gave him no credit for; and I have always thought of this little incident with pleasure. The snow was falling and the wind blowing outside the mountain pavilion, but within all was warmth and laughter. They were happy, for they loved each other, and did not mind the snow. None of us mind it in youth, when those we love are beside us. As we grow old they leave us sometimes, and the snow settles in our hearts——when we have a dreary time enough.

II

In the spring of 1773, which was the year after his marriage, Thomas Jefferson took his seat in the House of Burgesses. He was only about thirty, and therefore quite a young man still, but it soon became plain that he would be one of the greatest leaders of the Revolution. He was a very poor speaker, and it is doubtful whether he ever made a regular speech in his life; but he was an excellent writer, and this was the foundation of his fame. He wrote a pamphlet on the subject of the quarrel between England and America, which was so defiant that he was declared a traitor by the English government. But this had no effect upon him. He said what he thought, and men like himself are always ready to support their opinions.

He was heart and soul for resistance to England, and now became the author of one of the greatest of all plans for uniting the colonies. This was a "Committee of Correspondence", whose duty it was to write to similar committees to be formed in other parts of the country, by which means each colony would know what the rest were ready to do. Jefferson proposed this, and the committee was appointed. The effect was soon seen. From the North to the South the scattered colonies formed one country in their resistance to oppression; and through their committees they made an arrangement to meet in Congress at Philadelphia.

In these movements at Williamsburg, Patrick Henry and Thomas Jefferson were the great leaders. Each had his peculiar gift. Jefferson could not speak, but was a powerful writer. Henry could not write, but was a wonderful orator. Thus each did his part, and urged resistance as the only course now left. The Burgesses followed their suggestions, and the English governor dissolved them, as it was called; but they determined to meet at the Raleigh Tavern, in the "Apollo Room", and did so. Here they consulted as to the next step. Jefferson was among them. He must have looked around him, and remembered the days of his youth, when he was so well acquainted with the old apartment. He had danced many a set with "Belinda" and other young ladies in this very room, when he was a thoughtless young man; and now he was a grave statesman, organizing revolution on the same floor which he had danced upon. He must have closed his eyes sometimes, and fancied he heard the music again; for even the busiest men find time to go back in this way often, and return in memory to the happy days of their youth.

I have mentioned the General Congress of the colonies which met at Philadelphia. Jefferson was one of the delegates to it, and in the year 1776 he became immortal in American history as the author of the Declaration of Independence. In May of that year, Virginia suggested that this declaration should be made, and directed Richard Henry Lee, one of her most distinguished patriots, to move the resolution. He did so, and Congress resolved that the declaration should be made; after which they looked about for a person to write it.

The choice fell upon Jefferson. He had scarcely risen in Congress since he had been a delegate, for he was nothing of a public speaker, as I have said, and left debating to others. But his powers as a writer were well known. His style was plain, vigorous, and went straight to the point. What he had to say he said clearly always, and he knew well what to say. The colonies meant in this great paper to declare themselves independent, and give the reasons for doing so; and, sitting down in an old house in Philadelphia, Jefferson wrote the Declaration.

It was then offered to Congress, and a hot debate took place upon it. Jefferson had no share in this; he left the struggle to the great John Adams and other friends, who fought like giants for it. Many were opposed to it, and did all they could to defeat it, but failed. The time had come to declare that the colonies were independent, and Congress resolved that this declaration should be made in the terms used by Jefferson. It was passed with a few changes which did not alter the meaning, and was the crown of Jefferson's fame as a statesman.

It was natural that he should be proud of it, and he seems to have been so. By his own request, the words "Author of the Declaration of American Independence" were cut upon his tombstone.

III

I cannot tell you, in his short story, of Jefferson's long and famous career as a statesman and ruler. He became President of the United States, and the head of a great party; and his fame as an upholder of democracy extended throughout the world. For good or evil——and there are different opinions as to that——he left a powerful impress on the country; and his name will probably last as long as its history.

He passed his last days at "Monticello", where he and his bride had spent that snowy night so long before. He was old, but still active. The University of Virginia was established by him, and he spared no exertions in his last years to make a great institution of it, in which he succeeded.

He wrote many letters, and still watched political affairs keenly; but his chief sources of happiness were literature and the society of his family.

He was happy in his home. His family loved him tenderly, for he was kind and affectionate. His neighbors liked him, for he was extremely hospitable and cordial whenever they came to see him, and he entertained so many visitors that it nearly ruined him. These came to see him from all parts of the world, and especially from France, when he had been minister and was exceedingly popular. One and all were met with a warm welcome and smiles; and they went away and said that the "Sage of Monticello" was one of the most agreeable as well as one of the greatest men in the world.

He still remained busy. Such a man, with a mind so keen and active, never rests. He labored to establish firmly the great University of Virginia. He wrote thousands of letters to people on politics or other subjects. He read and studied, and wrote for many hours every day, and took a very deep interest in everything relating to Virginia. He had himself, you know, played a great part in her history. He and Edmund Pendleton had rewritten the laws, and Jefferson had overturned with his own hand the old order of things, and made all new. He had put everybody on a level. The old religious intolerance was swept away by his exertions, and, in spite of Edmund Pendleton's opposition, he had destroyed the old system of giving the land to the eldest son, which kept up distinctions in society. This quite altered the State, and he was not much liked by the old planters for it; but the people in general were delighted, and said he was the defender of the "rights of man".

He was very fond of farming operations, and would go into the harvest-field in the hottest part of the day to see his cradlers cut the wheat. He also took a deep interest in stock, and raised blooded horses and fine breeds of cattle. He was an excellent rider. Even when he was an old man and very feeble, he would mount the most spirited horses, and control them with ease. To the last his seat in the saddle was erect and firm, and he continued to ride out on his high-mettled horses when his servants had to lead them up to the porch for him to mount them.

These little details will give you an idea how Thomas Jefferson passed the evening of his life at "Monticello". His sun was setting gradually, and all eyes were fixed upon it as it sank. At last it began to descend below the horizon, as you may have seen the large red orb of the real sun touch the blue mountains in the west and slowly disappear. In the year 1826, he was taken sick and went to bed. His family and friends gathered around him, and were deeply distressed, but he himself was entirely resigned. He did not seem afraid to die. But he gradually sank; and on the night of the third of July, those at his bedside saw that he was dying. Very singularly, the famous John Adams, who had been his friend and supporter in the great struggle over the Declaration of Independence, was dying at the very same time, far off in Massachusetts. He remembered his old friend in Virginia, and was heard to say to himself,

"Thomas Jefferson still lives!"

Just as midnight struck, Jefferson roused himself, and his lips moved. Those beside him bent over him and heard him murmur, in a low voice,

"This is the fourth of July!"

He lived until twelve o'clock in the day. He then said, in a feeble voice,

"I resign myself to my God, and my child to my country!"

After uttering these words, he expired; and John Adams died on the same evening. Fifty years before, almost hour for hour, these two great men had placed their names to the Declaration of Independence in Philadelphia.

(John Esten Cooke)

译文

托马斯·杰斐逊：革命的文学斗士

I

帕特里克·亨利发表他伟大的反《印花税法》演说的那天，许多来自威廉与玛丽学院的学生都站在门口聆听。其中一名22岁的年轻人，专注地沉浸在每一个字里。后来被问及这场争论时，他形容其“十分杀气腾腾”。虽然他那时还不为人所知，但却注定会成为和亨利一样的名人，因为这个年轻人的名字叫托马斯·杰斐逊。

1743年4月，他出生于弗吉尼亚阿尔伯马尔县一个富裕的农民家庭。长大后，他被送去威廉斯堡的威廉和玛丽学院上学。这在当时是很流行的做法。杰斐逊在威廉和玛丽学院度过了一段努力学习的时光。在不那么忙的时候，他会和年轻女士约会。据说，女士们都很喜爱他。虽然他长得高且不那么优雅，还有一头浅茶色头发，但他富有才智，风趣幽默，而且喜爱跳舞和其他娱乐活动。我们没有理由相信他会因为这群年轻女士而耽误学业，但他确实享受着那一份环绕着他的乐趣和欢闹。这是他自己告诉我们的。他曾给一位名叫约翰·佩奇的朋友写过很多信。约翰·佩奇后来当上了弗吉尼亚州州长，这些信也被公开出版了。在这些信里，杰斐逊透露了不少日常生活的细节，读起来非常有趣。在一封信里，他描述了一个在乡下老房子里度过的夜晚：漏进来的雨水滴到他的手表上，老鼠吃光了他的笔记本；在另一封信里，他谈到了“在‘阿波罗’和贝琳达跳舞”，并告诉他的朋友说当时他是多么幸福。

“阿波罗”是威廉斯堡老罗利酒馆的一个大房间。作为爱国者聚会的场所，它后来变得与波士顿的法尼尔厅一样有名，然而早期它仅仅被当成一个舞厅使用；这名年轻人提及的“贝琳达”则是他所爱的一位年轻女士，他的信里满满都是她的身影。看到未来会成为美国总统的重要人物发出这种“和她跳舞感到非常快乐”的感叹，实在很有趣。他们不曾结婚，年轻的杰斐逊并没有表现得或是假装表现得伤心欲绝。他说他打算组装一条船开往欧洲，并在海外待上两年。但这可能只是一句玩笑话，他的注意力很快就转向了其他地方。

不久，他离开了大学，开始从事法律行业。他直到将近三十岁才结婚。杰斐逊结婚时发生了有趣的一幕，这能让我们清楚地了解他无忧无虑的性情。我将在下文讲到这一点。

他的新娘是查尔斯城县一名年轻貌美的寡妇，人们叫她斯凯尔顿夫人。她大约二十三岁，住在一个叫“森林”的地方。因为她非常富有，并且拥有很多爱慕者，不过在这些人中，她偏爱的是托马斯·杰斐逊先生。1772年1月，他们在“森林”举行婚礼。这是一个老式的弗吉尼亚派对：成群结队的亲朋好友，腾空呼啸的盛大烟火，以及音乐和舞会。结婚派对整整持续了一个通宵。第二天一早，新郎和新娘登上了一辆四匹马拉着的马车，动身前往杰斐逊居住的山间。然后，他们的麻烦开始了。

正值隆冬季节，天空开始下起一场暴雪。他们停在了卡特上校的住所“布伦海姆”，这里离他们的目的地并不太远。但由于卡特一家不在家，他们决定继续赶路，争取在天黑之前抵达杰斐逊的居所“蒙蒂塞洛”。因此他们就继续上路了，但后来的事证明这是个糟糕的决定。大雪持续下个不停，山路上积满了雪，他们根本无法前进。马儿陷进雪里，不耐烦地喷着鼻息；马车左右摇晃，艰难向前；看起来他们很可能在没有食物和火的情况下，不得不在野外或是森林里过夜。这考验着年轻女士的勇气，但她一路笑着，保持着良好的精神状态。最后，马车向前猛冲，攀上了通向“蒙蒂塞洛”的崎岖山路。

眼前是一片沉闷景象。大雪覆盖了整座山，看不到一点灯光或是火光。但这并没有影响到这对年轻的夫妇。杰斐逊打开一个小小的帐篷，领着他的新娘进去。接着，他点燃一堆火，从搁架上放着的书后面拿出一瓶红酒和一些饼干。然后他们吃了晚饭，笑着，唱着，好似回到了童年时代，快乐地嬉戏玩闹。

这是众多小事中的一件。我挑选了本身并不很重要的小事来讲，是希望从中让我们能看出杰佛逊的性格。准确地说，这才是我们希望实现的目的。杰斐逊在这一场合下的良好心境，展现出他性格中的一种特质。虽然很多人并不认为他就是这样的人，但我总是带着愉快的心情回想这个小插曲。山上的帐篷之外，大雪纷飞狂风呼啸，而帐篷里则充满了笑声和温暖。他们很幸福，因为他们深爱对方，毫不在意风雪。年轻时候，当所爱的人就在身边，我们谁都不会在意风雪。但随着年纪渐长，爱的人也离开了我们，当我们觉得沉闷无聊时，就还会回想起那样的雪夜。

II

1773年春天，在他结婚后的第二年，托马斯·杰斐逊在下议院取得一个席位。他当时年仅三十岁，仍旧是个相当年轻的男人。但我们很快就会清楚地看到，他将成为美国独立革命中最伟大的领袖之一。他是个很糟糕的演说者，人们怀疑他终其一生都没有发表过一次合格的演说。但是，他的写作能力却极其优秀，这也是奠定他显赫声名的基石。他写过一本针对英美之间争论的小册子，用词非常犀利大胆，以至于英国政府宣布他是叛国者。不过，这并没有对他造成任何影响。他畅所欲言，而和他志同道合的人们总是时刻准备着支持他的观点。他全心全意投入到反英斗争中，那时他成了一个殖民地联合方案的发起人。该方案可以说是所有殖民地联合方案中最伟大的方案之一，它就是“通讯委员会”。所谓“通讯委员会”，就是在全国各地建立相似的委员会并互写通讯信息。通过这种方式，殖民地之间就能知道各方在准备做些什么事。杰斐逊提出了这一建议，随后委员会成立了。“通讯委员会”的效果立竿见影，分散在南北方的殖民地在共同反抗压迫的过程中形成了一个国家，他们通过委员会商定在费城召开殖民地联合会议。

帕特里克·亨利和托马斯·杰斐逊是威廉斯堡这些革命运动的杰出领袖。他们各有各的特殊天赋。杰斐逊不善于演说，但他写出的文章充满力量；亨利不善于写作，但他发表的演说精彩绝伦。如此这般，两人各司其职，共同推进反抗斗争。议员们追随着他们的脚步，而英国政府宣称“解散”他们。他们决定到罗利酒馆的“阿波罗房间”碰头，事实上他们确实这么做了。他们在这里商议下一步的计划，杰斐逊就在他们当中。在他如此熟悉的这个旧房间里，他一定会环顾四周，想起他的青年时代。当他还是个无忧无虑的年轻人时，他和“贝琳达”以及其他年轻女士在这个房间跳过许多支舞。而现在，他成了一名重要的政治家，正在他曾经跳过舞的同一块地面上组织着革命斗争。他有时候一定会闭上眼想象他重又听见音乐声，因为即使是最忙碌的人，也要经常以这种方式找时间回到过去，回到记忆中他们那些年轻时的幸福时光。

杰斐逊是我之前提到的费城殖民地会议的代表之一。1776年，他以《独立宣言》起草人的身份成为美国历史上流芳百世的作家。那年五月，弗吉尼亚州建议制定这份宣言，并委派该州最杰出的爱国者之一理查德·亨利·李去推动决议的进行，他做到了。会议决定要起草宣言，然后他们开始四处寻找起草这份宣言的人。

任务落到了杰斐逊身上。我之前说过，他不是一个会在公开场合演说的人，因此自从当上会议代表后，都是其他人在激烈辩论，而他几乎从来没有站起来发言。但作为一名写作者，他的能力广为人知。他的写作风格平实、有力，直击要害，总能把他要说的话说明白，而他也很清楚该说些什么。殖民地联邦打算在这篇重大的文章中宣布独立，并告诉人们他们这么做的依据。于是，杰斐逊坐在费城的一所老房子里撰写了这份宣言。

这份宣言被提交给了联合会，然后代表们围绕它展开了一场激烈的争辩。杰斐逊没有参与辩论，他把斗争留给了伟大的约翰·亚当斯及其伙伴，他们像巨人一般为它奋斗。很多人对宣言表示反对，并想方设法要驳倒它，但都没有成功。宣布殖民地独立的时机到了，联合会决定就以杰斐逊的措辞制定宣言。最终，《独立宣言》被批准通过，只做了一点无伤主旨的改动，它让杰斐逊身为一名政治家的声望达到了巅峰。

他自然会以此为荣，他也确实以此为荣。按照他的要求，“美国独立宣言的起草人”的字样被刻在他的墓碑上。

III

在这个短短的故事里，我没法完全告诉你杰斐逊那漫长又声名显赫的政治统治者生涯。他成了美国总统，成了一个伟大政党的领袖。作为一名民主制的支持者，他的声名传遍世界各地。他在这个国家刻下了深深的个人印记，虽然人们对此有不同的看法，但不论好坏，他都将会名垂青史。

杰斐逊在“蒙蒂塞洛”度过了最后的时光。很久之前，他和他的新娘在这里度过了一个下雪的夜晚。他虽已年老，但仍旧充满活力。他创办了弗吉尼亚大学，在人生的最后几年里，他为了让这所大学变成首屈一指的教育机构而费尽心血，最终他成功了。他写了很多信，仍然密切关注政治事件，不过他快乐的源泉主要来自于文学和家庭。

他在家中很幸福。他和蔼又慈爱，家人们都温柔地爱着他；他诚恳又热情，邻居们也都喜欢他。他热情款待无数来访的人，几乎累垮了身体。这些人来自世界各地，特别是法国来的人最多，因为他曾是一名极受欢迎的驻法大使。杰斐逊总是带着笑容去迎接他们，而他们离开之后总会说，"蒙蒂塞洛的圣人"不仅是世界上最伟大的人之一，也是世界上最有礼貌的人之一。

他仍然很忙，像他这样一个思维敏捷活跃的人是从不会休息的。他努力巩固弗吉尼亚大学的地位；他就政治和其他话题给人们写成千上万封信；他读书，学习，每天写作很长时间，对涉及弗吉尼亚的每一件事都深感兴趣。你知道，他在弗吉尼亚的历史上起到了重要作用。他和埃蒙德·彭德尔顿重新修订了法律。杰斐逊亲手推翻了旧秩序，建立了新秩序。他使每个人都平等地站在同一条水平线上。经过他的努力，那些老旧的宗教禁忌被一扫而空，并且他不顾埃蒙德·彭德尔顿的反对废除了古老的长子继承制，在社会上引起了强烈反响。这在相当程度上改变了美国，他也因此为守旧的农场主们所不喜，但大多数人很高兴，称他为"人权"的捍卫者。

他很喜爱农事，会在天气最热的日子里到丰收的田野里去，看他的工人用镰刀割麦子；他对家畜也很感兴趣，会饲养纯种马和良种的牛。他是一名优秀的骑手，即便他年老体弱，仍能骑上最烈的马并轻松地驾驭它们。直到最后一刻，他马鞍上的座位依然牢牢安在马上，即使为了他得以继续骑上他那狂野不羁的马，仆人们不得不把马儿牵到门廊处让他骑上去。

想象下面这个场景，你就能明白托马斯·杰斐逊在"蒙蒂塞洛"的最后时刻是怎样度过的。他生命的太阳正在渐渐落山，所有的目光都在注视这渐落的夕阳。最终，它开始滑下地平线，就像你可能见过的真正的太阳一样，又大又红的圆球触碰到西边蓝色的山峰，然后慢慢消失了。1826年，杰斐逊生病在床。他的亲朋好友环绕在他身边，非常伤心难过，但他自己却异常从容，看上去并不害怕死亡。他的生命力渐渐离他而去，7月3日夜里，人们在他身边看着他走向死亡。奇异的是，著名的约翰·亚当斯也在同一个时间走向死亡。他远在马萨诸塞州，是杰斐逊的朋友，也是捍卫《独立宣言》的伟大的斗争者。他记起了他在弗吉尼亚的老朋友，人们听见他自言自语地说：

"托马斯·杰斐逊还活着！"

就在午夜来临的时候，杰斐逊苏醒过来，颤动着双唇。他身边的人弯身去听，听到他用很低的声音喃喃说道：

"现在是7月4日了！"

他坚持活到了那天的午夜12点，然后气息奄奄地说：

"我把自己献给上帝，把孩子献给我的国家！"

说完这些话，他与世长辞。而约翰·亚当斯也在同一天晚上逝世。五十年前的费城，这两名伟人几乎同时在《独立宣言》上签下了他们的名字。

（约翰·埃斯滕·库克）

A Breakfast with Elia

预习

aeronaut /ˈerənɔːt/ 气球驾驶员

duplicated /duːplɪˈkeɪtɪd/ 复制的

mentality /menˈtæləti/ 心理状态

statoscope /ˈstætəˌskoʊp/ 气压计

Invited to breakfast with a gentleman in the Temple to meet Charles Lamb and his sister——"Elia and Bridget Elia!" I never in my life had an invitation more to my taste. The Essays of Elia are certainly the most charming things in the world, and it has been for the last ten years my highest compliment to the literary taste of a friend to present him with a copy. Who has not smiled over the humorous description of Mrs. Battle? Who that has read Elia would not give more to see him than all the other authors of his time put together ?

I arrived a half hour before Lamb, and had time to learn some of his peculiarities. He lives a little out of London, and is very much of an invalid. Some family circumstances have tended to depress him very much of late years, and unless excited, he scarcely shows a trace of what he was.

There was a rap at the door at last, and enter a gentleman in black, short and very slight in his person, his head set on his shoulders with a thoughtful, forward bent, his hair just sprinkled with gray, beautiful deep-set eyes, aquiline nose and a very indescribable mouth. Whether it expressed most humor or feeling, good nature or a kind of whimsical peevishness, or twenty other things which passed over it by turns, I cannot in the least be certain.

His sister, whose literary reputation is associated very closely with her brother, and who, as the original of Bridget Elia, is a kind of object of literary affection, came in after him. She is a small bent figure, evidently a victim to illness, and hears with difficulty. Her face has been, I should think, a fine and handsome one, and her bright gray eyes are full of intelligence and fire.

They both seemed quite at home in our friend's chambers, and as there was to be no one else, we immediately drew around the breakfast table. I had set a large arm-chair for Miss Lamb. "Don't take it, Mary," said Lamb, pulling it away from her very gravely, "it appears as if you were going to have a tooth drawn." Nothing could have been more delightful than the kindness and affection between the brother and sister, though Lamb was continually taking advantage of her deafness to mystify her with the most serious gravity upon every topic that was started.

The conversation turned upon literature after a while, and our host, the Templar, could not express himself strongly enough in admiration of Webster's speeches, which he said were exciting the greatest attention among the politicians and lawyers of England. Lamb said, "I don't know much of American authors. Mary, there, devours Cooper's novels with a ravenous appetite, with which I have no sympathy. The only American book that I ever read twice was the 'Journal of John Woolman', a Quaker preacher and tailor, whose character is one of the finest I ever met with."

My friend spoke of buying a book of Lamb's a few days before, and I mentioned my having bought a copy of Elia the last day I was in America to send as a parting gift to one of the most lovely women in our country.

"What did you give for it?" said Lamb.

"About seven and six pence."

"Permit me to pay you that," said he, and with the utmost earnestness he counted the money upon the table.

"I never yet wrote anything that would sell," he continued.

"I am the pub lisher's ruin. My last poem won't sell a copy. Have you seen it, Mr. Willis? "

"I have not."

"It is only eighteen pence, and I'll give you six pence toward it," and he described it to me, where I should find it sticking up in a shop window in the Strand.

Lamb ate nothing and complained of the veal pie. There was a kind of potted fish, which he expected our friend would secure for him. He inquired whether there was not a morsel left, perhaps, in the bottom of the last pot. Our host was not sure.

"Send and see," said Lamb, "and if the pot has been cleaned, bring me the cover. I think that the sight of it would do me good."

The cover was brought, upon which there was a picture of the fish. Lamb kissed it with a reproachful look at his friend, and then left the table and began to wander around the room with a broken uncertain step, as if he almost forgot to put one foot before the other. His sister arose after a while, and commenced walking up and down very much in the same manner on the opposite side of the table, and in the course of half an hour they took their leave.

To any one who loves the writing of Charles Lamb with but half of my own enthusiasm, even these little particulars of an hour passed in his company will have an interest. Wreck as he certainly is and must be, of what he was, I would rather have seen him for that single hour than the hundred and one sights of London put together.

(Nathaniel Parker Willi)

译文

和伊利亚共进早餐

我被邀请到法学院里同一位绅士共进早餐，其间能见到查尔斯·兰姆和他的姐姐——“伊利亚和布丽姬特·伊利亚”！我这辈子还没有收到过如此合心意的邀请。《伊利亚随笔》毋庸置疑是世上最美妙的书了，我过去十年内对喜欢文学的朋友的最高奖赏就是赠予他这本书。谁能不对那关于巴特尔太太的诙谐描述会心一笑呢？读过《伊利亚随笔》的人，谁不愿来见见作者呢？哪怕要花上见其他所有作者加起来这么多的时间也好啊。

我比兰姆早到半小时，所以有时间了解下他的一些特点。他住在伦敦市外不远的地方，身体虚弱。近年来，他常常因家事而感到沮丧，除非比较激动，他很少表露出真实的自我。

终于，有人来敲门了。一位身着黑色衣服的绅士进了门。他身材矮小，十分瘦削。他的脑袋微微前倾，仿佛若有所思地搭在肩膀上，他的头发已有几缕灰白，他有迷人而深邃的眼睛、鹰钩鼻和一张难以形容的嘴。他那张嘴不知道是要开玩笑还是表达感情，不知道是显得好脾气还是带一种坏脾气……或者其他什么二十余种东西会一句句从这张口中吐露，我都丝毫无法确信。

他的姐姐随他之后进来，她在文学上的声誉与他紧密相连，并且作为布丽姬特 · 伊利亚的原型人物，某种程度上也是他文学作品中的情感对象。她体型弱小，身子弯曲着，显然深受疾病的困扰，而且她的听力有问题。我想，她的面容原是姣好而端庄的，她明亮的灰色眼睛里闪耀着智慧和激情。

在我朋友的房间里，他们看上去像在自己家里一样舒适自在。因为不会再有其他人来，所以我们立刻围向了早餐餐桌。我为兰姆女士安置了一个大的扶手椅。“别坐那儿，玛丽。”兰姆说道，同时很严肃地把扶椅从她身边拉开，“看上去你像是要去拔牙一样。”没什么比姐弟之间的温情和爱护更令人愉快了，即使兰姆不断地在开始每个话题时表现得郑重其事来迷惑姐姐，利用她的听力不佳。

不久，话题转向了文学方面。我们的东道主是名法学家，他没能强有力地表达自己对韦伯斯特的演讲的赞美之情，韦伯斯特的演讲正吸引着英格兰政客和律师的高度关注。兰姆说：“我并不了解美国作家。你瞧，库珀的小说很对玛丽的胃口，她看起书来废寝忘食，但我就不是很认同她的品位。我唯一读过两遍的美国书籍就是《约翰 · 伍尔曼日记》，他是贵格会的传教士，也是个裁缝，是我见过的性格最好的人之一。”

我的朋友谈及前几天买了本兰姆的书，我便说起自己曾在美国的最后一天买过一本《伊利亚》，还把它作为告别礼物，送给了我们那里最可爱的女人。

“你花了多少钱？”兰姆问。

“大概六便士吧。”

“请准许我把这些钱还给你。”他说，然后用最诚挚而认真的态度在桌上数起钱来。

“我从未写过任何能卖得好的作品。”他继续说，“我就是出版商的灾星。我最新的诗歌一本都卖不了。您看过吗？威利先生？”

“没看过。”

“只卖区区十八个便士，我给你六便士去买这本书。”然后他向我描述，河岸街的哪家商店的橱窗里，能找到被竖立摆放着的这本书。

兰姆什么都没吃，还抱怨了牛肉馅饼。他希望我们的朋友能为他拿一种罐装鱼，询问是不是他们把上一罐鱼全吃完了，一点没剩。我们的东道主无法确定。

“派人去看看，”兰姆说，“如果罐子里的鱼被吃得干干净净，就把罐子盖拿给我。我想看过之后我会好受一点。”

罐子盖拿来了，上面画着一张鱼的图像。兰姆轻抚盖子，责备地看了一眼他的朋友，然后起身离开桌子，开始在房间里脚步凌乱地走动起来，似乎忘记了该先伸出哪只脚似的。过了一会，他的姐姐也站起来，开始用同样的方式在桌子的对面走来走去，之后的半小时里，他们离开了。

对于任何一个哪怕只有我一半热情而深爱查尔斯·兰姆的文字的人来说，在与他共度的一小时里，即使是这些小细节也颇具趣味。他的身心确实极度受损，但这也造就了他。我与他相见的那一小时胜过我看到的无数伦敦风光的总和。

（纳撒内尔·帕克·威利）

作者介绍

纳撒内尔·帕克·威利，美国作家、诗人，出生于缅因州波特兰市。他在耶鲁大学读书时便开始写诗，毕业后投身于各种新闻事业工作中。他曾泛游国外，在《闲游》《我邂逅的那些人》《那些闻名的人们和地方》以及其他著作中写下了许多优美而有趣的见闻。

Liberty and Independence

There was tumult in the city,
In the quaint old Quaker town,
And the streets were rife with people,
Pacing restless up and down;
People gathering at corners,
Where they whispered each to each,
And the sweat stood on their temples,
With the earnestness of speech.
As the black Atlantic currents
Lash the wild Newfoundland shore,
So they beat against the State House,
So they surged against the door;
And the mingling of their voices
Made a harmony profound,
Till the quiet street of Chestnut
Was all turbulent with sound.
"Will they do it?""Dare they do it?"
"Who is speaking?""What's the news?"
"What of Adams?""What of Sherman?"
"Oh, God grant they won't refuse!"
"Make some way, there!""Let me nearer!"
"I am stifling""Stifle, then:
When a nation's life's at hazard,
We've no time to think of men!"
So they beat against the portal,——
Man and woman, maid and child;
And the July sun in heaven
On the scene looked down and smiled,
The same sun that saw the Spartan
Shed his patriot blood in vain,

Now beheld the soul of freedom
All unconquered rise again.
Aloft in that high steeple
Sat the bellman, old and gray;
He was weary of the tyrant
And his iron-sceptered sway;
So he sat with one hand ready
On the clapper of the bell,
When his eye should catch the signal
Of the glorious news to tell.
See! See! the dense crowd quivers
Through all its lengthened line,
As the boy beside the portal
Looks forth to give the sign!
With his small hand upward lifted,
Breezes dallying with his hair,
Hark! with deep, clear intonation,
Breaks his young voice on the air.
Hushed the people's swelling murmur,
List the boy's strong joyous cry!
"Ring!" he shouts aloud, "Ring! Grandpa!
Ring! Oh, ring for Liberty!"
And straightway, at the signal,
The old bellman lifts his hand,
Forth he sends the good news, making
Iron music through the land.
How they shouted! What rejoicing!
How the old bell shook the air,
Till the clang of Freedom ruffled
The calmly gliding Delaware!
How the bonfires and the torches
Shone upon the night's repose,
And from the flames, like Phoenix,

Fair Liberty arose!
That old State House bell is silent,
And hushed is now its iron tongue,
But the spirit it awakened
Still is living-ever young.
And while we greet the smiling sunlight
On the fourth of each July,
We'll never forget the bellman,
Who, twists the earth and sky,
Rang out our independence,
Which, please God, shall never die!

(Selected)

译文

自由与独立

城市中充满喧嚣，
在宁静而古老的贵格镇，
街道上人群拥挤，
来去匆匆，步履不停；
街角处人们聚集，
轻声窃窃私语，
太阳穴爬满了汗珠，
仍继续他们认真的谈话。
就像黑色的大西洋洋流席卷而来
冲刷着荒无人烟的新大陆海岸，
他们猛击着州议会会场，
他们狂奔着涌向大门；
这些声音交汇混杂
构成一首深邃的协奏曲，

安静的栗树街
渐渐被各种声音充斥演变成骚动。
“他们会行动吗？”“他们敢吗？”
“谁说的？”“有什么新闻？”
“亚当斯怎么样？”“谢尔曼呢？”
“噢，上帝保证他们不会拒绝！”
“让一让！”“让我靠近点！”
“我快窒息了。”“窒息，那么：
当国家的命运危在旦夕，
我们没有时间考虑个人！”
所以他们冲击大门，
有男人和女人，也有女仆和孩子；
七月，天空中艳阳高照
俯视一切，露出微笑，
相同的太阳曾见证斯巴达人
为了国家，徒劳地抛洒热血，
而现在目睹了自由的灵魂
所有未被打倒的人又重新站起。
在那高高的尖塔之上
坐着一位敲钟人，年长，白发；
他厌倦了专制者
摇动手中的铁杖；
他端坐着，一只手时刻准备着
敲响钟，
一旦他的目光捕捉到了信号
便会将这一惊人的好消息向全世界宣告。
看！快看！密密的人群人头攒动
排列在长长的延长线上，
大门边上的男孩
张望着准备传达这个信号！
高高举起他的小手，

徐徐微风拂过他的头发，
听！一个低沉、清晰的声音，
他年轻的声音撕裂空气。
人们喧嚣的低吟声渐渐平息，
倾听着男孩强劲且兴奋的哭喊声！
“铃声！”他大声喊道，“铃声！爷爷！铃声！噢，这是自由之声！”
很快，在信号台，
年迈的敲钟人举起他的手，
接着，传达出这个好消息，
大地充满铜铃声，仿佛美妙的音乐。
他们高喊欢呼！多么高兴！
古老的钟声响彻天空，
自由的铿锵声撼动着，
渐渐沸腾的特拉华州！篝火和火炬
照亮了宁静的黑夜，
如凤凰般，浴火重生，
光明的自由冉冉升起！
那座古老的议会会场钟声沉默，
铜铃声现在也安静了下来，
但革命的精神已被唤醒
尽管依旧年幼。
当我们与微笑的晨光相遇
在七月四日那天。
我们将永远铭记敲钟人，
是他，扭转了天地，
敲响了独立的钟声，
上帝啊，独立之魂将世代留存！

（节选）

Dedication of the Washington Monument

No sum could now be made of Washington's character which would not exhaust language of its tributes and repeat virtue by all her names. No sum could be made of his achievements which would not unfold the history of his country and its institutions, the history of his age and its progress, the history of man and his destiny to be free. But whether character or achievement be regarded, the riches before us only expose the poverty of praise.

So clear was he in his great office that no ideal of the leader or ruler can be formed that does not shrink by the side of the reality. And so has he impressed himself upon the minds of men, that no man can justly aspire to be the chief of a great free people who does not adopt his principles and emulate his example. We look with amazement on such eccentric characters as Alexander, Casar, Cromwell, Frederick, and Napoleon, but when Washington's face rises before us, instinctively mankind exclaims, "This is the man for nations to trust and reverence and for rulers to follow."

Drawing his sword from patriotic impulse, without ambition and without malice, he wielded it without vindictiveness and sheathed it without reproach. All that humanity could conceive he did to suppress the cruelties of war and soothe its sorrows. He never struck a coward's blow. To him age, infancy, and helplessness were ever sacred. He tolerated no extremity unless to curb the excesses of his enemy, and he never poisoned the sting of defeat by the exultation of the conqueror.

Peace he welcomed as a heaven-sent herald of friendship; and no country has given him greater honor than that which he defeated; for England has been glad to claim him as the scion of her blood, and proud, like our sister American States, to divide with Virginia the honor of producing him.

Grand and manifold as were its phases, there is yet no difficulty in understanding the character of Washington. He was no Veiled Prophet.

He never acted a part. Simple, natural, and unaffected, his life lies before us, a fair and open manuscript. He disdained the arts that wrap power in mystery in order to magnify it. He practised the profound diplomacy of truthful speech, the consummate tact of direct attention.

Looking ever to the All-Wise Disposer of events, he relied on that Providence which helps men, by giving them high hearts and hopes, to help themselves with the means that their Creator has put at their service. There was no infirmity in his conduct over which charity must fling its veil; no taint of selfishness from which purity averts its gaze; no dark recess of intrigue that must be lit up with colored panegyric; no subterranean passage to be trod in trembling lest there be stirred the ghost of a buried crime.

A true son of nature was George Washington——of nature in her brightest intelligence and noblest mold; and the difficulty, if such there be, in comprehending him, is only that of reviewing from a single standpoint the vast procession of those civil and military achievements which filled nearly half a century of his life, and of realizing the magnitude of those qualities which were requisite to their performance; the difficulty of fashioning in our minds a pedestal broad enough to bear the towering figure, whose greatness is diminished by nothing but the perfection of its proportions.

If his exterior——in calm, grave, and resolute repose——ever impressed the casual observer as austere and cold, it was only because that observer did not reflect that no great heart like Washington's could have lived unbroken unless bound by iron nerves in an iron frame. The Commander of Armies, the Chief of a People, the Hope of Nations, could not wear his heart upon his sleeve; and yet his sternest will could not conceal its high and warm pulsations.

Under the enemy's guns at Boston he did not forget to instruct his agent to administer generously of charity to his needy neighbors at home. The sufferings of women and children thrown adrift by war, and of his bleeding comrades, pierced his soul. And the moist eye and trembling voice with which he bade farewell to his veterans bespoke the underlying tenderness of his nature even as the storm wind makes music in its undertones.

When Marathon had been fought and Greece kept free, each of the victorious generals voted himself to be first in honor, but all agreed that Miltiades was second. When the most memorable struggle for the rights of human nature of which time holds record was thus happily concluded in the monument of their preservation, whoever else was second, unanimous acclaim declared that Washington was first.

Nor in that struggle alone does he stand foremost. In the name of the people of the United States, their President, their Senators, their Representatives, and their Judges do crown today with the grandest crown that veneration has ever lifted to the brow of glory, him whom Virginia gave to America, whom America has given to the world and to the ages, and whom mankind with universal suffrage has proclaimed the foremost of the founders of the empire in the first degree of greatness; whom liberty herself has anointed as the first citizen in the great Republic of Humanity.

(John Warwick Daniel)

译文

华盛顿纪念碑献词

若不去穷尽所有致敬的语言，若不去说尽所有美德的名字，我们就形容不出华盛顿高尚的人格。若不去翻开他的国家的历史，看清其体制的来龙去脉；若不去翻开他的时代的历史，看清其前进的步步艰难；若不去翻开人类的历史，看清其迈向自由的曲折命运，我们就形容不出华盛顿取得的成就。然而，无论是考虑其人格还是考虑其成就，他所呈现在我们面前的财富只能暴露出我们语言赞美的贫乏。

他虽身居高位，但两袖清风。现实中，没有哪个领导人或统治者的形象被塑造得如此毫无瑕疵。他在人类的思想上刻下了自己深深的印记，以至于没有谁会只想着成为一个伟大自由民族的领袖，而不去接纳他的准则，不去效仿他的榜样。我们用惊叹的目光看待那些如亚历山大、凯撒克伦威尔、弗雷德里克及拿破仑一样性格独特的人物，但当华盛顿的面孔浮现在我们面前时，人类发自内心地大声宣告："这就是国民信任尊重而统治者竞相追随的人！"

出于爱国的激情，他拔出权力之剑，没有半点野心，不存丝毫祸心。他掌权用剑时，心中没有报复之情；他还剑入鞘时，心中没有怨怼之情。他做了人类所能想到的一切去制止残酷的战争，并抚平由它带来的悲痛。他从没有打过一场懦夫般的仗。对他来说，老人、婴儿和无助之人在任何时候都是值得尊重的。他忍辱负重，直到敌人放肆的行为得到遏制；他尊重他人，从不以征服者的得意戳失败者的痛处。

他欢迎和平，将它视为上天赐予的友谊大使。他打败了英国，然而没有哪个国家比英国赋予他的荣耀更高，因为她曾愉悦地宣称他是她的血脉后裔，并像我们的姐妹美国各州一样，自豪地与弗吉尼亚分享孕育他的荣耀。

虽然华盛顿性格在各个面上都显得伟大而多元，但了解起来却并不困难。他不是什么蒙着面纱的神秘先知，他也从不扮演这样的角色。他的生活像一本公开而清晰的手稿般摊开在我们面前，简单、自然，毫无掩饰。他不屑于去做那些用神秘感包装以夸大其神奇力量的行为。他诚实的言谈之下包含着诚实的行为，他的关怀中蕴藏着无上的机智。

在那些他曾经指望得上的众神中，他信赖的是帮助人类的神灵。它赋予人类高尚的心灵和崇高的希望，令他们用造物主赐予他们的方法自力更生。他的品行中，没有掩藏的弱点需要仁慈揭开它的面纱；没有自私的污点需要纯洁避开它的目光；没有阴谋的黑洞需要以文过饰非的颂词来照亮；没有隐藏的道路需要在颤抖中踏过，唯恐惊动被掩埋罪行的幽灵。

乔治·华盛顿是人类天性的赤子，他具备这种天性最超群的智慧和最高贵的人格。如果理解他确实存在什么难题的话，那就是我们难以站在个人的立场去回顾他一生中在近半个世纪里取得的内政及军事上的成就，难以去了解那些成就背后所必需的品质的重要性，难以在我们的思想中给这位高不可攀的伟人足够高的位置。没有什么可以削弱他的伟大，除了伟大自身的完美程度。

如果他所表现出来的镇定、严肃和彻底的平静曾经给旁观者留下严厉、冷酷的印象的话，那只是因为旁观者没有深入思考，如果不覆盖着钢铁的外衣，不束缚于坚韧的意志，没有哪颗心灵能像华盛顿一般坚不可摧。身为军队的统帅、人民的领袖和民族的希望，他不可能让感情外露。但是，他坚定至极的意志并不能掩盖其崇高温暖的情感悸动。

在波士顿敌军的枪口下，他也没有忘记指示他的代理人给家乡贫穷的邻居们送上慷慨的捐助。因战争而流浪的妇女儿童以及流着鲜血的战友所遭受的苦难撕扯他的灵魂。当他向老兵们告别时，那湿润的眼眶和颤抖的声音显示出他天性中深藏的温柔，正如狂风也会低声吟唱。

马拉松之战胜利后，希腊保住了国家的独立。虽然每一名打了胜仗的将军都认为自己才是最大的功臣，但他们都一致同意米太亚得是第二号功臣。与此相似的是，时光会铭记这场最值得纪念的斗争，它捍卫了人类天然的权利，从纪念这些权利保护的丰碑中我们可以轻松地断定，无论谁是第二号功臣，众口一词的赞美已经表明华盛顿是最大的功臣。

在这场斗争中，他不是独自一人站在最前方。以美国人民的名义，他们的总统、参议员、议员和法官确实在以最辉煌的王冠为他加冕——他们用尊敬将它举起到光荣的眉梢。他是弗吉尼亚给予美国的，是美国给予世界和时代的；他是拥有普选权的公民公开承认的伟大开国元勋中的第一名，是自由本身所选定的伟大人类共和国中的首席公民。

（约翰·沃里克·丹尼尔）

作者介绍

约翰·沃里克·丹尼尔1842年出生于弗吉尼亚的林奇堡。他在南北战争期间服役于北弗吉尼亚联盟军，此后在出生地林奇堡践习司法。他曾服务于弗吉尼亚的参议院和众议院以及美国的参议院和众议院。这是一篇发表于1885年2月21日华盛顿纪念碑的落成典礼上的演说词，选自《世界著名演说集》。该书由查尔斯·莫里斯选辑，由费城的约翰·C. 温斯顿公司出版。

朗读

The Washington Monument

Straight soars to heaven the white magnificence,
Free as man's thought, high as one lonely name;
True image of his soul,——serene, immense,
Mightiest of monuments and mightiest fame.

译文

华盛顿纪念碑

白色的华表高耸入云，
自由如人类的思想，崇高如孤独的姓名；
他灵魂的真身安详而浩渺，
不巧的丰碑传颂不朽的声名。

预习

beaten /ˈbiːtn/ 被击败的

moderate /ˈmɑːdərət/ 适度的

staid /steɪd/ 保守的

sublunary /sʌbˈluːnərɪ/ 世俗的

translate /trænsˈleɪt/ 解释

Dickens

Let me speak today of Dickens in his youth. How well I recall the bleak winter evening in 1842 when I first saw the handsome, glowing face of the young man who was even then famous over half the globe! He came bounding into the Tremont House, fresh from the steamer that had brought him to our shores, and his cheery voice rang through the hall, as he gave a quick glance at the new scenes opening upon him, in a strange land.

"Here we are!" he shouted, as the lights burst upon the merry party just entering the house, and several gentlemen came forward to greet him. Ah, how happy and buoyant he was then! Young, handsome, almost worshiped for his genius, belted round by such troops of friends as rarely ever man had, coming to a new country to make new conquests of fame and honor——surely it was a sight long to be remembered, and never wholly to be forgotten.

The splendor of his endowments and the personal interest he had won to himself called forth all the enthusiasm of old and young America, and I am glad to have been among the first to witness his arrival. You ask me what was his appearance as he ran, or rather flew up the steps of the hotel, and sprang into the hall. He seemed all on fire with curiosity, and alive as I never saw mortal before.

From top to toe every fibre of his body was unrestrained and alert. What vigor, what keenness, what freshness of spirit, possessed him! He laughed all over, and did not care who heard him! He seemed like the Emperor of Cheerfulness on a cruise of pleasure, determined to conquer a realm or two of fun every hour of his overflowing existence. That night impressed itself on my memory for all time, so far as I am concerned with things sublunary.

It was Dickens, the true "Boz" in flesh and blood, who stood before us at last, and with my companions, three or four lads of my own age, I determined to sit up late that night. None of us then, of course, had the honor of an acquaintance with the delightful stranger, and I little thought that I should afterwards come to know him in the beaten way of friendship, and live with him day after day in years far distant; that I should ever be so near to him that he would reveal to me his joys and his sorrows, and thus that I should learn the story of his life from his own lips.

About midnight on that eventful landing,"Boz,"——everybody called him "Boz" in those days,——having finished his supper, came down into the office of the hotel, and, joining the young Earl of M——, his fellow-voyager, sallied out for a first look at Boston streets. It was a stinging night, and the moon was at the full. Every object stood out white and glittering, and "Boz" muffled up in a shaggy fur coat, ran over the shining frozen snow, wisely keeping the middle of the street for the most part. We boys followed cautiously behind, but near enough not to lose any of the fun. Dickens kept up one continual shout of laughter as he went rapidly forward, reading the signs on the shops, and observing the "architecture" of the new country into which they had dropped as if from the clouds.

The great event of Boz's first visit to Boston was the dinner of welcome tendered to him by the young men of the city. It is idle to attempt much talk about the banquet given on that Monday night in February, twenty-nine years ago. Papanti's Hall was the scene of that festivity. It was a glorious episode in all our lives, and whoever was not there has suffered a loss not easy to estimate.

We younger members of that dinner-party sat in the seventh heaven of happiness, and were translated into other spheres. Accidentally, of course, I had a seat just in front of the honored guest; saw him take a pinch of snuff out of Washington Allston's box, and heard him joke with old President Quincy. Was there ever such night before in our staid city? Did ever mortal preside with such felicitous success as did Mr. Quincy?

How he went with his delicious compliments to our guest! How he reveled in quotations from "Pickwick" and "Oliver Twist" and "The Curiosity Shop"! And how admirably he closed his speech of welcome, calling up the young author amid a perfect volley of applause! "Health, Happiness, and a Hearty Welcome to Charles Dickens!" I can see and hear Mr. Quincy now, as he spoke the words. Were ever heard such cheers before?

And when Dickens stood up at last to answer for himself, so fresh and so handsome, with his beautiful eyes moist with feeling, and his whole frame aglow with excitement, how we did hurrah, we young fellows! Trust me, it was a great night; and we must have made a mighty noise at our end of the table, for I remember frequent messages came down to us from the "Choir" begging that we would hold up a little and moderate if possible the rapture of our applause.

译文

狄更斯

今天，让我和大家聊一聊年轻的狄更斯吧！我仍清楚地记得，在1842年一个寒冷的冬日夜晚，我第一次见到了狄更斯，他是个帅气的小伙子，脸上容光焕发，那时的他已经红透了半个世界。他乘坐轮船来到我们国家，刚从船上下来，就直奔特里蒙特饭店，他快乐的声音响彻整个大厅，同时他匆匆扫了一眼面前这陌生土地上的新环境。

“我们来啦！”狄更斯一走进饭店就大声喊道，欢乐的派对上瞬间灯火通明，还有几位绅士前来迎接他。瞧！他多么风光啊！那时的狄更斯朝气蓬勃，英俊潇洒，才华横溢，交际广泛，朋友之多极为罕见，他来到一个新的国家，希望在这儿也能大受欢迎，收获更多的荣光——这个场景绝对让人铭记一生，永世不忘。

狄更斯天资聪颖，拥有独特的人格魅力，这燃起了美国老老少少对他的热情，而我因能成为首批迎接他的人之一备感荣幸。狄更斯一路急行，跨上台阶，蹦蹦跳跳地进入大厅，对于这一幕，我仍记忆犹新。当时，他非常兴奋，对周围充满好奇，我从没见过如此活跃的人。

狄更斯全身上下，从头顶到脚趾，每个细胞都是那么飞扬放纵、灵活机敏。多么活力四射！多么激情澎湃！多么精神焕发！他四处大笑，毫不在意谁会听见！他看上去就像是正在快乐巡游的喜剧之王，拥有着强大的气场，决心要时时刻刻以他激情四溢的存在去征服一两块乐土。只要我还存于世间，那个夜晚就一直深深刻在我的脑海里。

那天晚上，我和三四个同龄的夫人聚在一起，坐在我们对面的正是狄更斯，真的是那位笔名叫“博兹”的大作家，于是我决定多坐一会儿。当然，那时我们还没有荣幸到能结识这位眉开眼笑的陌生人，未曾想过会在往后的时光里，会以这种不同寻常的方式结下友谊，并在很远的将来和他日日生活在一起，也未曾想过能和他如此亲密，听他吐露所有的快乐悲伤，更没有想到我会因此从他口中了解他的人生故事。

那个时候，大家都以“博兹”来称呼狄更斯。就在他到来那天的午夜，“博兹”吃完夜宵，走下楼，来到了酒店大堂，和他的同行者M伯爵会面，一起出发，这是他们俩第一次欣赏波士顿的街景。那是一个激情澎湃的夜晚，月色正满，白雪覆盖了一切，闪闪发光，在这冰天雪地里，“博兹”披着一件松垮垮的毛皮大衣，在马路中央的冰雪上尽情奔跑。我们虽然小心翼翼地跟在后面，但却靠得足够近，不至于错失任何一件趣事。狄更斯一边笑个不停，一边飞快地跑着，阅读沿街商铺的店标，观察街上的“建筑”。在这个崭新的国度里，对于他而言，一切都很神奇。

博兹第一次来到波士顿时，让他印象最深刻的一件事情，是二月份的一个星期一的夜晚，有一群年轻小伙子在帕潘提斯会所为他准备了欢迎晚宴。那是二十九年之前，再多的文字都无法形容那场晚宴，那是我们一生当中最美妙的经历，对于那些没能参加的人来说，绝对是一个巨大的损失。

在那场晚宴中，我们年轻一辈宛如身处极乐世界一般，换句话说，我们在那儿度过了最难忘的时光。我偶然发现坐在我身后的，是一位尊贵的客人。他从华盛顿·奥尔斯顿的箱子里拿出一小撮鼻烟，还拿前总统昆西开玩笑。在这座死气沉沉的小镇里，我们有过这样的夜晚吗？我们这种老百姓，有过与昆西共享晚宴的机会吗？

他多么用心地赞美我们的客人啊！他引用了多少《匹克威客》《雾都孤儿》和《老古玩店》里的名句啊！他是多么出色地讲完了欢迎词，在一阵雷鸣般的掌声中请出了这名年轻的作家，“祝在座的各位身体健康，万事如意。让我们衷心欢迎查尔斯·狄更斯！”昆西说这句话的场景现在仍历历在目，我们曾经听过如此激昂的致辞吗？

最后，狄更斯起身发言。欣喜若狂，他美丽的眼睛里饱含深情，朝气蓬勃，潇洒英俊，浑身燃烧着激情。我们这帮年轻人是多么兴奋啊！我想我们一定是制造了极为巨大的噪音，因为我记得，经常有来自合唱队的口信，请求我们收敛一点，尽量节制鼓掌时的狂热激情。相信我，那个夜晚真的很精彩！

（詹姆斯·托马斯·菲尔兹）

Pocahontas

At last I was ushered into the presence of Powhatan, and found him seated before a fire, on a seat somewhat resembling a bedstead, covered with a great robe made of raccoon-skins, with all the tails hanging thereto.

On either hand did sit a young wench of sixteen or eighteen years, and along each side of the house were two rows of men, and behind them as many women, all with their heads and shoulders painted red; many of their heads were bedecked with the white down of birds, but every one wore something in the hair, and great chains of white beads about necks.

When I made my entrance before the king, all the people gave a great shout, and, to do me honor, the Queen of Appamatuck was appointed to bring me water wherewith. I might wash my hands, and another brought me a bunch of feathers wherewith to dry them, instead of a towel; and then they feasted me in the best manner they could; which, after all, was but barbarous.

Then they held a great consultation about me, which I could not altogether understand, but the conclusion was that I was to die; a fate which, in truth, was near coming to pass, but for God's goodness, as you shall hear. And, indeed, it did seem as if my last hour was at hand, for as many of the savages as could laid hold of me, and, having brought two great stones, which they placed before Powhatan, they dragged me to them, and laid my head thereon, making ready with their clubs to beat out my brains.

But now, mark the mercy of God towards me when in this evil case, for surely it was his handiwork. Their clubs were raised, and in another moment I should have been dead, when Pocahontas, the king's dearest daughter, finding no entreaties could prevail to save me, darted forward, and, taking my head in her arms, laid her own upon it, and thus prevented my death. She thus claimed me as her own, and for her sake Powhatan was contented that I should live, and that I should henceforth spend my time in making him hatchets and bell and beads and copper ornaments for Pocahontas. They made no manner of doubt but that I could make all these things, for in that country the men are of all handicrafts; nay, even the king himself will make his own robes, shoes, bows and arrows, or pots; plant, hunt, and do the same as his subjects.

(Captain John Smith)

译文

宝嘉康蒂

最终，我还是被带到了波瓦坦的面前，他正坐在火炉旁，而他坐的那个椅子倒是有点像个床架，铺着一大块浣熊皮制成的毯子，下摆随意地垂着。

另一边坐了个姑娘，看着十六或十八岁的样子。屋子的两边站着两列男人，他们的后面还有些女人。这些人的头和肩部都被染成了红色，有许多人头上还装饰着白色的鸟毛；不过，他们每个人的头发上都戴着点什么，脖子上也都戴着白色的项链。

我还没走到国王面前，所有人都欢呼起来向我致敬。阿波马托克斯的王后给我拿了些水用来洗手，另一个人给我拿了束羽毛代替毛巾用来把手擦干。他们用最讲究的方式款待了我——虽然看起来有点野蛮。

之后他们就我的问题，进行了一番热烈的讨论，虽然我基本不懂他们说的话，但我知道最终的结论无非就是我被判了死刑，说真的，就像是一种快要到来的宿命，而我只因为上帝的一点垂怜，才听见了死亡的脚步声。事实上，我的时间似乎是真的所剩无几了。这些野蛮的家伙蜂拥而上，一把抓住我，然后拿了两个大石头放在了波瓦坦面前，他们把我拖到石头边，把我的头摁在上面，做好了随时让我的脑袋开花的准备。

但就在这一切发生之际，上帝向我显示了慈悲，阻止了惨剧的发生——这件事无疑就是他的手笔。他们高高举起了棍棒，转瞬之间我将必死无疑。这时，波瓦坦最疼爱的女儿宝嘉康蒂发现想靠劝说保我一命毫无可能，于是她飞奔到我身旁，抱住我的脑袋，用自己的身体挡在前面，让我免于脑袋开花，并声称我是她的。因为她，波瓦坦决定让我活着，要我从今而后，所有的时间将用来为他制作舱门、门铃、床，为宝嘉康蒂制作铜饰品。他们毫不怀疑我能制作所有这些东西，因为这个国家的男人手艺都很精巧。不仅如此，就连国王也和他的臣民一样，种植、打猎，自己制作长袍、鞋子、弓箭和水壶。

（约翰·史密斯上校）

作者介绍

对美国的学生们而言，约翰·史密斯上校可是个很熟悉的名字，他们对约翰·史密斯上校生平的了解，基本都是来自他自己的作品。他出生于英格兰，就读于公立学校。后来，他在贸易行业当学徒，但在十五岁那年，在一次国外冒险时他逃跑了。在英国与其他国家常年战争期间，他被抓去当了奴隶。不过很快，他就逃到了俄罗斯，之后又回到了英格兰，加入了英国去美洲的远征军，在弗吉尼亚建立了殖民地。这一年是1606年，史密斯上校刚满二十七岁。文内印第安首领波瓦坦的女儿宝嘉康蒂救史密斯的事情发生在殖民地刚建立的时候，本文选自史密斯上校《弗吉尼亚简史》中对该事件的自述。

Webster's School Days

In 1791, when Daniel had just turned nine, a new honor, which deeply affected his later career, came to his father. The many evidences of confidence and esteem a gratified community had bestowed on Ebenezer Webster in the dark days of the Revolution did not cease with the war. The leader in strife remained a leader in peace, was sent year after year first to one and then to the other branch of the Assembly, was a delegate to the convention which ratified the Federal Constitution, and finally, in 1791, was placed on the bench of the Court of Common Pleas for the county in which he resided.

These courts were composed of a presiding judge, always an able lawyer, and of two side justices, usually laymen of hard common sense and sterling integrity; and it was to one of these side justiceships that Ebenezer Webster was appointed. The office was one of honor and dignity, and carried with it an annual salary of several hundred dollars, just enough to enable the father to go on with his long meditated plan for the education of Daniel.

Of his five sons, Ebenezer, David, and Joseph had grown to manhood, were settled in life, and long past the school age. To educate the two remaining, Ezekiel and Daniel, was beyond his means. But if his longing to see at least one son rise above the humble calling of a farmer was to be gratified, it must be one of these, and to choose which cost the father a bitter struggle. He met it with the unfaltering courage that marked the man, made his decision, and one day in 1795 announced his determination.

"On a hot day in July," said Webster, describing the scene many years later, "it must have been in one of the years of Washington's administration, I was making hay with my father, just where I now see a remaining elm-tree. About the middle of the forenoon the Hon. Abiel Foster, M.C., who lived in Canterbury, six miles off, called at the house and came into the field to see my father. When he was gone, my father called me to him and we sat down beneath the elm.

"He said, 'My son, that is a worthy man; he is a member of Congress; he goes to Philadelphia and gets six dollars a day, while I toil here. It is because he had an education which I never had. If I had had his education, I should have been in Philadelphia in his place. I came near it as it was. But I missed it, and now I must work here.'

"'My dear father,' said I, 'you shall not work; brother and I will work for you, and we will wear our hands out, and you shall rest.' And I remember to have cried, and I cry now at the recollection.

"'My child,' said he, 'it is of no importance to me. I now live but for my children. I could not give your elder brothers the advantages of knowledge, but I can do something for you. Exert yourself, improve your opportunities, learn, learn, and when I am gone you will not need to go through the hardships which I have undergone, and which have made me an old man before my time.'"

Almost a year passed, however, before the plan so long cherished was fairly started, and Daniel, dressed in a brand-new, home-made suit and astride a side-saddle, rode with his father to Exeter to be entered at the famous academy founded by John Phillips. The principal then and forty years thereafter was Dr. Benjamin Abbot, one of the greatest teachers our country has yet produced. As the doctor was ill, the duty of examining the new pupil fell to Joseph S. Buckminster, then an usher at the academy, but destined to influence strongly the religious life of New England.

It was the custom of the doctor, we are told, to conduct the examination of applicants with pompous ceremony, and that, imitating him, young Buckminster summoned Webster to his presence, put on his hat, and said, "Well, sir, what is your age?"

"Fourteen," was the reply.

"Take this Bible, my lad, and read that chapter."

Young Webster was equal to the test, and read the whole passage to the end in a voice and with a fervor such as Master Buckminster had never listened to before.

"Young man," said he, "you are qualified to enter this institution," and no more questions were put to him.

The voice and manner so famous in later life were even then strikingly manifest. But one other gift of nature still lay dormant——he could not declaim. Long after he had become the greatest orator of the day, he said to a friend, "I could not speak before the school. Many a piece did I commit to memory and rehearse in my room over and over again, but when the day came, and the school-master called my name, and I saw all eyes turned upon my seat, I could not raise myself from it. When the occasion was over, I went home and wept bitter tears of mortification."

His stay at the academy was short. At the close of the year he was at home again, teaching a small class of boys and girls at his uncle's house on the North Road, and while so engaged he made the acquaintance of the Rev. Samuel Wood, minister at Boscawen. Dr. Wood was also an educator, and took charge of Webster's Latin. A young senior from Dartmouth taught him some Greek, and in August, 1797, Webster became a freshman in Dartmouth College.

He had now reached a turning point in his career. Save during the nine months spent at Phillips Exeter, he had never been so far from home, had never been so completely thrown upon his own resources, nor brought in close contact with so many young men of his own age and generation. He was free to make of himself what he pleased. He read widely in English literature and in history, acquired a familiarity with Latin and with Latin authors, never forgot anything once acquired, was always able to display his knowledge to the best advantage, was in no sense a student or a scholar, but became the best-informed man in college, and impressed all who met him as a youth of uncommon parts, with promise of being a great man.

"So much as I read," says he, "I made my own. When a half-hour, or an hour at most, had elapsed, I closed my book, and thought over what I had read. If there was anything peculiarly interesting or striking in the passage, I endeavored to recall it and lay it up in memory, and commonly could effect my object. Then if, in debate or conversation afterward, any subject came up on which I had read something, I could talk very easily so far as I had read, and there I was careful to stop."

As time passed, this wide reading stood him in good stead, and for a year he paid his board by aiding in editing a weekly newspaper for which he made selections from books and contemporary publications, now and then writing a few paragraphs himself. Nor were his physical characteristics less striking. College-mates never forgot his deep-set eyes, the solemn tones of his voice, the dignity of his carriage, and, above all, his eloquence. The old shyness that tormented him so at the academy was gone. At last the greatest of his natural gifts was developing rapidly and was used freely.

(John Bach McMaster, adapted)

译文

韦伯斯特的学校岁月

1791年，丹尼尔的父亲在他刚满九岁时得到了一份新的殊荣，而这也深深地影响了小丹尼尔日后的人生。在独立战争的黑暗岁月中，埃比尼泽·韦伯斯特建立起了自信和能够聚拢一群人的领导力。这些能力并没有随着战争的结束而消失。如同在斗争时期那样，他在和平时期依然是个领导者，一年年任职于州议会众议院不同的部门。他曾作为代表参加了制定联邦宪法的大会，并最终于1791年在他居住的郡就任民事上诉法庭法官。

这些法院一般由一名能干的律师担任首席法官，再配上两名助理法官，他们通常是那些对于常理一丝不苟而又品格正直的外行人。埃比尼泽·韦伯斯特被任命为的正是这样的助理法官。这是一个光荣而又高贵的职位，每年有七百美元的收入，刚好够埃比尼泽·韦伯斯特实行那个已经考虑了很久的丹尼尔教育计划。

他五个儿子中，埃比尼泽、大卫和约瑟夫已经长大成人，各自的生活已经安顿下来了，且早已过了上学的年龄，而教育其余两个孩子——伊齐基尔和丹尼尔，则超出了他的财力所及。但如果他对至少有一个儿子要摆脱农夫这一卑微职业的渴望能够实现的话，那就必定是这两人中的一个。然而，选择哪一个着实让父亲苦恼地纠结了一阵，他最终以自己那坚定的勇气做出了决定，并在1795年的某一天宣布了他的决定。

“在一个七月的大热天，”韦伯斯特多年后如此描述那个场景，“肯定是在华盛顿总统任职的某一年。我和父亲一起晒着干草。那个地方有一棵榆树。大约是上午过半时，家住一万米外坎特伯雷的国会议员埃比尔·福斯特访问了我家并到田里来找我的父亲。他走后父亲将我叫到身边，我们便在榆树下坐了下来。

“他说：‘我的孩子，那是一个可敬的人。他是国会的一员，去费城一天可以赚到六美元，而我只能在这里劳作，这是因为他受过了我所没有受过的教育。如果我接受那样的教育，那我就会在费城干他所干的活。我曾经有机会那么做，但我错过了，所以现在只能在这里工作。’

“‘亲爱的父亲，’我说道，‘你不用干活了，我和哥哥们会替你干，而且尽全力干，那样你就可以休息了。’我记得那时我哭了，现在回想起这件事还是会哭。

“‘孩子，’他说道，‘这对我来说不重要，我现在只是为孩子们而活着。我没能给予你的哥哥们知识上的优势，但我可以为你做点什么。努力吧，改善你的机遇，学习再学习。那样的话，当我离开人世时，你就不用再遭受我所吃过的苦，那让我未老先衰的苦。’”

然而直到差不多一年后，这个酝酿长久的计划才得以正式实施。丹尼尔穿着家里缝制的崭新衣服，跨坐在侧鞍上同父亲一起骑马去了埃克塞特一所由约翰·菲利普斯创立的著名高中。从那个时候开始乃至以后的四十年间，这所学校的校长都是本杰明·阿博特博士，他是美国当时培养出来的最伟大的教师之一。由于博士生病了，审核入学新生的任务被交给了当时还是助理教员的约瑟夫·S. 巴克明斯特，但他注定会对新英格兰的宗教生活产生重大影响。

我们被告知，按照博士的惯例，申请者会经过繁杂环节的测试。随后，年轻的巴克明斯特效仿博士那样，把韦伯斯特叫到跟前，戴上帽子对他说道：“先生，你几岁了？”

“十四岁。”他回答。

“我的孩子，请拿着这本圣经朗读那一章节。”

年轻的韦伯斯特很适合这样的考试，他以一种巴克明斯特从来没有听到过的声音满含热情地读完了整篇文章。

他说："年轻人，你被这所学院录取了。"他没有被问到更多的问题。

韦伯斯特日后那著名的声音和仪态在此刻已经明显地展现了出来。但他的另一个天赋还没有萌发——他还无法大声朗诵。他在成为当时最伟大的演说家之一很久之后对朋友说过："我无法在学校的众人面前演说。好几次我已经牢牢记住了内容，并事先在自己的房间里排练了一遍又一遍。但到了当天，学校里的先生叫我名字时，看到所有的眼睛转向我的座位，我连站都站不起来。这一切结束、回到了家中后，我会为之屈辱而流下痛苦的眼泪。"

他在高中学校里待的时间很短，年末时又回到了家中，在北路他叔叔的家中教一个小班级的孩子们。在忙碌中他结识了博斯考恩的主持牧师塞缪尔·伍德。伍德博士也是个教育家，他教了韦伯斯特拉丁文。一个来自达特茅斯的年轻学长教了他一点希腊文。1797年8月，韦伯斯特成了达特茅斯学院的一名新生。

他现在迎来了生涯中的一个转折点。除了在菲利普斯埃克塞特度过的九个月，他从来没有离家如此遥远，从来没有如此彻底地自力更生；从来没有如此密切地和那些年轻的同龄人进行交流，他可以自由地做想做的事。他广泛地阅读了英国文学和历史并精通了拉丁文，熟悉了那些拉丁文作者。他一旦学会了什么就不再会遗忘，总是能够充分地展现自己的学识。他已经不只是一个学生或是一个学者，而是学院里最有学识的人。每一个遇到他的人都会留下深刻印象，认为他将来必成大器。

"我读了很多，并把它们转化为了自己的东西，"他说道，"每读半小时或者最多一小时后，我会合上书重新考虑一下我所读到的内容。如果文章中有什么特别有趣或惊人的东西，我会尽力回忆并把它保留在记忆中，而它们常常会对我的思想产生影响。如果在以后的辩论探讨中出现了我曾阅读过的主题，只要是我读到过的，我就可以非常轻松地发表意见，而对于别的我就会谨慎地闭口不谈。"

随着时间的流逝，这种广泛的阅读对他大有裨益。有一年他曾替一家周报做编辑，从书中和当时的刊物中摘录节选文章给它供稿，同时自己也不时写一些文章，以此来支付膳宿费用。他的模样同样引人注目，大学同学们永远不会忘记他那深陷的双眼、庄重的声调、高贵的举止，还有那最突出的雄辩的口才。高中阶段折磨着他的那种旧日的害羞已经消失了，最终那最伟大的天赋飞速发展，并能被他运用自如了。

（约翰·巴赫·麦克马斯特，有删改）

作者介绍

约翰·巴赫·麦克马斯特是一名史学家，1852年出生于纽约的布鲁克林。从纽约城市学院毕业后，他曾从事土木工程行业，并在1877年普林斯顿大学的项目中担任了指导员。1883年，他接受了宾夕法尼亚大学的美国历史教授职位。他的著述包括很多美国的历史，比如《文人本杰明·富兰克林》和《丹尼尔·韦伯斯特》。后者是由世纪公司出版的，本文正是经得作者和出版公司的慷慨允许而从此书中节选出来的。

Chapter 2

Views | 各地风物

A Louisiana Sugar Plantation of the Old Regime

The Bore plantation was situated on the left bank of the Mississippi, about six miles above New Orleans, taking as a point of departure the Cathedral, then the center of the city, and following the public road that ran along the river in all its windings. Indigo had been the principal staple of the colony, but at last a worm which attacked the plant and destroyed it, through consecutive years, was reducing to poverty and to the utmost despair the whole population.

Jean Etienne de Bore determined to make a bold experiment to save himself and his fellow citizens, and convert his indigo plantation into one of sugar cane. In these critical circumstances, he resolved to renew the attempt that had been made to manufacture sugar. He immediately prepared to go into all the expenses consequent on so costly an undertaking.

His wife warned him that her father had in former years vainly made a similar attempt. She represented that he was hazarding on the cast of a die all that remained of their means of existence; that if he failed, as was probable, he would reduce his family to hopeless poverty; that he was of an age, being over fifty years old, when fate was not to be tempted by doubtful experiments, as he could not reasonably entertain the hope of a sufficiently long life to rebuild his fortune if once completely shattered; and that he would not only expose himself to ruin, but also to a risk much more to be dreaded, that of falling into the grasp of creditors.

Friends and relatives joined their remonstrances to hers, but could not shake the strong resolve of his energetic mind. He had fully matured his plan, and was determined to sink or swim with it. Purchasing a quantity of cane from two men, who cultivated it only to sell as a dainty in the New Orleans market and to make coarse syrup, he began to plant in 1794, and to make all the other necessary preparations, and in 1795 he made a crop of sugar which sold for twelve thousand dollars, a large sum at that time.

Bore's attempt had excited the keenest interest. Many people had frequently visited him during the year to witness his preparations; gloomy predictions had been set afloat, and on the day when the grinding of the cane was to begin, a large number of the most respectable inhabitants had gathered in and about the sugar house, to be present at the failure or success of the experiment.

Would the syrup granulate? Would it be converted into sugar? The crowd waited with eager impatience for the moment when the man who watched the coction of the juice of the cane should determine whether it was ready to granulate. When the moment arrived, the stillness of death came among them; each one holding his breath, and feeling that it was a matter of ruin or prosperity for them all.

Suddenly the sugar-maker cried out with exultation, "It granulates!" Inside and outside of the building one could have heard the wonderful tidings flying from mouth to mouth, and dying in the distance, as if a hundred glad echoes were telling it to one another. Each one of the bystanders pressed forward to ascertain the fact through the evidence of his own senses, and when it could no longer be doubted, there came a shout of joy, and all flocked around Etienne de Bore, overwhelming him with congratulations and almost hugging the man.

This plantation was sagaciously and tastefully laid out for beauty and productiveness. The gardens occupied a large area, and at once astonished the eye by the magnificence of their shady avenues of orange trees. Unbroken retreats of myrtle and laurel defied the rays of the sun. Flowers of every description perfumed the air. Extensive orchards produced every fruit of which the climate was susceptible. By judicious culture there had been obtained remarkable success in producing an abundance of juicy grapes, every branch of which, however, when they began to ripen, was enveloped in a sack of wire to protect it against the depredations of the birds.

The fields were cultivated with so careful an observance of successive seasons, that there was no such thing known as short or half crop, or no crop at all. This was reserved for much later days. But under the administration of Etienne Bore, during a period of about twenty-five years from the first ebullition of a sugar kettle, in 1795, to the time of his death in 1820, every crop was regularly the same within a few hogsheads.

It was a self-sufficient little domain, exporting a good deal and importing but meagerly, so that the balance was very much in its favor. It was largely supplied with sheep and their wool, with geese, ducks, turkeys, Guinea fowls, and every variety of poultry, without stint. Eggs were gathered by the bushel. Pigeons clouded the sun, and when the small black cherries were ripe, those feathered epicures ate them voraciously.

A numerous herd of cattle, under the inspection of old Pompey and a black youngster, pastured luxuriously and grew fat. What a quantity of fresh butter, rich cheese, milk, cream, and clabber! Vast barns gorged with corn, rice, and hay, hives bursting with honey, vegetables without measure, and so luscious; a varied and liberal supply of carriages always ready for use, horses for the saddle or for driving, all glossy and sleek, and spirited mules, well fed and well curried, the pride of the field hands.

Bore had made of his estate both a farm and a plantation. Every day before dawn cart-loads departed for New Orleans with diversified produce, most of which was handed over, when it reached its destination, to two old women, Agathe and Marie, who were the occupants and the guardians of the town house of Bore.

They admirably understood the art of selling, and were well known to the whole population whose confidence they possessed. Going to market with baskets full, they generally brought them hack empty. Josephine, a handsome mulattress, with an assistant of a darker color, sold the milk and butter with wonderful rapidity, and both were back at the plantation at half-past ten in the morning, with the mail and daily papers, and whatever else they had to bring. It was clock work in everything on that plantation of the old regime.

(Charles Etienne Arthur Gayarre)

译文

路易斯安那州的老式甘蔗园

博尔的种植园位于密西西比河左岸，距离南部的新奥尔良一万米远，邻近大教堂、市中心还有沿河蜿蜒的公路。在殖民时期，靛蓝属植物曾是人们的主食，但是最终由于害虫连年的侵蚀，毁坏了植被，让民众困苦不堪，陷入绝望之中。

为了让自己和其他百姓渡过难关，简·埃蒂安·博尔曾下定决心，做一个大胆的尝试，把靛蓝种植园变为甘蔗种植园。在这个紧要关头，他又毅然决然地重拾起制糖的想法。他立刻着手准备投入全部的身家在这个耗资不小的工程上。

博尔的妻子警告他，她的父亲早些年在类似的投资上失手过。她告诉博尔，他现在正冒着失去全家赖以生存的一切的风险，一旦失败了，就很有可能把家人都推入绝望的深渊里，苦不堪言，而且他已经五十多岁了，冒不起这个风险，如果他倾家荡产了，很难想象在残烛之年他还能东山再起。若投资失利，他不但会让自己破产，更可怕的是，还会落入负债累累的险境。

尽管亲朋好友加入她的规劝中，但也无法动摇雄心勃勃的博尔，他心意已决。博尔不断完善他的计划，不管成败与否，他都下定了决心。博尔从两个男人手中买来一批甘蔗苗，那两个男人种的甘蔗不是在新奥尔良市场上作为美味出售，就是用来制作粗劣的糖浆。1794年，博尔开始种植甘蔗，并做好了完全的准备。1795年，他生产了大量的糖，并把这些糖卖了12,000美元。这在当时来说是一笔巨款了。

博尔的尝试激起了民众极大的兴趣。这一年的时间里，许多人时不时前来拜访他，看一看他的准备过程，那些不看好的声音烟消云散。在碾磨甘蔗的这一天，制糖的房子里里外外挤满了德高望重的居民，他们想见证这一尝试的成败与否。

糖浆会是颗粒状的吗？糖浆会变成白糖吗？围观的人们急不可耐地等待着这一刻，而博尔盯着沸腾的甘蔗汁，判断是否有颗粒出现。最关键的一刻来了，现场静如死灰，每个人都屏住呼吸，宛如是和他们所有人生死攸关之事一般。

突然，博尔兴高采烈地喊道：“有颗粒出现啦！”叫喊声响彻屋里屋外，老百姓将这喜讯一传十,十传百，仿佛有许多的回声，不断地将这个消息传播出去，一直到很远的地方。每一个路人都争先恐后地挤进制糖的房子里，想亲眼目睹这一切。他们验证这是真的之后，立刻欢呼雀跃。大家都围着埃蒂安·博尔，他沉浸在大家的祝贺声中，几乎要被大家抱起来。

种植园的设计精妙绝伦，高贵典雅，既富于美感，又不妨碍生产。花园占地宽敞，漫步于此，你立刻会对植满橘子树的林荫大道惊叹不已。香桃木和月桂树的遮蔽连绵不断，足以抵挡阳光。各种各样的花儿散发出香气，弥漫在空气里。无边的果园里满是各种应季的水果。在栽种者的精心培育下，种植园产出了大量的多汁葡萄，收获颇丰。不过，在每串葡萄快要成熟的时候，栽种者就要给它们套上金属丝做成的袋子，以防鸟类啄食。

园内的种植严格遵循四季变换的规律，从没有发生过低产或停产的事情，这样的传统一直延续了很久。但是，从1795年制糖成功到1820年博尔逝世的二十五年间，埃蒂安·博尔一直管理着种植园，每种作物的收成一般都固定在几大桶以内。

这不是一个自给自足的产业，种植园出口量大而进口量少，因此收入是非常可观的。种植园大量供应绵羊及羊毛、鹅、鸭子、火鸡、几内亚鸡等，总之可以无限量地供应各种家禽。鸡蛋按蒲式耳（容量单位，等于三十升）收集。鸽子多到可以遮蔽天空，每当黑色的小樱桃成熟时，这些会飞的家伙就开始肆无忌惮地开吃了。

园子里还有一位名叫庞培的老人和一位黑人小伙子，他们饲养了一群牛，让牛尽情地享用牧草，长得壮实肥硕。这样可以制出多少新鲜的黄油、美味的奶酪、牛奶、奶油和凝乳啊！宽敞的谷仓里堆满了玉米、大米、干草、富含蜂蜜的蜂巢还有无公害的蔬菜，让人感到多么愉快！还有很多随时候命、型号多样、数量充足的马车，有用于乘坐或骑用的马匹，全都油光水亮，膘肥体壮；还有生气勃勃的骡子，被喂养得很好，刷得很干净。它们是工人们的骄傲。

博尔打造的产业包括了一个种植园和一个农场。每天天还没亮，几马车品种繁多的货物就运往新奥尔良。到了目的地后，这些货物就转手给两个老夫人，一个是阿加莎，一个是玛丽，她们俩住在博尔镇上的房子里，看守着这套房子。

她们深知买卖的艺术，在老百姓中知名度很高，获得了大家的信任。每次她们带着满满的一筐商品去市场，一般都会卖空。约瑟芬是一位帅气的穆拉托人，皮肤黝黑，他很快就能卖光黄油和牛奶。于是，他们全都会在每天早上十点半回到种植园，带上信件、日报和其他需要的东西。这就是老式的种植园，一切工作都得按时进行。

（查尔斯·埃蒂安·亚瑟·加亚雷）

South Carolina and Massachusetts

I have sometimes fancied South Carolina and Massachusetts, those two illustrious and heroic sisters, instead of sitting apart, one under her palm-trees and the other under her pines, one with the hot gales from the tropics fanning her brow, and the other on the granite rocks by her ice-bound shores, meeting together, and comparing notes and stories as sisters born of the same mother compare notes and stories after a long separation. How the old estrangements, born of ignorance of each other, would have melted away.

They would have found much, these two sisters, to talk about of a later time. South Carolina would have talked of her boy, Christopher Gadsden, who, George Bancroft said, was like a mountain torrent dashing on an overshot wheel. And Massachusetts would try to trump the trick with James Otis, that flame of fire, who said he seemed to hear the prophetic song of the sibyl chanting the springtime of the new empire. They might dispute a little as to which of these two sons of theirs was the greater. I do not know how that dispute could be settled, unless by Otis's own opinion. He said that "Massachusetts sounded the trumpet. But it was owing to South Carolina that it was assented to. Had it not been for South Carolina, no Congress would have been appointed. She was all alive, and felt at every pore." So perhaps we will accept the verdict of the Massachusetts historian, George Bancroft. He said that "When we count those who above all others contributed to the great result of the Union, we are to name the inspired madman, James Otis, and the unwavering lover of his country, Christopher Gadsden." It is the same Massachusetts historian, George Bancroft, who says that "the public men of South Carolina were ever ruled by their sense of honor, and felt a stain upon it as a wound."

"Did you ever hear how those wicked boys of mine threw the tea into the harbor?" Massachusetts would say. "Oh, yes," South Carolina would answer, "but not of mine was willing to touch it. So we let it all perish in a cellar."

I should like to have a chance to hearken to their talk. Why, their gossip would almost make up the history of liberty! How they would boast to each other, as sisters do, of their children, their beautiful and brave children! How many memories they would find in common! How the warm Scotch-Irish blood would stir in their veins! How the Puritan and the Presbyterian blood would quicken their pulses as they recounted the old struggles for freedom to worship God! What stories they would have to tell each other of the day of the terrible knell from the bell of the old tower of St. Germain de L'Auxerrois, when the edict of Nantes was revoked and sounded its alarm to the Huguenot exiles who found refuge, some in South Carolina and some in Massachusetts! You have heard of James Bowdoin, of Paul Revere, and Peter Faneuil, and Andrew Sigourney. These men brought to the darkened and gloomy mind of the Puritan the sunshine of beautiful France, which South Carolina did not need. They taught our Puritans the much-needed lesson that there was something other than the snare of Satan in the song of a bird or the fragrance of a flower.

The boys and girls of South Carolina and the boys and girls of Massachusetts went to the same school in the old days. Their schoolmasters were tyranny and poverty and exile and starvation. They heard the wild music of the wolves' howl, and the savages' war-cry. They learned in that school little of the grace or the luxury of life. But they learned how to build States and how to fight tyrants.

For myself, I believe that whatever estrangements may have existed in the past, or may linger among us now, are born of ignorance and will be dispelled by knowledge. I believe that of our forty-five States there are no two who, if they could meet in the familiarity of personal intercourse, in the fullness of personal knowledge, would not only cease to entertain any bitterness, or alienation, or distrust, but each would utter to the other the words of the Jewish daughter, in that most exquisite of idylls which has come down to us almost from the beginning of time: "Entreat me not to leave thee, or to return from following after thee; for whither thou goest, I will go; and where thou lodgest, I will lodge; thy people shall be my people, and thy God my God. Where thou diest, will I die, and there will I be buried; the Lord do so to me, and more also, if aught but death part me and thee."

The American people have learned to know, as never before, the quality of the Southern stock, and to value its noble contribution to the American character; its courage in war, its attachment to home and States, its love of rural life, its capacity for great affection and generous emotion, its aptness for command; above all, its constancy, that virtue above all virtues, without which no people can long be either great or free. After all, the fruit of this vine has a flavor not to be found in other gardens. In the great and magnificent future which is before our country, you are to contribute a large share both of strength and beauty.

Let us not be misunderstood. I am not myself a descendant from the Pilgrims. Every drop of my blood through every line of descent for three centuries has come from a Puritan ancestor. I am ready to do battle for the name and fame of the Massachusetts Puritan in any field and against any antagonist. Let others, if they like, trace their lineage to Norman pirate or to robber baron. The children of the Puritan are not ashamed of him. The Puritan, as a distinct, vital, and predominant power, lived less than a century in England. He appeared early in the reign of Elizabeth, who came to the throne in 1558, and departed at the restoration of Charles II, in 1660. But in that brief period he was the preserver, aye, the creator of English freedom. By the confession of the historians who most dislike him, it is due to him that there is an English constitution. He created the modern House of Commons. That House, when he took his seat in it, was the feeble and timid instrument of despotism. When he left it, it was what it has ever since been——the strongest, freest, most venerable legislative body the world has ever seen. When he took his seat in it, it was little more than the register of the King's command. When he left it, it was the main depository of the national dignity and the national will. King and minister and prelate who stood in his way he brought to the bar and to the block. In the brief but crowded century he made the name of Englishman the highest title of honor upon the earth.

A great historian has said, "The dread of his invincible army was on all the inhabitants of the island. He placed the name of John Milton high on the illustrious roll of the great poets of the world, and the name of Oliver Cromwell highest on the roll of English sovereigns." The historian might have added that the dread of this invincible leader was on all the inhabitants of Europe.

And so, when a son of the Puritans comes to the South, when he visits the home of Rutledges and the Pinckneys and of John C. Calhoun, if there be any relationship in heroism or among the lovers of constitutional liberty, he feels that he can——Claim kindred there and have the claim allowed.

(George Frisbie Hoar, adapted)

译文

南卡莱罗纳州与马萨诸塞州

有时候，我会有这样一种幻想，南卡莱罗纳州与马萨诸塞州，这两座恢弘英勇的姐妹城，不再是遥遥相望，而是一个坐在棕榈树下，一个站在松树林中，一个带着自额前拂过的热带地区的暖风，另一个从冰封的海岸边的花岗岩上走来，相聚于此，就像是久别重逢的亲生姐妹一般，交换着彼此的印记与故事。即使她们在诞生后就未曾谋面，已有深深的隔阂，那么此时也将烟消云散。

关于以后，这对姐妹花将会有聊不完的话题。南卡莱罗纳州会谈起自己的孩子，克里斯朵夫·加兹登，乔治·班克罗夫特曾评价他是如同击打在水车上的山洪。而马萨诸塞州则会打出詹姆斯·欧蒂斯这张王牌，他就像一团火焰，人们说他似乎能听到女巫颂扬新帝国之春的预言之歌。这两姐妹或许会为谁的儿子更为出色而争辩。我不知道如何才能止息这场辩论，除非让欧蒂斯自己来做决断。他说道："马萨诸塞州听起来似乎更胜一筹。可胜者应当是南卡莱罗纳州。如果不是南卡莱罗纳州，国会就不会成立。她全身上下都是生机勃勃的。"因此，我们可能就要听一听马萨诸塞州的一位历史学家，乔治·班克罗夫特的观点。他说："当我们细数是什么造就了我们国家如今的辉煌成就的时候，我们就要呼唤出这位才华横溢的奇人，詹姆斯·欧蒂斯，以及对祖国有着深切的热爱的克里斯朵夫·加兹登。”而还是这位来自马萨诸塞州的历史学家乔治·班克罗夫特，他说道：“南卡莱罗纳州的公众人物充满荣誉感，感觉对荣誉的损害是一种耻辱。”

“你可曾听说过我那几个顽皮的孩子将茶扔进了海湾里？”马萨诸塞州说。“哦，是的，”南卡莱罗纳州回答说，“可是我的孩子没有一个愿意去碰那些东西。所以我们让它们全部腐烂在了地窖中。”

我应当找个机会倾听一下她们的谈论。为什么？因为她们的闲话几乎就构成了自由的历史！她们像姐妹一样，向对方夸耀自己的孩子，多么美丽，多么勇敢！她们将发现彼此有多少共同的回忆！有多少温暖的苏格兰与爱尔兰人的血液融合在了一起！当说起过去那些为自由崇拜上帝而做出的斗争时，又有多少清教徒与长老会教徒燃起兴奋之情！当南特赦令取消并对胡格诺派的流亡者发出警告，她们将如何对彼此叙述从圣日耳曼奥赛尔教堂传来可怕的丧钟鸣响的那一天？他们的庇护所要么在南卡莱罗纳州，要么在马萨诸塞州！你可曾听说过詹姆斯·鲍登、保罗·列维尔、皮特·法尼尔，还有安德鲁·西格尼。这些人将南卡莱罗纳州并不缺少的美丽的法国的阳光带进了清教徒黑暗混沌的思想中。他们教会了我们的清教徒急需了解的一课，那就是在鸟鸣与花香中不是只有撒旦的圈套。

昔日里南卡莱罗纳州的男孩和女孩以及马萨诸塞州的男孩女孩们上的是同样的学校。他们的老师就叫作专制，叫作贫穷，叫作流放，叫作饥饿。他们所听的狂野乐曲是狼嚎，是敌人的呐喊。他们在那所学校没有领略到一丁点儿生活的优雅与富足。但是他们学会了怎样建造我们的国家，如何抵御暴君专政。

对我而言，我相信无论从前隔阂有多深，如今依旧存在于我们之中，它自蒙昧中产生，也会随智慧而消失。我相信我们的四十五个州，如果可以在亲密的人际交流中，在丰富的人类智慧中聚在一起，没有哪两个州之间会仅仅只是停止对痛苦、离间或是怀疑的抱怨，而不是用从创世之初传承至我们身上的最优美的田园诗，去向对方诉说犹太教女儿的话语：“祈求我不要离开你，祈求我不要从对你的追随中回头；因为无论你要去哪里，我就去哪里；你在哪停留，我就在哪停留；你的子民就是我的子民，你的上帝就是我的上帝。你在哪里死去，我也会在哪里消逝并埋葬；祈求上帝这样对我，祈求除了死亡，没有什么能将你我分离。”

美国的人民前所未有地深深地了解到了南方人血液里流淌的品质，并肯定了这种品质在美国特质中的重要贡献：面对战争的胆量豪情，对家乡国土的依恋，对田园生活的热爱，还有装满深情与慷慨的广阔胸怀以及领导力；尤其是，那种坚定不移，应是百德之首，如果没有这种品质，那么没有谁能够成为伟大的人或是自由的人。毕竟，不是每个花园的藤上都能找到如此美味的果实。你要为我们的国家恢宏而壮丽的未来贡献很多力量，把它塑造得更美。

让我们不要再产生误解了。我并不是清教徒的后裔。可是三百年来，我每根血管中的每一滴血都来自一位清教徒祖先。我已经做好准备，去为马萨诸塞州的清教徒的名誉一战，无论战场在哪儿，无论敌人是谁。如果其他人愿意，就让他们去追溯诺曼强盗或是盗贼男爵的血统吧。清教徒的孩子们是不会感到羞耻的。清教徒，作为一种独特而重要且颇有影响力的力量，在英格兰存在尚未超过一百年。他在1558年伊丽莎白坐上王位开始统治的时期出现，又于1660年查理二世的复辟王朝离开。但是在那段短暂的历史中，他是英国人自由的保护者、拥护者以及创造者。透过那些最厌恶他的历史学家的忏悔来看，正是因他才有英国宪法的建立。他创建了新式的下议院。当他在下议院占据一席之地时，也就是专制政权式微之际。当他离开时，那里依然是世界上一直以来亘古未有的最强大的、最自由的、最不容侵犯的立法机关。当他在下议院取得席位之时，那里仅仅只是一个国王命令的登记簿；当他离开下议院时，那里已是国家尊严与国家意志的重要储备处。若是国王、大臣或主教挡了他的路，他将把他们带到法庭上。在这个短暂而又忙乱的世纪中，他赋予了英国人在这个世界上最高的荣誉头衔。一位伟大的历史学家曾说过：“他那不可征服的军队依靠的就是这座岛上的全部居民，他将约翰·弥尔顿的名字放在了世界伟大诗人名册的前列，将奥利弗·克伦威尔放在了英国元首名册的第一位。”这位历史学家或许补充说这位战无不胜的领导者依靠的就是欧洲的所有人民。

因此，当一个清教徒的后裔来到南方，当他造访劳特里奇和平克尼还有约翰·C.卡尔霍恩的故乡时，如果说他和这些英雄或是宪法自由的拥戴者之间有什么关联，那就是他觉得他可以将血脉亲缘昭告天下，并让这昭告得到认可。

（乔治·弗里斯比·霍尔）

A Flower in the Window

预习

lateral /ˈlætərəl/ 侧面的

supersede /ˌsuːpərˈsiːd/ 取代

uncongenial /ˌʌnkənˈdʒiːniəl/ 不合适的

vernacular /vərˈnækjələr/ 方言

Why does not every one who can afford it have a geranium in his window, or some other flower? It is very cheap; its cheapness is next to nothing; if you raise it from seed or from a slip; and it is a beauty and a companion. It sweetens the air, rejoices the eye, links you with nature and innocence, and is something to love.

But, pray, if you choose a geranium or possess but a few of them, let us persuade you to choose the scarlet kind, the "old original" geranium, and not a variety of it,——not one of the numerous diversities of red and white, blue and white, or ivy-leaved. Those are all beautiful, and very fit to vary a large collection; but the race is to run the hazard of preferring the curious to the beautiful, and costliness to sound taste.

It may be taken as a good general rule, that the most popular plants are the best; for otherwise they would not have become such. And what the painters call "pure colors" are preferable to mixed ones, for reasons which Nature herself has given when she painted the sky of one color, and the fields of another, and divided the rainbow itself into a few distinct colors, and made the red rose the queen of flowers.

Variations in flowers are like variations in music, often beautiful as such, but almost always inferior to the theme on which they are founded——the original air. And the rule holds good in beds of flowers, if they are not very large, or in any other small assemblage of them. Nay, the largest bed will look well, if of one beautiful color, while the most beautiful varieties may be inharmoniously mixed up.

Contrast is a good thing, but we must observe the laws of harmonious contrast, and unless we have space enough to secure these, it is better to be content with unity and simplicity, which are always to be had. We do not, in general, love and honor any one single color enough, and we are instinctively struck with a conviction to this effect, when we see it abundantly set forth.

The other day we saw a little garden wall completely covered with nasturtiums, and felt how much more beautiful they were than if anything had been mixed with them; for the leaves and the light and shade offer variety enough. The rest is all richness and simplicity united, which is the triumph of an intense perception. Embower a cottage thickly and completely with nothing but roses, and nobody would desire the interference of another plant.

Everything is handsome about the geranium, not excepting its name; which cannot be said of all flowers, though we get to love ugly words when associated with pleasing ideas. The word "geranium" is soft and pleasant; the meaning is poor, for it comes from a Greek word that signifies a crane, the fruit having the form of a crane's head or bill. Cranesbill is the English word for geranium, though the learned appellation has superseded the vernacular. But what a reason for naming a flower! As if the fruit were anything in comparison, or anyone cared about it.

Such distinctions, it is true, are useful to botanists; but as a plenty of learned names are sure to be reserved for the freemasonry of the science, it would be well for the world at large to invent joyous and beautiful names for these images of joy and beauty. In some instances we have them; such as hearts-ease, honeysuckle, marigold, mignonette (little darling), daisy (day's eye). And many flowers are so lovely, and have associated names, otherwise unmeaning, so pleasantly with one's memory, that no new ones would sound so well, or seem even to have such proper signification.

In pronouncing the words lilies, roses, tulips, pinks, jonquils, we see the things themselves, and seem to taste all their beauty and sweetness. Pink is a harsh, petty word in itself, and yet assuredly it does not seem so; for in the word we have the flower. It would be difficult to persuade ourselves that the word rose is not beautiful. Pea is a poor Chinese monosyllable and brier is rough and fierce, as it ought to be; but when we think of sweet-pea and sweet-brier, the words appear quite worthy of their epithets. The poor monosyllable becomes rich in sweetness and appropriation; the rough dissyllable, also; and the sweeter for its contrast.

The names of flowers, in general, among the polite, are neither pretty in themselves nor give us information. The country people are apt to do them more justice. Goldy-locks, ladies-fingers, rose-a-ruby, shepherd's-clock, shepherd's-purse, sauce-alone, scarlet-runners, sops-in-wine, sweet-william, and many other names, give us some ideas, either useful or pleasant.

But from the peasantry come many uncongenial names, as bad as those of the botanist. It is a pity that all fruits and flowers, and animals, too, except those with good names, could not be passed in review before somebody with a genius for christening, as the creatures were before Adam in Paradise, and so have new names given them worthy of their creation.

Suppose that flowers themselves were new! Suppose that they had just come into the world, a sweet reward for some new goodness, and that we had not yet seen them quite developed; that they were in the act of growing; had just issued, with their green stalks, out of the ground, and engaged the attention of the curious. Imagine what we should feel on seeing the first lateral stem bearing off from the main one, or putting forth a leaf.

How we should watch the leaf gradually unfolding its little graceful hand; then another, then another; then the main stalk rising and producing more; then one of them giving indications of astonishing novelty——a bud! Then this mysterious bud gradually unfolding like a leaf, amazing us, enchanting us, almost alarming us with delight, as if we knew not what enchantment were to ensue, till at length, in all its fairy beauty, shone forth "the bright consummate flower"!

Yet this phenomenon, to a person of any thought and lovingness, is what may be said to take place every day; for the commonest objects are wonders at which habit has made us cease to wonder, and the marvelousness of which we may review at pleasure, by taking thought.

(Leigh Hunt)

译文

窗台边的花

为什么不是每一个买得起天竺葵的人都会买一朵天竺葵，或者其他什么花摆在窗台上呢？它很便宜，便宜到几乎不要钱。如果从种子或者幼枝开始养，就会是一幅美景，一种陪伴。它芳香四溢，赏心悦目，使你和纯朴的大自然相联系，而且它还需要爱护。

但是，拜托，如果你要挑选一株天竺葵，或者养几株，请你一定要选深红色的、"元老级"的天竺葵，而不要买那种五花八门的——各色各样、数不胜数的红白相间、蓝白混杂或是常青藤叶的天竺葵。那些都很漂亮，十分适合扩充大量收集品的多样性；但这些品种是给愿意冒险去满足对漂亮事物好奇心的偏好，并高调彰显自己品位的人准备的。

这可能是一条好用而普遍的潜规则，即最广受欢迎的植物就是最好的，不然怎么会那么受欢迎呢？而画家们说的"纯色"也比混色略胜一筹，因为大自然都是用一种颜色绘出了天空，用另一种颜色画出了大地，把彩虹本身分成几个分明不同的色彩，还把红玫瑰冠为百花之后。

花的多样性就和音乐的多样性一样，都是如此美妙，然而几乎都逊色于它们所发源的基调——那最初的旋律。而且这条规律也适用于那些不怎么大的小花坛或是小花坛的组合。不仅如此，大型花坛也是只种一种美丽颜色的花好看，如果混杂多种颜色的话，就算是最漂亮的花也会显得不协调。对比反差是个好东西，但我们必须遵循和谐对比的原则。除非有足够大的空间确保这些，我们最好还是知足于长久存在的统一和朴素。一般而言，我们并没有足够喜爱和仰慕任何一种单色，因此，当大量单色物体展现在我们眼前时，我们本能地感到震撼。

前几天，我们看到一个小花园的墙面上爬满了旱金莲，都感慨没有其他物种混杂的它们美丽得多，因为叶子和光影形成了足够的变幻。叶子以外的其他部分则集华美与朴素于一体，给人留下强烈的印象。倘若一间小木屋完全隐匿于玫瑰深处，谁都不希望再有其他植物来干扰吧。

天竺葵的一切都是这么端庄大方，名字也不例外；这么说并不适用于所有花种，尽管我们确实能通过联想好的寓意来爱上一些丑陋的词。“天竺葵”一词就给人以清雅和愉悦之感；其含义却略为贫瘠，因为这个词源于希腊词汇，表示鹤类或有着鹤的脑袋或喙形状的水果。在英语词汇中，老鹳草就是指天竺葵，只是后来学名取代了俗称。但是对花的命名哪有什么理由呢？相比之下仿佛果实是什么重要的东西而人人都在意似的！

这样明显的区别，确确实实，对植物学家而言是有用的；但这么大量的学名一定会伴随着科学的发展被保留下来，因此为这些美好的化身创造美好的名字，对整个世界来说，也会是件好事。在有些名字中，我们拥有这种美好，譬如三色堇、忍冬、金盏花、木犀草（小宝贝）、雏菊（日之眼）。许多花都很漂亮，也有相应的名字，虽然在其他方面并无意义，但因为人们对此充满愉快的回忆，觉得没有任何新名字听起来有这么好听，有这么合适的意义。

透过这些名称的读音，百合、玫瑰、郁金香、石竹、黄水仙，我们能看到它们的样子，似乎还能品尝到它们的芳香和美丽。石竹这个词听起来坚硬而不足为奇，但它看上去肯定不是这样的；简而言之，因为我们会养花，所以要说服自己玫瑰这个词不美自然很困难。豌豆的英文读法在汉语中不过是一个单音节词，而蔷薇则是粗糙而野性的，正如它原本应有的样子。而当我们想到甜豌豆和野蔷薇时，这些词显得名副其实。在加上词语后缀并置于语境之中后，贫乏的单音节词变得充实起来；简陋的双音节词也是如此，因为单音节词的对比而显得更讨人喜爱。花名一般较为文雅，本身既不会很好看也不能给我们传达信息。而乡村的人们就善于更加直观妥当的取名。“金锁”

（金凤花）、“淑女指”（秋葵）、“红宝石玫瑰”、“牧人的钟”（蓝繁缕）、“牧人的钱包”（荠菜）、“独一无二的刺激”（药用蒜芥）、“红色舞者（南美菜豆）、“泡酒花片”（康乃馨）、“甜蜜威廉”（须苞石竹）以及很多其他俗称，带给我们有用又有趣的意象。

但是农民们也给植物取了很多不适合的名字，糟糕程度堪比植物学家的取名。遗憾的是，所有果实、花卉，还有动物，除了具备好听名字的那些，都逃不过拥有取名天赋的人的眼睛，正如伊甸园里亚当面前的生物一样，因此与它们的存在价值相称的新名字就诞生了。

假设花卉本身就是一种新的物种；假设它们刚刚来到这个世界，是上天对善意的甜蜜奖励，我们也从未见过它们成熟的模样；假设它们不断长大，嫩绿的茎秆刚刚破土而出，引来人们好奇的目光。想象一下，当我们第一次看到主茎上抽出的侧枝，或是生出的一片叶子的时候会是什么感觉？

我们应该如何观察那片叶子逐渐展开它优雅的小手；又一片；再一片；然后主茎继续生长并长出更多的叶片；再然后其中的一片叶子会有产生令人惊异的新事物的迹象——一个花蕾！这个不可思议的花蕾像叶片一样缓缓展开，惊艳而迷人，一股喜悦将我们打动，仿佛我们不知道会有什么魅力接踵而至，直到最后，“绚丽完美的花朵”闪耀着它全部的优雅之美。

此情此景，对任何一个关心且钟情于花的人来说，可能是每天都在上演的事；最常见的花朵本身就是奇迹，但司空见惯使我们忽略了它的魅力，要想在愉悦的回忆中感受到它的惊艳，唯有通过思考。

（雷欧·亨特）

In the Wheat Field

When the lids of the virgin Dawn unclose,
When the earth is fair and the heavens are calm,
And the early breath of the wakening rose
Floats on the air in balm,
I stand breast-high in the pearly wheat,
That ripples and thrills to a sportive breeze,
Borne over the field with its Hermes feet,
And its subtle odor of southern seas;
While out of the infinite azure deep,
The flashing wings of the swallows sweep,
Buoyant and beautiful, wild and fleet,
Over the waves of the whispering wheat.

(Paul Hamilton Hayne, adapted)

译文

麦田

当晨曦浅浅划开一道口子，
当大地平静，天空晴朗，
刚睡醒的玫瑰呼吸着，
空气中弥漫着香气，
我站在齐胸的闪着珍珠光泽的麦田中
调皮的微风吹起阵阵涟漪波动，
田野上空迎来这远方的信使，
带来淡淡的南方大海的味道；
虽然这里不是无垠的蔚蓝深海，
燕子却挥舞着翅膀划过，

轻快优雅，狂野疾驰，
飞过这细语呢喃的滚滚麦浪。

（保罗·汉密尔顿·海恩斯，有删改）

作者介绍

保罗·汉密尔顿·海恩斯来自英国，家世显赫，殖民时期居住在南卡罗莱纳。他毕业于查尔斯顿学院，很早便投身于文学事业当中，其诗歌的思想性和表现力都极为罕见。

Broek

预习

automatons /ɔːˈtɒmətənz/ 自动机器

bas-relief /ˌbæsrɪˈliːf/ 浮雕

caricature /ˈkærɪkətʃər/ 笨拙的模仿

ennui /ɑːnˈwiː/ 怠倦

imbecility /ˌɪmbəˈsɪləti/ 愚钝

importunity /ɪmpəˈtjuːnətɪ/ 胡搅蛮缠

invective /ɪnˈvektɪv/ 恶言谩骂

odious /ˈoʊdiəs/ 可憎的

superfluous /suːˈpɜːrfluəs/ 不必要的

Imagine the most childish eccentricity to which the name of village can be given and you will form a vague idea of Broek.

All the houses are surrounded by gardens, and separated from the street by sky-blue palings in the shape of a balustrade or a railing, with wooden fruits, apples or oranges, stuck on the points of each pale. The streets that have these palings on either side are very narrow, paved with small bricks of different colors placed sideways, and arranged in all manner of designs, so that from a distance they seem to be streets covered with Turkish shawls.

The greater number of the houses are of wood, only one story in height and very small. Some are rose-color; others black, gray, purple, light blue, or the color of mountain grass.

Their roofs are covered with varnished tiles arranged like a chess-board; the gutters are ornamented with a sort of wooden festoon perforated like lace; the pointed facades are surmounted with a small weathercock, a little lance, or something which looks like a bunch of flowers; the windows have panes of red or blue glass, and are adorned with curtains, embroideries, ribbons, nets, fringes, tassels, and trifles; the doors are painted and gilded and decorated with all sorts of bas-reliefs representing flowers, figures, and trophies, in the midst of which the name and profession of the proprietor can be read. Nearly every house has two doors, one in front and one behind, the last for every-day entrance and exit, and the former opened only on great occasions, such as births, deaths, and marriages.

The gardens are as peculiar as the houses. They seem to have been laid out for dwarfs. The paths are hardly wide enough to walk in; one could embrace the flower-beds; the arbors would barely hold two persons closely curled up; the myrtle hedges would scarcely reach to the knees of a four-year-old child.

Between the arbors and the flower-beds run little canals which seem made to float paper boats. They are crossed by superfluous wooden bridges with colored pillars and parapets; there are ponds the size of a bath, which are almost concealed by lilliputian boats tied with red cords to blue stakes; tiny staircases, miniature kitchen-gardens, crossways, bowers, little doors, and tiny gates. Everything could be measured with the hand, crossed at a leap, and demolished by a blow. Moreover, there are trees cut in the shape of fans, plumes, disks, trapezes, with their trunks colored white and blue, and here and there wooden kennels for the domestic animals painted and decorated like royal doll palaces.

After looking at the first houses and gardens, I entered the village. There was not a living soul in the street or at the windows. All the doors were closed, all the curtains drawn, all the canals deserted, all the boats motionless. The village is built on such a plan that one cannot see more than four or five cottages from any one spot, and as one advances, a house disappears, another is partly revealed, and a third shows itself entirely, and everywhere among the trunks of trees stripes and touches of the brightest color shine forth and vanish, like a troop of masqueraders who are playing at hide-and-seek.

At every step one discovers another stage effect, a fresh combination of hues, some new absurdity. It seems as though every moment a population of automatons must issue from the doors with Turkish cymbals and tabors in their hands, like the figures that play on the street-organs. Fifty steps take one round a house, over a bridge, through a garden, across a street, and back where one started. A child seems a man, and a man a giant. Everything is minute, compact, affected, painted, imitated, unnatural, and childish. At first, it makes one laugh;then one gets vexed at thinking that the inhabitants of the village will imagine that strangers consider it beautiful. The caricature appears odious, and one would like to accuse all the masters of the houses of imbecility; one feels a desire to declare to them that their famous Broek is an insult to art and nature, and that they have neither good sense nor good taste. But when one has let off steam in invectives, one begins to laugh again, and laughter prevails.

There was a time when all the houses and gardens in Broek were like this. But now not only the appearance of the village, but the population, is in great part changed. In former times Broek was called the village of millionaires, because nearly all its inhabitants were wealthy merchants who settled there for the love of retirement and peace. Little by little, ennui, the ridicule to which their houses and they themselves were subjected, the importunity of travelers, the desire for more beautiful places, drove away nearly all the rich families, and the few who remained ceased from the emulation which all these childish marvels had created, and allowed the old order to disappear. Now [1894] Broek has about a thousand inhabitants, of whom the greater number make cheese, and the others are shopkeepers, farmers, and mechanics who live on their incomes.

Although Broek has declined, it is still visited by almost all strangers who travel in Holland. In one room of a house I went into there was an enormous book containing thousands of cards and autographs of visitors from every country. The greatest number of the visitors were Englishmen and Americans, the smallest number Italians, and these few were almost all members of the nobility of Southern Italy. Among many illustrious names I saw those of Victor Hugo and Walter Scott. Among the souvenirs there is a paper-weight presented by the Emperor and Empress of Russia to a citizen of Broek as a sign of their gratitude for the hospitality he had offered the Grand Duke Nicholas Alexandrovitch.

(Edmondo De Amicis)

译文

布鲁克

想一想这个村子孩子气的古怪名字，你就会对布鲁克有一个模糊的印象。

所有的房子都被花园环绕，与街道间用天蓝色的栅栏隔开，这些栅栏外形像一个个栏杆，每个栅栏上都插着木制的水果，以苹果、橘子为主。街道两边都是栅栏，因此这些街道普遍都很窄。街道上横向铺满了各种颜色的小砖块，这些小砖是按各式各样的图案摆置的，所以从远处看过去，街道像是披上了土耳其风格的围巾。

这里的大部分房子都是木屋，只有一层高，面积也很小。有的是玫瑰色，还有的是黑色、灰色、紫色、浅蓝色，或是草绿色。

这里房子的房顶都铺着上了漆的瓦片，摆放的方式看着很像棋盘；排水渠则用一些彩色镂空的木头装饰，远望倒是很像五颜六色的缎带；房屋立面的尖顶处挂着小小的风向标、枪矛，或其他像花束的东西；窗户上镶嵌的是红色或蓝色的玻璃，在窗帘、绣品、缎带、网眼花边、流苏、小穗子和其他小装饰品的映衬下格外惹人喜爱；门上画了各种流线型的装饰画，又用各式各样形状的浮雕作为装饰，描绘着花朵、数字和战利品雕饰，在浮雕中间可以看到这家主人的名字和职业。几乎每栋房子都有两扇门，一扇在前，一扇在后，后门主要用于日常进出，而前门只在一些重要场合，如生日宴会、葬礼和婚宴上才会打开。

这里的花园也像房子一样独特。她们看上去像是为了小矮人而设计的。小径窄得根本走不进去；花坛一个人就能圈起来；凉亭小得勉强能容纳两个近乎蜷曲着的人；香桃木的树篱矮得连四岁小孩子的膝盖都不到。

花坛和凉亭中间流淌着一条小水渠，看上去似乎只能飘个纸船。水渠间搭建了略显多余的木桥，桥下的柱子和桥上的栏杆都是彩色的；花园里有数个浴缸大小的池塘，它们几乎完全被小船掩盖住了，这些小船都被红色的绳子拴在蓝色的桩子上；花园里还有一些小楼梯、小菜园、小岔路、凉亭以及各种小门。总之，所有的东西小得用手就能量出来，一步就能跨过去，一阵风就能摧毁它们。不仅如此，花园里还有不少树，这些树被修剪得有的像扇子，有的像羽毛，有的像圆盘，还有的像秋千架，树干则被染成了白色和蓝色；花园里还零星散布着不少为家养动物制作的木窝，装扮得犹如皇家玩偶的宫殿。

等看完这些房子和花园，我踏入了这个村庄。整个街道和窗口都看不到一个活物。所有的门都紧闭着，窗帘也都拉着，水渠都干涸了，船也都一动不动。当初在建这个村庄时，就设计成了无论站在村庄的哪个地方，一个人能同时看到的房子至多不超过五个，每前进一步，就会有一栋房子从视野消失，一栋房子露出一角，还有一栋则能完整映入眼帘。树干与树干之间的每一处都间以鲜艳的色彩，时而闪耀，时而黯淡，像一群戴着假面的人在玩捉迷藏。

每走一步，就又是另一番天地，你会看到全新的、不可思议的色彩组合。就好像那些在自动管风琴上演奏的小人一样，这里一定也会有一群自动人偶，每时每刻都会从门里出来，手上拿着土耳其铜钹和手鼓，五十步就能绕着屋子走完一圈，踏过一座桥，穿过花园和街道，然后回到起点。小孩子看着像大人，而大人看着则像巨人。一切都是那么微小、紧凑、做作，充满虚饰、仿造、反常和孩子气。最初，它可能会让你大笑，但过了一会儿你就开始烦恼，是不是在村民的想象中初来这里的人会觉得这样的搭配很美？实际上这种拙劣的模仿实在令人厌恶，有人可能会指责所有的房主都很愚蠢；还有人可能恨不得去跟他们说，他们这所谓的布鲁克是对艺术和自然的侮辱，着实没有鉴赏力，也没有品位。但当人们在恶言谩骂中出尽了怒气，他们又再次笑了起来。这时，笑声占据了上风。

布鲁克的房子和花园曾经有段时间是这样的。但现在，不仅是村庄的外观，连居住的村民也都有了很大变化。以前，布鲁克被称为百万富翁之村，因为居住在这里的几乎都是有钱的商人，他们想在退休后找一个平静祥和的地方居住，所以便搬来了这里。但是渐渐地，他们厌倦了总是受到人们对他们的房子和自身的嘲笑，胡搅蛮缠的游客以及对更美风景的渴望，驱使几乎所有的富裕家庭离开了这里，而少数留下来的住户也停止了对那些傻气景色的竞相效仿。于是，旧风气也慢慢消失了。1894年，布鲁克有将近一千名住户，其中大部分人都是做奶酪的，其余的则是些店主、农民以及手艺人，他们靠着收入维持生活。

虽然布鲁克的吸引力在减弱，但几乎所有来荷兰旅行的人仍旧会参观这里。我进去参观的房间里有一本很大的书，书中集有几千张来自不同国家的游客写下的卡片以及他们的亲笔签名。游客当中最多的是英国人和美国人，最少的是意大利人，而这少数的意大利人中，又以意大利南部的贵族为主。我还在当中看到了很多众所周知的名字，比如维克多·雨果、沃尔特·斯科特。在纪念品当中有一个由俄国皇帝和皇后赠送的镇纸，他们曾在布鲁克居住过，这个镇纸就是为了感谢大公爵尼古拉斯·亚历山德罗维奇对他们的热情招待而赠送的礼物。

（埃迪蒙托·德·亚米契斯）

作者介绍

埃迪蒙托·德·亚米契斯是一位意大利作家，他关于旅行的书曾被译为好几种语言。他几乎走遍了世界上的所有国家，他描写旅程的语言总是栩栩如生、妙不可言。除了这一篇，他还创作了举世闻名的儿童文学《爱的教育》，书里详细地讲述了一个小学生在学校的日常生活。本文选自埃迪蒙托的《荷兰》，由约翰·C.威斯汀公司许可授权。

Mardi-Gras

预习

Krewe 为狂欢节组织游行或是舞会的组织。

Mardi-Gras "忏悔星期二"，狂欢节的最后一天，是大斋节前一个星期新奥尔良和许多其他国家都会庆祝的节日。

cairn /kern/ 石堆纪念碑

concourse /ˈkɑːŋkɔːrs/ 大厅；广场

cortege /kɔːˈteɪʒ/ 行列

elemental /ˌelɪˈmentl/ 基本的

inter /ɪnˈtɜːr/ 埋葬

lush /lʌʃ/ 苍翠繁茂的

tarn /tɑːrn/ 山中小湖

timothy /ˈtɪməθɪ/ 猫尾草

It was Mardi-Gras night in New Orleans. Canal Street, as far as the eye could reach in either direction——out towards the river or back in the direction of the swamp lands——was a surging mass of people.The deep balconies, the galeries of the old French town, overhanging the banquettes on either side the way, were crowded beyond their strength, and many would have fallen but for the temporary support of heavy timbers put in for the occasion.

Above the heads of the crowds little street urchins, newsboys, beggars, gamins——white, black, yellow, brown, and all the shades between——sat perched like chattering sparrows on every available projection of lamp-post or tree, many even clinging about the tops of street cars. Others, mounting the granite pedestal of Henry Clay's statue at the corner, steadied themselves by embracing the statesman's legs; while one or two of the more adventurous had even scaled his lofty figure and sat astride his broad bronze shoulders.

The occasional turning of the great electric searchlight in the Pickwick Club building revealed a ripping sea of happy smiling faces along the line of galeries opposite, all wearing, no matter what their race or condition, the holiday expression which showed them in touch with the Carnival spirit.

The great "Mystick Krewe" had already passed along the street and disappeared, but it would soon come again in another direction. Presently there was a restless movement on all the galeries——a concerted bending forward of bodies and inquiring questions: "Which way?" "Where?" "Who says so?"

"Oh, pshaw!" "Nothing but some persons trying to raise an excitement."

But no! A sudden hurrying and scurrying, hither and thither, of now loud-laughing and talking crowd afoot; now two or three mounted police slowly, carefully, clearing the way; and now——a blaze of light! "Ah-h-h-h!" "Oh-h-h-h!" "Ah-h-h-h!" The exclamation passes like a great wave from one gallery to another, until its echoes are drowned by the stirring music of the band.

The Krewe has come again. The first float passes; another, and yet another, and still they come, until—what is this? Bows, hand-kisses, a shower of candies——real French bonbons——from the merry maskers of a special car over the shoulders and into the laps of the children. And here they come again; and once more——dragees, marsh-mallows, "kisses," crystallized figs, thrown backward this time for the float has passed, and still they fall with true aim into the hats and over the faces of the now merrily laughing and waving group.

Other candies were flying in other directions to other people or to anybody. Float followed float. The procession represented "The Five

Senses", and it was from the fruit-laden float following in Ceres' train that the greatest shower of candies had come. The Sense of taste had been elaborately illustrated by a profusion of such things as delight the palate.

While from one float animated mushrooms, asparagus, and common vegetables without number bowed and waved to admiring multitudes, on another were gleeful figs, waddling watermelons, frisking cantaloupes, and a rollicking lot of oranges, lemons, and smaller fruits.

Presently the procession was only a pillar of fire moving slowly out Canal Street, and soon that disappeared. It had been a gorgeous pageant, but Mardi Gras, the mad festival, excepting to such as followed the maskers into theatre and ball-room, was over——over for another year. And now for getting home.

(Ruth Mcenery Stuart)

译文

新奥尔良狂欢节

这是新奥尔良的狂欢之夜。放眼望去，运河街——无论是眺望河水的方向，还是回望沼泽地的方向——人山人海。这座古老的法国小城（最初的新奥尔良是法国的殖民地）在宽敞的露台和眺台上朝各个方向搭建了向外突出的便道，拥挤的人群使得露台和眺台不堪重负，要不是有临时用来支撑加固的木材，恐怕许多人会掉下去。

人群的头顶之上，街头流浪儿、报童、小乞儿和顽童们——有白色、黑色、黄色、棕色，肤色各异，深浅不一——像一群叽叽喳喳的麻雀一样坐在灯杆和树枝上，许多孩子甚至爬上有轨电车的车顶上。其他的孩子，爬到了角落里的亨利·克莱雕像的大理石底座上，为站稳而紧紧抱着这位政治家的腿，还有一两个胆大的，甚至爬上这座高耸的伟人雕像，骑在他宽广的青铜色肩膀上。

匹克威客俱乐部大楼临时开启了大型电气探照灯，照亮了对面那排便道里的灿烂笑脸，如同一片欢乐的海洋。不论什么种族，也不论什么身份，人人都露出节日的欢颜，沉浸在狂欢节的情绪里。

“神秘克鲁”已经沿街游行过了，消失在人海中，但是很快，它又会在另一个地方和大家见面。此时，新奥尔良的大街小巷里，熙熙攘攘，人流朝着同一个方向涌动，为了能看到“克鲁”的下一次游街，人们都在问着：“往哪个方向走？”“在哪个地方？”“这是谁说的？”

“啊！哼！”“有些人只是想让大家高兴些！”

但是！不！突然，大家匆匆忙忙地跑了起来，人潮攒动，笑声、说话声震耳欲聋。两三名骑警只能放慢脚步，小心翼翼地清空路面。一束光瞬间出现了！“啊！啊！啊！”“哇！哇！哇！”“啊！啊！啊！”一阵一阵的尖叫声如浪潮般袭来，充斥着整个街道，直到乐队奏起激动人心的音乐，才慢慢盖住人们的叫喊声。

“克鲁”再次出现。第一场演出结束，接着第二场、第三场，他们会一直表演，直到——这是什么？在一辆特别的花车上，戴着面具的表演者热情洋溢，不断向人群鞠躬、飞吻，还向孩子们的衣兜里抛洒了一阵糖果雨，这可是正宗的法国软糖。瞧！他们又来了，再一次向观众洒下糖李子、棉花糖、好时巧克力和蜜饯无花果，这一次他们在花车经过时向后抛洒，这些糖果从此时兴高采烈、激动不已的人群面前飞过，准确地落在了他们的帽子里。

还有些糖果往另一个方向洒去，飞向其他人群或者任何人。花车一辆接着一辆。伴随谷物女神队伍中的硕果花车抛洒的最大一阵糖果雨，游行队伍表现了“感官五重奏”。人们通过这些大量愉悦口味的东西精巧地表现出了“味觉”。

一辆花车装点着蘑菇、芦笋等无数常见的蔬菜，演员们向赞叹的人群鞠躬、挥手；另一辆花车上则满载着快乐的无花果、摇摆的西瓜、跳动的哈密瓜和许多欢欣的橘子、柠檬等小水果。

现在，游行队伍正缓慢离开运河街，人们只能看到一条火柱，但它很快也消失在人们的视线里。这是一场盛大的游行，但是除非你就这样跟着戴面具的表演者进入剧院和舞厅，否则这个疯狂的节日就到此结束了，因为新的一年即将到来。而现在，该是回家的时候了。

（鲁思·麦克内里·斯图尔特）

October in Tennessee

Far, far away, beyond a hazy height,
The turquoise skies are hung in dreamy sleep;
Below, the fields of cotton, fleecy-white,
Are spreading like a mighty flock of sheep.
Now, like Aladdin of the days of old,
October robes the weeds in purple gowns;
He sprinkles all the sterile fields with gold,
And all the rustic trees wear royal crowns.
The straggling fences all are interlaced
With pink and purple morning-glory blooms,
The starry asters glorify the waste,
While grasses stand on guard with pikes and plumes.
Yet still amid the splendor of decay
The chill winds call for blossoms that are dead,
The cricket chirps for sunshine passed away,
The lovely summer songsters that have fled.
At last, November, like a conqueror, comes
To storm the golden city of his foe;
We hear his rude winds like the roll of drums,
Bringing their desolation and their woe.
The sunset, like a vast vermilion flood,
Splashes its giant glowing waves on high,
The forest flames with blazes red as blood,
A conflagration sweeping to the sky.
Then all the treasures of that brilliant state
Are gathered in a mighty funeral pyre;
October, like a king resigned to fate,
Dies in the forests with their sunset fire.

(Walter Malone, adapted)

译文

十月的田纳西

在很远、很远的地方，远至朦胧的天际，
蓝绿色的苍穹悬挂在人们的睡梦中；
苍穹下是片片棉花田，宛如羊毛般洁白，
遍布大地，就像成群的绵羊。
此刻，好似回到阿拉丁的古老年代，
十月给野草披上了帝王的衣袍；
他给贫瘠的土地饰以黄金，
给粗糙的树木佩戴皇冠。
蔓生的篱笆上层层叠叠，
粉色和紫色的牵牛花在盛放，
星星点点的紫苑惊艳了这片荒原，
小草用刺刀和盔甲站岗放哨。
在腐朽的壮丽中，
凉风呼唤着枯萎的花朵绽放生姿，
蟋蟀因阳光的流逝哀鸣，
夏日里可爱的歌唱者已消失不见。
终于，十一月到来了，就像一个侵略者，
狂风暴雨肆虐这座金色城池；
我们听到粗野的狂风怒吼，像鼓点般急促轰鸣，
带着他的荒芜和悲鸣席卷而来。
夕阳之光如同朱红色的洪水倾泻而下，
在高空中掀起一阵炽热的巨浪，
森林好似迸射出熊熊大火，变得如鲜血般绯红，
这团火焰一直延伸到苍穹。
那灿烂中蕴藏的所有珍宝
都融汇于此，化为灰烬；

十月，就像一位听天由命的帝王，
在森林里伴着落日余晖消亡。

（沃特·马龙，有删改）

November

The autumn air sweeps faint and chill
Across the maple-crested hill;
And on my ear
Falls, tingling clear,
A strange, mysterious, woodland thrill.
From utmost twig, from scarlet crown
Untouched with yet a tinct of brown,
Reluctant, slow,
As loath to go,
The loosened leaves come wavering down.

(Margaret Junkin Preston, adapted)

译文

十一月

秋风扫过，卷来微凉
风儿穿过那片满是枫叶的山丘；
我的耳朵战栗不已，
刺痛感是如此清晰，
陌生、神秘，是森林的气息。
从树梢的嫩枝，从那还未曾沾染一丝凋败枯黄的红色树冠，
勉勉强强，慢慢悠悠，
是如此不情不愿，
落叶摇曳着飘零。

（玛格丽特・琼金・普勒斯顿，有删改）

作者简介

玛格丽特·琼金·普勒斯顿（1820–1897）出生于费城，但却在弗吉尼亚州莱星顿度过了她的大半生。她最著名的诗歌是《杰克逊将军之墓》和《战死沙场》。

Home of the People

I went to the Washington the other day, and I stood on the Capitaol Hill; my heart beat quick as I looked at the towering marble of my country's capitol, and the mist gathered in my eyes as I thought of its tremendous significance, and the armies and the treasury, and the judges and the president, and the congress and the courts, and all that was gathered there. And I felt that the sun in all its course could not look down on a better sight than that majestic home of a republic that has taught the world its best lessons of liberty.

Two days afterward, I went to visit a friend in the country, a modest man, with a quiet country home. It was just a simple, unpretentious house, set about with big trees, encircled in meadow and field rich with the promise of harvest. The fragrance of the pink and hollyhock in the front yard was mingled with the aroma of the orchard and of the gardens, and resonant with the cluck of poultry and the hum of bees.

Inside was quiet, thrift, and comfort. There was the old clock that had welcomed, in steady measure, every newcomer to the family, that had ticked the solemn requiem of the dead, and had kept company with the watcher at the bedside. There were the big, restful beds, and the old, open fireplace, and the old family Bible, thumbed with the fingers of hands long since still, and wet with the tears of eyes long since closed, holding the simple annals of the family, and the heart and the conscience of the home.

Outside, there stood my friend, the master, a simple, upright man, with no mortgage on his roof, no lien on his growing crops, master of his land and master of himself. There was his old father, an aged, trembling man, but happy in the heart and home of his son. And as they started to their home, the hands of the old man went down on the young man's shoulder, laying there the unspeakable blessing of the honored and grateful father, and ennobling it with the knighthood of the fifth commandment.

And as they reached the door, the old mother came with the sunset falling fair on her face, and lighting up her deep, patient eyes, while her lips, trembling with the rich music of her heart, bade her husband and son welcome to their home. Beyond was the housewife, busy with her household cares, clean of heart and conscience, the buckler and helpmeet of her husband. Down the lane came the children, trooping home after the cows, seeking as truant birds do the quiet of their home nest.

I saw the night come down on that house, falling gently as the wings of the unseen dove. And the old man——while a startled bird called from the forest, and the trees were shrill with the cricket's cry, and the stars were swarming in the sky——got the family around him, and taking the old Bible from the table, called them to their knees, the little baby hiding in the folds of its mother's dress, while he closed the record of that simple day by God's benediction on that family and on that home. And while I gaze, the vision of that marble Capitol faded. Forgotten were its treasures and its majesty, and I said, oh, surely here in the homes of the people are lodged at last the strength and the responsibility of this government, the hope and the promise of this republic.

(Henry W. Grady)

译文

人民之家

前些天，我去了华盛顿，站在美国国会山上：当我看着高耸的大理石国会大厦时，我的心跳得飞快；当我想到它非凡的意义时，我的眼中噙满了泪水。不仅如此，美国军队、财政部、司法部、总统以及国会和法院，还有聚集在这里的其他所有为国家正常运转而服务的部门，都令我感慨万千。我感到日日东升西落的太阳也看不到比这庄严共和国更宏伟的景象了，它出色地教给了全世界什么是自由。

两天之后，我去拜访了一位乡下的朋友，他是一个谦逊的人，有着一间十分具有田园气息的屋子。这间屋子很简单，坐落在草丛中，周围环绕着参天大树，田地产量丰富，农作物长势大好，看来今年会大丰收。前院中，石竹花和蜀葵芳香四溢，与果园和花园传来的阵阵芳香融合。母鸡“咯咯”地叫着，蜜蜂“嗡嗡”地飞舞，好不热闹。

屋里装潢简约，安静舒适。屋里有一座古老的钟，“滴滴答答”，沉稳地响着，欢迎着每一位新的来宾。它“滴答滴答”地响着，为死去的人鸣响庄严的安魂曲，始终陪伴着床边的守灵人。屋内有几张给人休息的大床，一个古老、宽阔的壁炉和一本老旧的家庭圣经。这本圣经保存着简单的家族传承史，也保留着家庭的爱与善良，它早就被许多双手翻阅过，也早就被许多眼泪浸湿过。

屋外，站着我的牧师朋友，一位谦逊、节俭、正直的人，他没有抵押房屋，也没有抵押生长中的农作物，他完完全全拥有他的土地，也完完全全拥有自己。他的老父亲上了年纪，哆哆嗦嗦，但内心很幸福，对他儿子的家也很满意。他俩向家中走去，儿子背着父亲，老人的双手搭在儿子的肩上，这展现了父亲那无法用言语表达的福气——被尊重、被感恩，更以第五诫（圣经十诫，第五诫即“当孝敬父母”）的骑士精神让这种福气变得高尚尊贵。

当他们到达门口时，老母亲出来迎接他们。落日的余晖温柔得照在老母亲的脸上，照在她那深邃和蔼的眼睛上，闪闪发光，老母亲的嘴唇因由内心发出的喜悦而颤动着，欢迎着她的丈夫和儿子回到家中。老母亲的身后是牧师的贤内助妻子，妻子正忙着干家务活，心地纯洁善良，不仅是她丈夫坚强温暖的后盾，也是她丈夫一位知心的朋友。接着，孩子们从小巷中跑了出来，赶着牛群回家，像游荡的鸟儿一样寻求着家的宁静。

我看见夜色降临在那座房屋，像看不见的鸽子翅膀般轻柔降落。从森林中传出一只受惊鸟儿的叫声，树木间到处是蟋蟀连续不断的鸣响，夜空中挤满了繁星。老父亲将家人聚集在他周围，从桌上拿起老旧的圣经，吩咐他们跪下祷告，小婴儿就这样被遮盖在妈妈裙子的褶皱里。正是在这祈求上帝赐福家人及家庭的祷告中，平凡的一天结束了。此时，我凝视着眼前，美国国会大厦的景象渐渐褪去。我忘记了它的财富，忘记了它的威严。我得说，政府的力量和责任，共和国的希望和前途最终无疑体现在了人民的家中。

（亨利 · W.格雷迪）

作者介绍

亨利·伍德芬·格雷迪1852年出生于美国佐治亚州雅典区。从佐治亚大学毕业后，他从事记者工作，最后成为《亚特兰大宪法报》的编辑，并担任此职直到1889年去世。除了他为各种杂志就涉及南方的话题做出贡献外，格雷迪先生作为演说家也负有盛名。他最著名的演讲是《新南方》和《黑人的未来》。

讲解

1.指示代词是指代它所提及的名词或名称。指示代词有this，that，these，those。this和these指代近处的人或物，that和those指代远处的人或物。

例如：This is my book. That is your book. These are beautiful trees. Those are beginning to die.

2.不指代特定人或物的代词叫不定代词。不定代词有any，each，none，one，some等。

What Is Our Country?

We cannot honor our country with too deep a reverence; we cannot love her with an energy of purpose, or a faithfulness of zeal. And what is our country? It is not the East, with her hills and her valleys, with her countless sails, and the rocky ramparts of her shores. It is not the North, with her thousands of villages and her beautiful Ohio and her verdant Missouri. Nor is it yet the South, opulent in the mimic snow of the cotton, in the rich plantations of the rustling cane, and in the golden robes of the rice field. What are these but the sister families of one greater, better, holier family, our country?

(Thomas S. Grimke)

译文

我们有着怎样一个国家？

我们不能依靠盲目地崇拜敬仰我们的国家，我们不能依靠决心的力量或热情的信念来热爱她。那么我们有着怎样一个国家呢？这里不是东方，没有延绵的山脉，没有雄伟的峡谷，没有无尽的船只，没有岩石嶙峋的海岸。这里不是北方，没有成千上万的村庄，没有美丽动人的俄亥俄，没有青翠葱茏的密苏里。这也不是南方，没有洁白如雪的棉花，没有种植园里“沙沙”作响的茎秆，没有金色覆盖的稻田。那么我们到底有着怎样一个国家呢？她是一个各大姐妹州联合起来的，更伟大、更美好、更神圣的国家。

（托马斯·S. 格里姆克）

Chapter 3

Popularizing Science | 趣味科普

The Origin of Roast Pig

Mankind, says a Chinese manuscript, which my friend M. was obliging enough to read and explain to me, for the first seventy thousand ages ate their meat raw, clawing or biting it from the animal, just as they do in Abyssinia to this day. This period is not obscurely hinted at by their great Confucius in the second chapter of his Mundane Mutations, where he designates a kind of golden age by the term Cho-fang, literally the Cook's Holiday. The manuscript goes on to say that the art of roasting, or rather broiling, was accidentally discovered in the manner following.

The swineherd, Ho-ti, having gone out into the woods one morning, as his manner was, to collect mast for his hogs, left his cottage in the care of his eldest son, Bo-bo, a great lubberly boy, who, being fond of playing with fire, as youngsters of his age commonly are, let some sparks escape into a bundle of straw, which, kindling quickly, spread the conflagration over every part of their poor mansion, till it was reduced to ashes. Together with a cottage (a sorry makeshift of a building, you may think it), what was of much more importance, a fine litter of newborn pigs, no less than nine in number, perished.

China pigs have been esteemed a luxury all over the East, from the remotest periods that we read of. Bo-bo was in the utmost consternation, as you may think, not so much for the sake of the tenement, ——which his father and he could easily build up again with a few dry branches, and the labor of an hour or two, at any time, ——as for the loss of the pigs.

While he was thinking what he should say to his father, and wringing his hands over the smoking remnants of one of those untimely sufferers, an odor assailed his nostrils, unlike any scent which he had before experienced. What could it proceed from? ——not from the burnt cottage——he had smelt that smell before; indeed this was by no means the first accident of the kind which had occurred through the negligence of this unlucky young firebrand. Much less did it resemble that of any known herb, weed, or flower.

He knew not what to think. He next stooped down to feel the pig, if there were any signs of life in it. He burned his fingers, and to cool them he applied them in his booby fashion to his mouth. Some of the crumbs of the scorched skin had come away with his fingers, and for the first time in his life (in the world's life, indeed for before him no man had known it) he tasted—crackling! Again he felt and fumbled at the pig. It did not burn him so much now; still he licked his fingers from a sort of habit.

The truth at length broke into his slow understanding that it was the pig that smelled so, and the pig that tasted so delicious. Surrendering himself to the new-born pleasure, he fell to tearing up whole handfuls of the scorched skin with the flesh next it, and was cramming it down his throat in his beastly fashion, when his sire entered amid the smoking rafters, armed with a cudgel. Finding now affairs stood, he began to rain blows upon the young rogue's shoulders, as thick as hailstones, which Bo-bo heeded not any more than if they had been flies. His father might lay on, but he could not beat him from his pig, till he had fairly made an end of it, when something like the following dialogue ensued:

"You graceless whelp, what have you got there devouring? Is it not enough that you have burned down three houses with your dog's tricks, and be hanged to you! but you must be eating fire, and I know not what——what have you got there, I say?"

"O father, the pig, the pig! Do come and taste how nice the burnt pig eats."

The ears of Ho-ti tingled with horror. He cursed his son, and he cursed himself that ever he should have a son that should eat burnt pig.

Bo-bo, whose scent was wonderfully sharpened since morning, soon raked out another pig, and fairly rending it asunder, thrust the lesser half by main force into the fists of Ho-ti, still shouting out, "Eat, eat, eat, the burnt pig, father, only taste!" ——with such barbarous cries, cramming all the while as if he would choke.

Ho-ti trembled in every joint while he grasped the abominable thing, wavering whether he should not put his son to death for an unnatural young monster. But the crackling scorched his fingers, as it had done his son's; and applying the same remedy to them, he in his turn tasted some of its flavor, which, make what sour mouths he would for pretence, proved not altogether displeasing to him. In conclusion both father and son fairly sat down to the mess, and never left off till they had despatched all that remained of the litter.

Bo-bo was strictly enjoined not to let the secret escape, for the neighbors would certainly have stoned them for a couple of abominable wretched, who could think of improving upon the good meat which God had sent them. Nevertheless, strange stories got about. It was observed that Ho-ti's cottage was burned down more frequently than ever. Nothing but fires from this time forward. Some would break out in broad day, others in the night time. Ho-ti himself, which was the more remarkable, instead of chastising his son, seemed to grow more indulgent to him than ever.

At length they were watched, the terrible mystery discovered, and the father and son summoned to take their trial at Pekin. Evidence was given, the obnoxious food itself produced in court, and verdict about to be pronounced, when the foreman of the jury begged that some of the burnt pig, of which the culprit stood accused, might be handed into the box. He handled it, and the jury all handled it. They all burned their fingers as Bo-bo and his father had done before them, and nature prompted to each of them the same remedy. Against the face of all the facts, and the clearest charge which judge had ever given, ——to the surprise of the whole court, townsfolk, strangers, reporters, and all present, ——without leaving the box, or any manner of consultation whatever, they brought in a verdict of Not Guilty.

The judge, who was a shrewd fellow, winked at the unfairness of the decision; and when the court was dismissed went privily, and bought up all the pigs that could be had for love or money. In a few days his lordship's town house was observed to be on fire. The thing took wing, and now there was nothing to be seen but fire in every direction. Fuel and pigs grew enormously dear all over the district. The insurance offices one and all shut up shop.

People built slighter and slighter every day, until it was feared that the very science of architecture would in no long time be lost to the world. Thus this custom of firing houses continued, till in process of time, says my manuscript, a sage arose, who made a discovery, that the flesh of swine, or indeed of any other animal might be cooked (burned as they called it) without the necessity of consuming a whole house to dress it.

Then first began the rude form of gridiron. Roasting by the string or spit came in a century or two later. By such slow degrees, concludes the manuscript, do the most useful and seemingly the most obvious arts make their way among mankind.

(Charles Lamb)

译文

论烤猪

我的朋友M曾好意地读给我听一篇中国的文稿并向我讲解它的内容。据上面的记载，人类在起初七万年间是从动物身上撕咬下肉来生吃的，就像如今的阿比西尼亚人那样。他们那个伟大的孔夫子在他关于历史兴衰的书中毫不隐讳地提到过这个时期，在《春秋》的第二章中他还将一个黄金时代命名为“厨丰”，字面上的意思就是厨师的节日。这份文稿继续讲述了炙烤，或者不如说烧煮，这门手艺是如以下的记述那样，在无意间被发现的。

一天早上，养猪人何悌按照惯例去林子里为他的猪采集橡果，他把小屋留给大儿子波波来照看。波波是个胖乎乎的笨拙孩子，像同龄人一样喜欢玩火。他把一些火星溅到了稻草堆上，草立刻被点燃了。大火烧遍了小破屋的每个角落，直到将它烧为灰烬。一同烧毁的还有一间小房（你可以想象为一个临时搭起的简陋建筑），不过更为紧要的是，新生的可爱小猪，多达九只，也被烧死了。

据我们读到的记载，从远古时期开始，中国猪在整个东方已经被视为一种珍贵的食品。正如你想的那样，波波十分惊慌，倒也不是为了小屋——父亲和他能够随时花上一两小时用干草把它重新建起来，而是因为烧死了那些猪。

当面对一具还冒着烟的小猪的尸体，他搓着双手思考着如何向父亲解释时，一股从来没有闻到过的味道向他的鼻子袭来。它是从哪里来的呢？不是来自于烧毁的小屋——他以前就闻到过那种味道；事实上，这绝不是倒霉的小玩火者由于疏忽造成的第一起事故了。它也不像是那些已知的药、草和花的味道。

他想不出什么主意，便弯下腰摸了摸那只猪，看看还有没有活着的迹象。手指被烫着了，他就用那傻乎乎的方法把它们塞进嘴里来进行冷却。一些烧焦的猪皮碎屑粘在了手指上，他有生以来第一次（也是世界历史中的第一次，其实在他之前没有人知道这个）尝到了——烤脆的皮！他又去触摸摆弄那头猪，现在已经不那么烫了，但他还是习惯性地舔了舔手指。

最终他那迟钝的头脑弄明白了真相，是猪散发出了这个味道，而且吃上去美味的也是猪。他沉溺于这个新发现的愉悦中，大把大把地连带旁边的肉一起撕下烤熟的猪皮，用他那粗鲁的方式将它们塞进喉咙。这时，他的父亲手拿着棍子，穿过冒着烟的柱子走了进来。明白发生了什么事情后，责打就像冰雹一样落在了这个小淘气的肩上，然而波波却把它们当成苍蝇一般完全没在意。不管父亲怎么责打，他就是不离开那头猪，直到差不多吃完了为止。接着就发生了如下的对话：

“你这个粗野的小孩，你在那边吃什么？你用那些狗把戏烧毁了三座屋子还不够吗？真该把你吊起来！你居然在吃火，我都不知道，——我说，你到底在那里吃什么？”

“哦，爸爸，这头猪，这头猪！来尝尝这个烧熟的猪有多么美味吧。”

何悌害怕得耳朵“嗡”的一声，他咒骂儿子，也咒骂自己居然生了一个吃烤猪的儿子。

波波的嗅觉自早上以来就很灵敏，他立刻找到了另一只猪，把它撕成差不多的两部分并把较小的一半硬是塞进了何悌的手中，继续叫唤着：“吃吧吃吧，吃这个烤猪吧，爸爸，尝尝看！”——他一面粗野地叫着一面猛往嘴里塞，都快要噎住了。

何悌拿着这该死的东西，浑身上下每一个关节都在颤抖，他犹豫着要不要把他的儿子当作一个违背人伦的小怪物来处死。但烧脆的猪皮就像烫了他儿子那样，烫着了他的手指。他也同样地把手指放进嘴里尝到了味道。他虽然装出一副不好吃的样子，但明白这味道不差。最后父子俩都坐下吃了起来，直到把所有余下的都吃完，一点不剩为止。

波波被严格要求不要泄露这个秘密，要不然邻居们肯定会向他们投石子，把他们当作可恶的人，居然改变神灵赐予的好肉。然而，奇怪的传言还是传播了开来。有人看到何悌的小屋比以前烧毁得更频繁了。从那以后，他们家总是起火，有时是在大白天，有时是在晚上。更加引人注意的是，何悌并没有责打他的儿子，而且看起来越来越骄纵他了。

最终他们受到了监视，这个可怕的秘密被揭发了，父子俩被传唤到北京接受审问。证据提交了上去，那可憎的食物也在法庭上被制作出来。就在判决即将被宣布时，陪审长请求把据此指控罪犯的烤猪呈上陪审席。他摸了摸烤猪，陪审员们也都摸了摸烤猪。他们像波波和他的父亲以前一样被烫着了，然后自然地采用了相同的疗法。然后，不管眼前的所有事实，不管法官最明确的指控，让整个法庭、市民、外乡人、记者和所有在场者吃惊的是，他们没有离开陪审席，也没有进行任何讨论，就做出了无罪的判决。

法官是一个精明的人，默许了这个不正当的判决过程。退庭以后，他就暗中靠白要和用钱买拿走了所有的猪。没过几天，法官大人的公馆就着火了。这样的事飞速地传播着，如今到处都可以看到火烧。整个地区燃料和猪的价格涨得飞快，而保险公司却一个个都倒闭了。

一天天的，人们把房屋盖得越来越简陋，直到有人开始担心建筑科学不久就会从世上失传了。就这样，这种烧房子的习惯延续着。直到随着时间的流逝，如手稿记载那样出现了一个贤者，他发现不管是烹制（用他们的话来说就是烤熟）猪肉还是别的动物，根本无需花费整座房子来烤。

随后，先出现了烤肉架的原型，一两个世纪后又有了挂在绳子上或者串在铁叉上烤肉的方法。这部手稿最后写道：就这样，那些最有用也最平凡的手艺慢慢在世间一步步发展了起来。

（查尔斯·兰姆）

The Biography of a Beaver

预习

amateur /ˈæmətər/ 业余爱好者

apex /ˈeɪpeks/ 最高点

incisors /ɪnˈsaɪzəz/ 切牙

reconnoiter /ˌrekəˈnɔɪtə/ 勘测

vise /vaɪs/ 虎头钳

I

A broad, flat tail came down on the water with a whack that sent the echoes flying back and forth across the pond, and its owner ducked his head, arched his back, and dived to the bottom. It was a very curious tail, for besides being so oddly paddle-shaped it was covered with what looked like scales, but were really sections and indentations of hard, horny, blackish-gray skin. Except its owner's relations, there was no one else in all the animal kingdom who had one like it. But the strangest thing about it was the many different ways in which he used it. Just now it was his rudder——and a very good rudder, too.

In a moment his little brown head reappeared, and he and his brothers and sisters went chasing each other round and round the pond, ducking and diving and splashing, raising such a commotion that they sent the ripples washing all along the grassy shores, and having the jolliest kind of time. When the youngsters wanted a change, they climbed up on to a log, and nudged and hunched each other, poking their noses into one another's fat little sides, and each trying to shove his brother or sister back into the water. By and by they scrambled out on the bank, and then, when their fur had dripped a little, they set to work to comb it. Up they sat on their hind legs and tails——the tail was a stool now, you see——and scratched their heads and shoulders with the long brown claws of their small, black, hairy hands. Then the hind feet came up one at a time, and combed and stroked their sides till the moisture was gone and the fur was soft and smooth and glossy as velvet.

After that they had to have another romp. They were not half as graceful on land as they had been in the water. In fact they were not graceful at all, and the way they stood around on their hind legs, and shuffled and pranced and wheeled like baby hippopotami, and slapped the ground with their tails, was one of the funniest sights in the heart of the woods. And the funniest and liveliest of them all was the one now whom I shall call the Beaver——with a big B.

The first year of his life was an easy one, especially the winter, when there was little for anyone to do except to eat, to sleep, and now and then to fish for the roots of the yellow water-lily in the soft mud at the bottom of the pond. During that season he probably accomplished more than his parents did, for if he could not toil he could at least grow.

But later, on a dark autumn night, behold the young Beaver working with might and main. His parents have felled a tree, and it is his business to help them cut up the best portions and carry them home. He gnaws off a small branch, seizes the butt end between his teeth, swings it over his shoulder, and makes for the water, keeping his head twisted around to the right or left so that the end of the branch may trail on the ground behind him. Sometimes he even rises on his hind legs, and walks almost upright, with his broad, strong tail for a prop to keep him from tipping over backward if his load happens to catch on something. Arrived at the canal or at the edge of the pond, he jumps in and swims for town, still carrying the branch over his shoulder, and finally leaves it on the growing pile in front of his father's lodge.

These were his first tasks. Later on he learned to fell trees himself. Standing on his hind legs and tail, with his hands braced against the trunk, he would hold his head sidewise, open his mouth wide, set his teeth against the bark, and bring his jaws together with a savage nip that left a deep gash in the side of the tree. A second nip deepened the gash, and gave it more of a downward slant, and two or three more carried it still farther into the tough wood. Then he would choose a new spot a little farther down, and start a second gash, which was made to slant up toward the first. And when he thought that they were both deep enough he would set his teeth firmly in the wood between them, and pull and jerk and twist at it until he had wrenched out a chip——a chip perhaps two inches long, and from an inch to a quarter of an inch thick.

Chip after chip was torn out in this way, and gradually he would work around the tree until he had completely encircled it. Then the groove was made deeper. Little by little he dug away the tree's flesh until there was nothing left but its heart, and it began to creak and rend. The Beaver jumped aside to get out of the way, and hundreds of small, tender branches, and delicious little twigs and buds came crashing down where he could cut them off and eat them or carry them away at his leisure.

One night the Beaver came swimming down the pond, homeward bound, and as he dived and approached the submarine entrance of the lodge, he noticed some stakes driven into the mud——stakes that had never been there before. They seemed to form two rows, one on each side of his course, but as there was room enough for him to pass between them he swam straight ahead without stopping. His hands had no webs between the fingers, and were of little use in swimming, so he had folded them back against his body; but his big feet were working like the wheels of a twin-screw steamer, and he was forging along at a great rate. Suddenly, half-way down the line of stakes, his breast touched the pan of a steel trap, and the jaws flew up quick as a wink and strong as a vise. Fortunately there was nothing that they could take hold of. They struck him so hard that they lifted him bodily upward, but they caught only a few hairs.

A week later, however, he was really caught and lost his right hand. By the time the Beaver's wound was healed——Nature was good to him, and the skin soon grew over the torn stump——the pond was covered with ice. The beavers, only half as numerous as they had been a few weeks before, kept close in their lodges and burrows, and for a time they lived in peace and quiet, and their numbers suffered no further diminution. Then the trapper took to setting his traps through the ice, and before long matters were worse than ever. By spring the few beavers that remained were so thoroughly frightened that the ancient town was abandoned forever. The lodges fell to ruins, the burrows caved in, the dam gave way, the pond and canals were drained, and that was the end of the city.

II

The next city that claimed the honor of being our Beaver's home was a brand-new one. Let us see how it had its beginning. The Beaver got married about the time he left his old home. Except for his missing hand, his wife was so like him that it would have puzzled you to tell which was which. Do you want to know what they looked like? They measured about three feet, six inches, from tip of nose to tip of tail, and they weighed perhaps thirty pounds apiece. Their bodies were heavy and clumsy, and were covered with thick, soft, gray is under-fur, which in turn was overlaid with longer hairs of a glistening chestnut-brown, making a coat that was thoroughly water-proof as well as very beautiful. Their heads were somewhat like those of gigantic rats, with small, light-brown eyes,little round ears covered with hair, and long orange-colored incisors looking out from between parted lips. One portrait will answer for both of them.

They wandered about for some time, looking for a suitable location, and examining several spots along the beds of various little rivers, none of which seemed to be just right. But at last they found, in the very heart of the wilderness, a place where a shallow stream ran over a hard stony bottom, and here they set to work. Alder bushes laid lengthwise of the current were the first materials used, and for a time the water filtered through them with hardly a pause. Then the beavers began laying mud and stones and moss on this brush foundation, scooping them up with their hands, and holding them under their chins as they waddled or swam to the dam.

The first year the beavers did not try to raise the stream more than a foot above its original level. There was much other work to be done——a house to be built, and food to be laid in for the winter——and if they spent too much time on the dam they might freeze or starve before spring. A few rods upstream was a grassy point which the rising waters had transformed into an island, and here they built their lodge, a hollow mound of sticks and mud, with a small, cave-like chamber in the center, from which two tunnels led out under the pond. The walls were masses of earth and wood and stones, so thick and solid that even a man with an axe would have found it difficult to penetrate them. Only at the very apex of the mound there was no mud, nothing but tangled sticks through which a breath of fresh air found its way now and then. In all other respects the house was neat and clean. The floor was only two or three inches above the level of the water in the tunnels, and would naturally have been a bed of mud; but they mixed little twigs with it, and stamped and pounded it down till it was hard and smooth. With the ends of projecting sticks cut off to leave the walls even and regular, and with long grass carried in to make the beds, the lodge was finished and ready.

Five babies came in May, and they were very pretty children——about as large as rats, and covered with thick, soft, silky, reddish-brown fur, but without any of the longer, coarser, chestnut-colored hairs that formed their parents' outer coats. They were very playful, too, as the father and mother had been in their own youthful days. The old beavers brought in little twigs for them, about the size of lead-pencils; and if you had been there, and your eyes had been sharp enough to pierce the gloom, you might have seen the youngsters exercising their brand-new teeth, and learning to sit up and hold sticks in their baby hands while they ate the bark. And wouldn't you have liked to be present on the night when they first went swimming down the long, dark tunnel; and, rising to the surface, looked around on their world of woods and water——on the quiet pond, with its glassy smoothness broken only by their own ripples; on the tall trees, lifting their fingers toward the sky; and on the stars, marching silently across the heavens, and looking down with still, unwinking eyes on another family of babies that had come to live and love and be happy for a little while on God's earth?

Only once that year did a man come to town, and then he did not do anything very dreadful. He was not a trapper, he was only an amateur naturalist who wanted to see the beaver sat their work, and who thought he was smart enough to catch them at it. His plan was simple enough: he made a breach in the dam one night, and then climbed a tree and waited for them to come and mend it. It was bright moonlight, and he thought he would see the whole thing and learn some wonderful secrets.

The Beaver was at work in the woods not very far away, and presently he came down to the edge of the pond, rolling a heavy birch cutting before him. He noticed at once that the water was falling, and he started straight for the dam to see what was the matter. The amateur naturalist saw him coming, a dark speck moving swiftly down the pond, with a long V-shaped ripple spreading out behind him like the flanks of a flock of wild geese. But the Beaver was doing some thinking while he swam. He had never before known the water to fall so suddenly and rapidly; there must be a very bad break in the dam. How could it have happened? It looked suspicious. It looked very suspicious indeed; and just before he reached the dam he stopped to reconnoiter, and at once caught sight of the naturalist up in the tree. His tail rose in the air and came down with the loudest whack that had ever echoed across the pond, a stroke that sent the spray flying in every direction, and that might have been heard three-quarters of a mile away. His wife heard it, and paused in her work of felling a tree; the children heard it, and the neighbors heard it; they all knew it meant business.

The Beaver dived like a loon and swam for dear life, and he did not come to the surface again till he had reached the farther end of the pond and was out of sight behind a grassy point. There he stayed, now and then striking the water with his tail as a signal that the danger was not yet over. The naturalist roosted in the tree till his teeth were chattering and he was fairly blue with cold, and then he scrambled down and went back to his camp. He decided that watching beavers wasn't very interesting, anyhow——hardly worth the trouble it cost.

In the following year the population was increased to eighteen, for six more babies arrived in our Beaver's lodge, and four in his neighbors. In another twelve-month the first five were old enough to build lodges and found homes of their own; and so the city grew, and our Beaver and his wife were the original inhabitants, the first settlers, the most looked-up-to of all the citizens.

(William Davenport Hulbert)

译文

河狸传记

I

一条又宽又扁的尾巴重重拍打着水面，引得池塘上空水声缭绕不绝。尾巴的主人正低头弓背，向池底潜去。这是一条长得很奇怪的尾巴，不但形状像古怪的扁板，而且还覆盖着一层看上去像鱼鳞的东西。但实际上，这些类似鱼鳞的凹凸是由坚硬的黑灰色角质层构成的。除了尾巴主人的亲戚，整个动物王国都没有谁拥有这样一条尾巴了。不过最奇特的还是这条尾巴用途的多种多样。就在刚才，它变身成了主人的方向舵——而且是一个很棒的方向舵哦！

一会儿，他那小小的棕色脑袋又出现了，一圈又一圈地绕着池塘，和他的兄弟姐妹们追逐嬉戏。他们栽进水里，潜到水底，使得水面溅起高高的浪花。他们在水里造成的骚动激起了层层涟漪，拍打在绿草茵茵的池岸上。这是他们拥有的最快乐的时光。当这些小家伙们想要换个游戏时，他们就会爬到一根木头上，互相推推搡搡，把鼻子戳进对方胖乎乎的小小身体，试图将自己的兄弟姐妹们掀翻到水里。又过了一会儿，他们爬上了岸，等身上的皮毛滴干一点水分，就开始着手进行梳理的工作。他们直直坐在自己的后腿和尾巴上——这时候你会发现尾巴变成了一个凳子——用长长的棕色爪子在头上和肩膀上又抓又搔。这些爪子长在他们那小小的、黑色的而又多毛的手上。他们一次会抬起一只脚，不断梳理和抚顺体侧的毛，直到毛上的水分变干。这时，他的毛会变得又软又滑，像天鹅绒一样富有光泽。

然后他们又开始嬉戏玩闹。他们在陆地上的表现不及在水里表现的一半优雅。事实上，他们根本就一点儿都不优雅。他们用后腿站立，像河马宝宝一样闪躲跳跃、滚来滚去；他们还用尾巴拍打着地面。他们的这副模样是森林深处最有趣的场景之一，而他们之中最有趣、最有活力的就是这只现在被我称作比弗（Beaver，意为“河狸”）的河狸了。

在生命里的第一年，比弗过得十分舒适，特别是冬天的时候，除了吃饭、睡觉以及时不时地从池塘底部柔软的淤泥里捞取黄色水仙花的根以外，他也没什么可干的了。在那个季节，他或许比他的父母成就更多，因为就算他不能吃苦耐劳，他还可以长个子呀。

但到了后来，年轻的比弗就得在黑沉沉的秋夜里拼命工作了。他的父母已经放倒一棵树，而比弗的任务是帮助他们把树上最好的部分砍下来并运回家。他咬断一根小树枝，用牙齿衔着树枝的末端把它甩到肩膀上，然后朝着水边前进，他左右扭动着脑袋好让树枝跟在他身后在地面上拖动。有时候他甚至用后腿站起来直立行走，这时他那又宽又强壮的尾巴就成了一个支柱，让他不至于因为树枝碰巧刮到什么东西而向后翻倒。等到了沟边或是池岸，他就跳入水中游向居住的小镇，肩膀上仍旧扛着那根树枝，最后他把它留在了父亲屋子前不断增高的木头堆里。

这些是他刚开始的工作，之后他得学会自己砍树。他用后腿和尾巴站立，两手紧抱树干，把头歪向一边，张大嘴用牙齿对着树皮，然后上下颚猛然合拢，凶猛地咬了一口——树干上留下了一个深深的咬痕。接着，他咬了第二口，不但加深了原来的咬痕，而且更大程度上让它向下倾斜，然后他再咬上两三口，让这一咬痕继续向坚硬的木头内部推进。之后，他会选择一个靠下的新位置，开始制造向上倾斜的第二个咬痕。当他认为两个咬痕都足够深的时候，他会把牙齿牢牢地嵌入它们中间的木头，又推又拉又扭，直到他撕开一个缺口——这个缺口大约五厘米长，两厘米厚。

就这样，他撕开一个又一个缺口，绕着树一点点啃咬，直到绕完一圈。于是这个沟就越变越深。他一点一点挖走了树里的木头，到最后除了树心外什么都没剩下，这时树就会开始“嘎吱”作响，慢慢断裂。比弗跳到一边，好给倒下的树让出空间。成百上千的小树枝、美味的小嫩枝和叶芽“啪啦”一声掉落下来，他可以从容不迫地咬断它们、吃掉它们或者把它们带走。

一天晚上，比弗沿着池塘向下游，想要回家去。当他潜入水里并向屋子的水下入口靠近的时候，他注意到淤泥里插着一些木桩——那里以前从没有木桩。这些木桩排成两排，分别立在回家路上的两边。由于有足够的空间让他通过，所以他毫不停歇地径直向前游去。他的手指之间没有蹼，在游泳时起不了什么作用，于是他把它们合拢了背在身后；但他的脚很有作用，像拥有双推进器汽船的轮子一样推动他向前，他以一个很快的速度努力游着。当他游到木桩半当中的时候，他的胸膛突然碰到了一个捕兽夹的底盘。眨眼之间，捕兽夹的钢牙就飞速地咬合在一起，像老虎钳一般铿锵有力。幸运的是，它们什么都没有抓到，猛烈攻击时带起的水流将他整个身体抬了上去，使得它们只抓到了几根河狸毛。

然而一星期后，他果真被捕兽夹夹到了，结果失去了右手。等到比弗的伤口痊愈的时候——大自然待他很和善，他新长的皮肤很快就盖住了残肢上被撕扯的伤口——池塘的水面已经结成了冰。现在的河狸在数量上只有几星期前的一半多，他们紧紧挤在屋子和洞穴里，将过上一段安详平静的时光，他们的数量不用继续减少。然而，捕猎者开始在冰层下面设置捕兽夹，情况在短时间内变得前所未有的糟糕，只有几只河狸在春天来临的时候幸存了下来。他们是如此害怕，以至于永远遗弃了这个过去居住的小镇。木屋成了废墟，洞穴塌陷，堤坝垮掉，池塘和沟渠里的水被排得一干二净。河狸们建造的城市走向了终点。

II

下一个有幸成为比弗家园的城市是崭新的。让我们看看它是如何发端的。大约是在离开前一个家的时候，比弗结婚了。他的妻子长得非常像他，若不是因为他缺了一只手，你很难分得清他们谁是谁。你想知道他们长成什么样吗？从鼻子尖量到尾巴尖的话，他们大约有一两米长，并且每只大约有十几千克重。他们的身体笨重，紧挨着皮肤长着一层浓密柔软的浅灰色绒毛，绒毛上再覆盖上一层油亮的栗棕色长毛。这样他们就穿上了一件又漂亮又完全防水的外套。他们的脑袋有点儿像大鼠，有浅棕色的小眼睛、覆有毛发的小圆耳和微张的嘴唇中间露出来的染成橘色的长门牙。瞧，一幅肖像画就把他们俩都描绘出来了。

有一段时间他们四处游荡，想要寻找一个合适的地方建造城池。他们沿着多条小河的河床勘查了几个地点，但看上去没有一个地点合适。不过，最后他们在荒野的深处找到了一处地方，那里有一条浅浅的小溪从坚硬的石头河床上流过。于是他们开始了工作。沿着溪流纵向生长的杨木丛是最先被用到的材料，而长久以来水流都是毫不停歇地从它们当中穿过。河狸们开始在这个灌木基座上堆积泥土、石头和苔藓，好把它建成一座堤坝。他们先是用手挖出泥土、石头和苔藓，然后在下巴下方捧着它们，或者是蹒跚地走回堤坝，或者是顺畅地游回堤坝。

第一年的时候河狸们没有试图将小溪原有的水位抬到三十厘米以上，因为他们有很多其他的工作要做——要修建房子，要为过冬储存食物——如果他们在堤坝上花费太多的时间，在春天来临前他们很可能要挨饿受冻。小溪上游几十米远的地方绿草茵茵，不断升高的水域把它变成了一个小岛，他们在这里建造起房屋：一个由树枝和泥巴构成的空心土堆，中间有一个洞穴似的小小房间，两条地道从这里通向池塘的下方。房屋的墙壁堆集了大量的泥土、木头和石块，非常厚实也非常坚硬，就算是一个成年人用斧头都难以劈开它们。土堆的顶端是没有泥土的，除了纠缠在一起的树枝外什么都没有，这让新鲜的空气可以随时进入。除此之外，房屋又干净又整洁，地面仅比地道里的水位高五六厘米，自然而然就成了一张泥土做的床，但他们在泥土里混入了小细枝，“咚咚咚”地在上面踩来踩去，直到地面变得坚硬而平滑。

他们还会把突出的树枝末端切断，使墙面变得平坦整齐，然后再搬来长长的青草当作被褥铺在地上。这时候，屋子就建成并准备停当了。

五月里，五只小宝宝出生了，他们都是非常漂亮的孩子——大约和老鼠一般大，全身覆盖着浓密柔软、丝绸般光滑的红褐色皮毛，不过他们没有一根织成父母外套的那种又长又粗糙的栗色毛发。他们也很爱玩耍，就像父母幼年时一样。年长的河狸们给他们带来小嫩枝当作食物，这些小嫩枝全都和铅笔差不多大小。如果你在现场并且你的眼神犀利得足够穿透昏暗的话，你可能会看见小家伙们正在锻炼他们的新牙齿，并学习怎样在啃树皮的时候坐直身体并用小手抓住树枝。在某个夜晚，他们会第一次游过漫长阴暗的地道，浮到水面上环顾他们那由木与水构成的世界——平静的池塘，要不是水面泛起的丝丝涟漪，它平静得就像一面镜子；他们会张望高高的大树，看它们将枝桠伸向天空；他们会仰望星星，看它们无声地跨越天幕，看它们睁大眼睛静静俯视着池塘，这是天地间河狸宝宝们的又一个家园，他们已经在这里相亲相爱地生活了一段时间，倍感幸福快乐。

那一年，只有一个人来过这个河狸小镇一次，而且他并没有做什么特别糟糕的事情。他不是捕猎者，只是一名业余的博物学家，想要观察河狸如何工作，自认为能够聪明地捕捉到他们工作时的样子。他的计划相当简单：趁着夜色在堤坝上制造一个缺口，然后爬上树等待他们来修补。月光明亮，他觉得自己会看到整个过程并得知一些绝妙的秘密。

比弗正在不远处的树林里工作。不久，他滚着一根沉重的桦木回到池塘边，立刻注意到水流正在倾泻，于是径直奔向堤坝去看发生了什么事。这名业余博物学家看见他过来了，一个黑点迅速向池塘下方移动，身后扩散开长长的V形水纹，看上去就像一群人字形大雁的侧面。但比弗在游水的时候还在不停思考：他以前从没见过池水如此突然、急速地倾泻，堤坝上肯定有一个很严重的缺口。这一切是怎么发生的呢？看上去真可疑。唔，看上去确实非常可疑。于是，他在堤坝前停下来进行侦察，立即看到了树上的博物学家。他高高竖起尾巴，狠狠地击向水面，这一下激得水花四面飞溅，响亮的拍打声不断在池塘上空回响，大概一千多米之外都能听得见。他的妻子听到了，停下了砍树的工作；他的孩子和邻居也听到了。他们都清楚这意味着有事情发生。

比弗像一只潜鸟一样潜入水里，为了宝贵的生命而游着，一次都没有浮上水面，直到游到池塘远远的一端，消失在绿草地后面。他在那里停住了，不时地用尾巴击打着水面，以此告知大家危险还没有过去。博物学家藏在树上，冻得牙齿打颤全身发紫，然后他爬下树回到了野营地。他想清楚了，无论如何，观察河狸都不是一件非常有趣的事——这点趣味几乎无法抵消它所引起的麻烦。

随后的一年里，河狸的人口增加到了十八只，比弗家里又多了六只小河狸，而他的邻居家里多了四只小河狸。又过了一年，最初的五只小河狸已经发育得足够成熟，开始修建屋子，建立自己的家园，于是城市不断扩大。而比弗和他的妻子作为原始居民和首批移民，成了所有城市居民最尊敬的河狸。

（威廉姆·达文波特·赫尔伯特）

作者介绍

威廉姆·达文波特·赫尔伯特出生于密歇根的麦基诺岛。少年时期，他在水上花费了大量的时间，驾着小艇或是父亲的渔船在麦基诺海峡四处出没。后来，他在密歇根上半岛中心的林场生活了几年，林场附近有一个他称作“闪光玻璃”的美丽小湖。在这一时期，他开始创作有关树林及生活在树林中的野生动物的故事。这些故事最初投给了《芝加哥实录》，后来投给了《麦克卢尔》和其他杂志。本文选自《森林邻居》，该书是一本收录了这些故事的合集，由麦克卢尔公司出版。

The Perils and Pleasures of Ballooning

When I was a small boy, it was a favorite pastime of my companions and myself to climb high up in trees and swing from branch to branch. The tender pines which grew about my Georgia home would sway as we jumped, and I could make leaps of from twenty to thirty feet. I excelled at the sport, and none of my companions could catch me. I believe that in that squirrel-like amusement were born the wishes and ambitions that have led me since to go up some twelve thousand feet in the air, sailing through the clouds, seeing the glories of the sunset, high above the land, and spending fourteen hours in the midst of a terrific storm with the lightnings playing above and below me.

There is something about the start of a balloon ascension which gives a thrill that cannot be experienced on any other occasion. This is especially true of the one who is to be the navigator. He cannot delegate to others, entirely, the responsibility of seeing that the balloon is in perfect condition before he trusts his life to it. The valves must work properly; the cords must be strong; the bag itself must not leak; the net must be on correctly; the basket must be properly attached and stored with instruments, water, and food. It would take but a moment in the air to find out a mistake that might cost the navigator and his passengers their lives.

It takes hours to inflate the balloon, but there is plenty of work to do as the gas slowly lifts the limp bag and spreads it out into a firm sphere. When it is tense and tugs at the numerous sand-bags, the car is made ready, slipped under, and attached. After all is tested again, the navigator steps in, the bags are let loose, one by one, the assistants hang on for a minute, then let go, and soon the earth is far behind.

There is no fear as one sees the earth receding from under the balloon——at least, there was none with me. At the height of a few hundred feet, a sense of tranquillity comes over one, and, as the distance from the earth increases, a feeling of actual happiness is experienced.

The atmospheric pressure which the man on the earth is constantly enduring, diminishes as the balloon rises in the air. Physical and mental exhilaration follow. The muscles seem harder, the heart beats with more ease, and there is a sense of lightness and freedom that cannot easily be described. At the same time there is an awakening of the mentality. The senses are keener. Perception is increased; one thinks more quickly, and the thoughts are more exalted. The amount of nervous energy which one expends while in the air is enormous. It is not appreciated, of course, until the earth is reached again. But then the effects are severe, and often lasting.

One of the strangest sensations that a balloonist experiences is that of being lost in a fog. The absolute separation which one feels at such a time cannot be duplicated in any other human experience. There is no calculating of position; the statoscope tells whether the balloon is rising or falling, but beyond that there is no way of knowing east or west, north or south. When one can see, the drag rope, extending three hundred feet below the car, will tell by its swaying which way the balloon is proceeding. But in a fog this, of course, cannot be seen. The knowledge of the direction in which the balloon is drifting is of extreme importance to those who are in it.

The sea is the great danger of the aeronaut. It is the one dread thing that is always before him. The peril of being blown out over the ocean or other large body of water is over in his mind, and he is constantly calculating his position with this thought in view. To be lost in a fog, then, exposes him to his greatest enemy. The balloon has a tendency to revolve, and one cannot keep any sense of direction in his head. The compass is likewise useless, placing the aerial navigator at the mercy of the unfelt wind. In this situation there are sounds that resemble those of the sea, and occasionally the fog seems to part and open up the awful deep. It is strange how a man can face such moments with merely a fleeting sense of fear. What it would be to find oneself over the ocean can be easily imagined. Yet even when the terrible conviction comes, that below the fog is water, it is accepted, in the exalted state a man's mind is in when high in air, without disturbance, and the result is watched for with perfect tranquillity.

I remember we were lost in a fog on the long trip we took a few months ago, when we landed in Massachusetts near the coast of the Atlantic Ocean. The fog lasted for hours. At times we could hear the water under us, but did not know whether it was a river, that would be able to do us little harm if we landed in it, or the unfathomable ocean, that would mean death if we ever touched it. There is nothing for a balloonist to do in such a situation. If he fears that he is over the sea, he must stay up as long as he can or until the fog breaks and possibly relieves his suspense.

But far more wonderful than the fog or the loveliness of the cloud land, which looks like great white mountains floating around in space, and more impressive even than the broad expanse of land on a clear, sunny day, is a storm. To be in the lightning, to have it above and below, to hear the thunder crash about me, to see the clouds condense and the moisture gather on the bag of the balloon and fall down the sides until it was a perfect spout, pouring down on my head——this was an experience I once had that lasted for fourteen and a half hours.

The storm was so grand that in its horror it failed to terrorize. The lightning was not forked nor in streaks; there was simply an opening up of blue flame which extended on all sides. The electricity was so prevalent that the ropes snapped as I touched them. Yet the very fact that I was immediately in the storm, with the lightning completely surrounding me, prevented the gas-bag from exploding, as it would have done had a match been touched to it.

But it is neither in the storm nor in the unusual manifestations of the air that the real pleasure of a balloon trip is found. It is rather in the sailing over the earth, where city and country can be seen as a bird sees them, in watching the rivers that look like threads and the mountains that seem mere playthings below, and in being, in a way, a master of space, as man in all the ages has not been. And this, after all, is the exquisite joy of the balloonist——that he can claim to have found a sport with which none other can compare.

(Julian P. Thomas)

译文

热气球的危险与乐趣

我还是个小男孩时，我和小伙伴们最大的乐趣就爬到高高的树上，在树枝间荡来荡去。我在乔治亚州的家附近有株细细的小松树，我们在那蹦跳玩耍时它就会来回摇晃，那时我可以跳到六米多远。我擅长玩这项游戏，我的小伙伴们都抓不着我。我觉得正是我们这项像松鼠一样的游戏孕育了那些心愿和抱负，把我带到了三千多米的高空。我畅游在浮云间，欣赏夕阳的余晖，高高浮于大地上空，在可怕的暴风雨中待上十四小时，看闪电在我身边上蹿下跳。

热气球升空之际似乎能给人一种其他地方无法体验到的快感，尤其是对驾驶它的人来说。在决定把生命寄托于此之前，他完全不能把察看热气球是否完好无损的责任交付给他人。气阀必须正常工作；绳索必须很结实；球囊本身不能漏气；网必须正确地展开；吊篮必须连接良好，还要储存些工具、水和食物。在空中，发生一个足以葬送驾驶员和所有乘客的失误不过是一瞬间的事。

给气球充气需要几个小时，但在气体慢慢使又软又瘪的球囊浮起，并伸展成饱满结实的球体期间还有许多工作要做。等到热气球的绳子绷紧，拖着很多沙袋时，吊篮也就准备好，轻轻放到下方，并连接到气球上。一切都再次检查完毕后，驾驶员登了上去，沙袋被一个个解开，助手拉着绳子稍等片刻，之后再放手，不一会大地就被远远地抛在身后了。

看着地球在气球下方逐渐退远并不吓人——至少，我不觉得吓人。在五六百米的高空，你会有种平和宁静的感觉，而随着与大地距离的增大，还会体会到一种真切的幸福感。那在地面上不断压迫人的气压，随着气球在空中上升而逐渐降低，随之而来的，是身体和心理上的愉悦。肌肉似乎更加有力，心跳也变得更加舒缓，还有一种难以言表的轻松自如。与此同时，还会有种容光焕发的感觉。感官变得更敏锐，感知力也增强了；思维更加迅速，思想也更兴奋。你在空中消耗的神经能量难以估量。当然，在你再次到达地面之前不会有所察觉，但其影响却十分深刻、久远。

热气球驾驶员经历的最奇异的事就是在大雾里迷失方向。在那样一段时间内与世隔绝的感觉在其他任何的人类经历中都无法复制。你无法估算自己的位置。气压计能显示气球在上升还是下降，但除此之外，根本没有办法知道东南西北。一般情况下，你可以看到吊篮下面拖着的延伸下去百来米的绳子，并根据它的摆动可以判断出气球的前进方向。但是在大雾之中，显然就看不见了。对身处热气球中的人来说，知道热气球飘行的方向极其重要。

海洋，对驾驶员而言，是一个巨大的威胁。它是一个噩梦，并且它总能战胜驾驶员。那在大海或者其他存在大量水的地方被吹翻的危险时刻笼罩在他心头，而他也带着这念头不断地在看得见的地方计算自己的位置。在雾中迷失，便将他暴露在他最大的敌人面前。热气球仿佛要打转，让人难以维持方向感。指南针也形同虚设，让天空中的驾驶员任凭无情的狂风摆布。这种形势之下，有些听起来像是大海的声音，迷雾时不时像是要散开，然后打开一个可怕的深渊。奇异的是，面对这种时刻，一个人感觉到的竟然只是转瞬即逝的恐惧！那么当他发现自己飘飞在海上的时候会做何感受也就不难想象了。即使是厄运来临，迷雾下方即是滚滚海水之际，也能坦然接受。在百米高空，处于兴奋的状态下的人会很专注，没有一丝杂念，只静候结果。

我还记得几个月前的那次长途旅行中，我们在靠近大西洋海岸的曼彻斯特着陆时，在迷雾中迷失了方向。迷雾持续了数小时。那段时间里，我们能听到下方的水声，却不能确定那是不会对我们的降落造成影响的河流，还是一旦落上去就必死无疑的深海。面对这种情况，驾驶员也无可奈何。如果他担心底下是海，那么就必须尽其所能地保持气球的高度，直到浓雾散去，消除他的疑虑。

那些美丽的、仿佛飘浮在空中的白色群山的云景，比晴空下广袤的土地更令人难以忘怀，但是，暴风雨却比迷雾和云景更加奇妙。穿行在闪电中，听雷声在身旁轰鸣，看浮云压缩凝结，潮湿的小水滴在热气球的球囊上汇聚后从两侧滑落，像个喷嘴一样把水淋到我头上——这是我曾有过的经历，还持续了十四个半小时。

暴风雨实在是太宏伟壮丽，以至于它那恐怖的面目都失去了威慑力。闪电既非叉状也非线状，只是简单粗暴地放大那向四面八方扩张的蓝焰。电流四蹿，连我去触摸那些绳子都会噼啪作响。然而事实是，我正处于暴风雨之中，闪电环绕在身边，而我还要防止气袋像被火柴点着般爆炸。

然而，热气球飞行的真正乐趣既不在暴风雨中，也不在气象反常的高空里，而是在可以鸟瞰到那些城市和乡村、涓细的河流和玩具似的群山的飞行里；某种程度上说，还在成为一个各年龄段的人都不曾经历过的空中操纵师的过程里。归根结底，能骄傲地说自己找到了一项无人能比的运动，这就是一个热气球驾驶员的最大乐趣。

（朱利安·P. 托马斯）

作者介绍

知名的热气球驾驶员朱利安·P. 托马斯出生于乔治亚州。上述文章中，他略微提及了他是如何对空中航行产生兴趣的。就像他自己说的，他是在实验室中，通过研究和无数次实验，为了学习那些在空中才能观测到的现象，才去设法解决可能是当今知识界最大的难题，并非是出于心血来潮，或仅仅为了追求在空中上升的刺激。

On the Art of Flying

Among the artists that had been allured into the happy valley, to labor for the accommodation and pleasure of its inhabitants, was a man eminent for his knowledge of the mechanic powers, who had contrived many engines both for use and recreation. By a wheel, which the stream turned, he forced the water into a tower, whence it was distributed to all the apartments of the palace. He erected a pavilion in the garden, around which he kept the air cool by artificial showers. One of the groves appropriated to the ladies was ventilated by fans, to which the rivulet that ran through it gave a constant motion; and instruments of soft music were placed at proper distances, of which some played by the impulse of the wind, and some by the power of the stream.

The artist was sometimes visited by Rasselas, who was pleased with every kind of knowledge, imagining that the time would come when all his acquisitions would be of use to him in the open world. He came one day to amuse himself in his usual manner, and found the master busy in building a sailing chariot; he saw that the design was practicable on a level surface, and with expressions of great esteem solicited its completion. The workman was pleased to find himself so much regarded by the prince, and resolved to gain yet higher honors.

"Sir," said he, "you have been seen but a small part of what the mechanic sciences can perform. I have been long of opinion that instead of the tardy conveyance of ships and chariots, man might use the swifter migration of wings, that the fields of air are open to knowledge, and that only ignorance and idleness need crawl upon the ground."

This hint rekindled the prince's desire of passing the mountains; having seen what the mechanic had already performed, he was willing to fancy that he could do more, yet resolved to inquire further, before he suffered hope to afflict him by disappointment.

"I am afraid," said he to the artist, "that your imagination prevails over your skill, and that you now tell me rather what you wish than what you know. Every animal has his element assigned to him; the birds have the air and man and beasts the earth."

"So," replied the mechanist, "fishes have the water in which yet beasts can swim by nature, and men by art. He that can swim need not despair to fly; to swim is to fly in a grosser fluid, and to fly is to swim in a subtler. We are only to proportion our power of resistance to the different density of matter through which we are to pass. You will be necessarily up borne by the air, if you can renew any impulse upon it faster than the air can recede from the pressure."

"But the exercise of swimming," said the prince, "is very laborious, the strongest limbs are soon wearied; I am afraid the act of flying will be yet more violent, and wings will be of no great use unless we can fly further than we can swim."

"The labor of rising from the ground," said the artist, "will be great, as we see it in the heavier domestic fowls; but as we mount higher, the earth's attraction and the body's gravity will be gradually diminished, till we shall arrive at a region where the man will float in the air without any tendency to fall. No care will then be necessary but to move forwards, which the gentlest impulse will effect. You, sir, whose curiosity is so extensive, will easily conceive with what pleasure a philosopher furnished with wings, and hovering in the sky, would see the earth and all its inhabitants rolling beneath him and presenting to him successively, by its diurnal motion, all the countries within the same parallel. How must it amuse the pendant spectator to see the moving scene of land and ocean, cities and deserts. To survey with equal serenity the marts of trade and the field of battle, mountains infested by barbarians and fruitful regions gladdened by plenty and lulled by peace. How easily shall we then trace the Nile through all its passage, pass over to distant regions and examine the face of Nature from one extremity of the earth to the other."

"All this," said the prince, "is much to be desired, but I am afraid no man will be able to breathe in these regions of speculation and tranquillity. I have been told that respiration is difficult upon lofty mountains, yet from these precipices, though so high as to produce great tenuity of air, it is very easy to fall; therefore I suspect that from any height where life can be supported, there may be danger of too quick descent."

"Nothing," replied the artist, "will ever be attempted, if all possible objections must be first overcome. If you favor my project, I will try the first flight at my own hazard. I have considered the structure of all volant animals, and find the folding continuity of the bat's wings most easily accommodated to the human form. Upon this model I shall begin my task tomorrow, and in a year expect to tower into the air beyond the malice and pursuit of man. But I will work only on this condition, that the art shall not be divulged, and that you shall not require me to make wings for any but ourselves."

"Why," said Rasselas, "should you envy others so great an advantage? All skill ought to be exerted for universal good; every man has owed much to others and ought to repay the kindness he has received."

"If men were all virtuous," returned the artist, "I should with great alacrity teach them all to fly. But what would be the security of the good, if the bad could at pleasure invade them from the sky? Against any army sailing through the clouds, neither walls nor mountains nor seas could afford any security. A flight of northern savages might hover in the wind, and light at once with irresistible violence upon a capitol of a fruitful region that was rolling under them. Even this valley, the retreat of princes, the abode of happiness, might be violated by the sudden descent of some of the naked nations that swarm on the coast of the southern sea."

The prince promised secrecy and waited for the performance, not wholly hopeless of success. He visited the work from time to time, observed its progress, and remarked many ingenious contrivances to facilitate motion, and to unite levity and strength. The artist was every day more certain that he should leave vultures and eagles behind him, and the contagion of his confidence seized upon the prince. In a year the wings were finished, and on a morning appointed the maker appeared, furnished for flight, on a little promontory; he waved his pinions awhile to gather air, then leaped from his stand and in an instant dropped into the lake. His wings, which were of no use in the air, sustained him in the water, and the prince drew him to land, half dead with terror and vexation.

(Samuel Johnson)

译文

论飞行的技艺

欢乐谷吸引了一批能工巧匠前来，为了当地居民生活的便利和舒适而劳作，其中就有一位以机械动力方面的知识而闻名的工匠，他发明了很多用来干活和消遣的机器。他利用以蒸汽推动的轮子将水送上高塔，并将水从那里输送到宫殿的各个房间。他在花园里建起了一个大凉亭，并在周围用人造喷泉来降温。还有一个适合女士游玩的小树林，由穿行其间的溪流带动风扇来保持通风，不远处响起的轻柔音乐，有些是通过风吹来奏响的，有些则是借助蒸汽的力量奏响的。

拉塞勒斯有时会来拜访这位巧匠，他喜欢各种各样的知识，幻想着总有一天他的这些设计能在外面的世界中发挥作用。一天，他像往常那样前来消遣时光，发现这个工匠大师正忙于制作一辆风帆马车。他发现这个马车能够在水平面上行驶，于是带着深深的敬意，期待着工匠能把这个设计完成。这位手艺人发现自己被王子如此重视，感到非常高兴，于是下定决心要让他更看重自己。

“阁下，”他说道，“你只看到了机械科学所能够做的一小部分。长久以来我一直认为，人类可以用翅膀来进行快速移动，以此替代船和马车之类缓慢的交通工具。天空会向富有学问的人们敞开，只有那些愚昧和懒惰的人才会在地上慢慢前行。”

这个提议重新燃起了王子那跨越大山的渴求，他已经目睹了机器的力量，愿意想象这位工匠能够实现更了不起的成就。但他还是决定更深入地询问，免受期盼落空之苦。

他对那位巧匠说：“恐怕你的想象力已经超越了你的技术。你告诉我的这些与其说是你知道的，不如说是你希望的。每种动物都有它们各自的基本特性，鸟儿们占据天空，而人和野兽则拥有大地。”

“阁下，”巧匠回答，“如此说来占有水的应该是鱼，然而走兽们天生就会游泳，人类通过技巧也能做到这一点。会游泳的人不会对飞行感到绝望，游泳就是在一个更稠密的流体里飞行，而飞行只不过是在一种更稀薄的流体里游泳罢了。我们只需要根据穿行其间的不同密度的物质带来的阻力，按比例调整动力即可。如果我们给物体补充冲力的速度比它从空气中收回压力的速度更快，那么物体肯定会被空气托起。”

王子说：“但是游泳是非常费力的，即便拥有最强壮的四肢过不多久也会感到疲劳。恐怕飞行是一种更为剧烈的运动，除非我们能够飞得比游得更远，要不然翅膀就没多大用处。”

这名巧匠说道：“从我们所观察到的那些较重的家禽来看，从地上飞起来所需要的力量是很大的。但一旦我们爬得高高的，地球的吸引力和身体的重量就会渐渐减弱，直到我们能够到达某个高度，在那里人们会飘浮在空中而不会掉下来。那时我们只需要关心如何向前，而最轻微的冲力就能起作用。阁下你有广泛的好奇心，肯定能够很容易地想象出一个装有翅膀的哲人会感到多么欣喜：他翱翔在空中，看到地球和上面所有的居民都在身下缓慢地转动着，随着昼夜的交替接连不断地出现，所有的国家都是如此。那悬浮着的观众看到陆地、海洋、城市和沙漠移动的景象时会感到多么有趣。无论是贸易集市还是战场，是野蛮人出没的大山还是那些富饶的地区，这些地方因为富足而欢乐，因为和平而宁静。无论什么地方，我们都可以同样平和地俯瞰。我们可以多么容易地随着尼罗河穿越大地，跨越那遥远的地方，从地球的一头到另一头细细观察那大自然的真面目。”

王子说道：“所有你说的这些都是值得期待的，但是我担心没有人能够在这种想象中的安宁环境中呼吸。我听说在高山上呼吸会变得很困难。这些峭壁太高了，这使得上面的空气变得很稀薄，而且人还很容易掉下来。因此我怀疑在任何人类能够生存的高度，都存在着快速掉落的危险。”

巧匠回答说：“如果必须先排除所有可能的异议再开始，那就不会有任何尝试。如果你赞成这计划，我会自己承担风险尝试首次飞行。我已经研究过所有带翅膀的动物，发现蝙蝠那可折叠而且没有间隙的翅膀最容易和人的形体配合。我从明天起就基于这个模型开始工作，并计划一年之内飞向天空，远离人类的恶意和追逐。但我需要你答应一个条件才行，决不能把它泄露出去，而且你也不能让我为我们俩以外的其他人制作翅膀。”

“为什么？”拉塞勒斯说道，“你想拥有这个巨大的优势而让别人羡慕？一项技术应该推行开来，让大众都受益。每个人都受益于他人，他们应该为自己所受到的善意而做出回报。”

巧匠回答说：“如果人类都是善良的，我很乐意教所有的人飞行。但如果坏人能够随意地从空中入侵，那好人的安全如何得到保障呢？在那些云层间前行的军队面前，围墙、高山和大海都不能保证安全。北方的野蛮人会随风飞来，在他们身下的一片富饶地区的中心大厦处突然着陆，带来难以抵御的暴行。即便是这个王子隐居的、存留着幸福的山谷，也会被那些突然降落的，原本聚集在南方海滩边上的那些赤身裸体的外国人所破坏。”

王子承诺保守这个秘密，等待着计划的实行，对于成功并非不抱希望。他经常来察看这项工程，关注进展情况，并提出了许多新奇的想法来让机器能够运行，使它变得既轻巧又坚固。随着时间一天天地过去，这名能工巧匠越来越确信他将会把秃鹫和雄鹰甩在身后，而他的这份自信也感染了王子。一年后翅膀终于完成了，在一个约定好的早晨，制作者出现了，他在一个小海角为飞行做好了准备。他舞动了翅膀片刻来聚集空气，随后从站立的地点跳了起来，但马上便向下掉入了湖中。他的翅膀在空中一点用都没有，只是在水中将他支撑起来而已。王子将他拉回到岸上，他已经因为害怕和懊恼而奄奄一息了。

（塞缪尔·约翰逊）

作者介绍

尽管塞缪尔·约翰逊在他生命的最后二十五年间成了英国文坛最著名的人物，他的整个早年生活却极度贫困。《论飞行的技艺》选自《拉塞勒斯》，这本书是“花了一周的夜晚为了支付母亲葬礼的费用”而写成的。六卷本的博斯韦尔的《约翰逊传》完整地记述了他一生的故事。

The Sister Years

Last night, between eleven and twelve o'clock, when the Old Year was leaving her final footprints on the borders of Time's empire, she found herself in possession of a few spare moments, and sat down——of all places in the world——on the steps of our new City Hall. The wintry moonlight showed that she looked weary of body, and sad of heart, like many another wayfarer of earth. Her garments, having been exposed to much foul weather and rough usage, were in very ill condition; and as the hurry of her journey had never before allowed her to take an instants rest, her shoes were so worn as to be scarcely worth the mending. But, after trudging only a little distance farther, this poor Old Year was destined to enjoy a long, long sleep.

I forgot to mention, that when she seated herself on the steps, she deposited by her side a very capacious bandbox, in which, as is the custom among travelers of her sex, she carried a great deal of valuable property. Besides this luggage, there was a folio book under her arm, very much resembling the annual volume of a newspaper. Placing this volume across her knees, and resting her elbows upon it, with her forehead in her hands, the weary, bedraggled, world-worn Old Year heaved a heavy sigh, and appeared to be taking no very pleasant retrospect of her past existence.

While she thus awaited the midnight knell, that was to summon her to the innumerable sisterhood of departed Years, there came a young maiden treading lightsomely on tiptoe along the street, from the direction of the Railroad Depot. She was evidently a stranger, and perhaps had come to town by the evening train of cars. There was a smiling cheerfulness in this fair maiden's face, which bespoke her fully confident of a kind reception from the multitude of people, with whom she was soon to form acquaintance. Her dress was rather too airy for the season, and was bedizened with fluttering ribbons and other vanities, which were likely soon to be rent away by the fierce storms, or to fade in the hot sunshine, amid which she was to pursue her changeful course. But still she was a wonderfully pleasant looking figure; and had so much promise and such an indescribable hopefulness in her aspect, that hardly anybody could meet her without anticipating some very desirable thing from her kind offices.

The New Year——for this young maiden was no less a personage——carried all her goods and chattels in a basket of no great size or weight, which hung upon her arm. She greeted the disconsolate Old Year with great affection, and sat down beside her on the steps of the City Hall, waiting for the signal to begin her rambles through the world. The two were own sisters, being both granddaughters of Time; and though one looked so much older than the other, it was rather owing to hardships and trouble than to age, since there was but a twelvemonth's difference between them.

"Well, my dear sister," said the New Year, after the first salutations, "you look almost tired to death. What have you been about during your sojourn in this part of Infinite Space?"

"Oh, I have it all recorded here in my Book of Chronicles," answered the Old Year, in a heavy tone. "There is nothing that would amuse you; and you will soon get sufficient knowledge of such matters from your own personal experience. It is but tiresome reading."

Nevertheless, she turned over the leaves of the folio, and glanced at them by the light of the moon, feeling an irresistible spell of interest in her own biography, although its incidents were remembered without pleasure.

"Have you done much for the improvement of the City?" asked the New Year. "Judging from what little I have seen, it appears to be ancient and timeworn."

"I have opened the Railroad," said the elder Year, "and half a dozen times a day you will hear the bell (which once summoned the monks of a Spanish Convent to their devotions) announcing the arrival or departure of the cars. Old Salem now wears a much livelier expression than when I first beheld her. Strangers rumble down from Boston by hundreds at a time. New faces throng in Essex Street. Railroad-hacks and omnibuses rattle over the pavement. There is a perceptible increase of oyster-shops, and other establishments for the accommodation of a transitory diurnal multitude. But a more important change awaits the venerable town. An immense accumulation of musty prejudices will be carried off by the free circulation of society. A peculiarity of character, of which the inhabitants themselves are hardly sensible, will be rubbed down and worn away by the attrition of foreign substances. Much of the result will be good. Whether for better or worse, there will be a probable diminution of the moral influence of wealth, and the sway of an aristocratic class which, from an era far beyond my memory, has held firmer dominion here than in any other New England town."

The Old Year, having talked away nearly all of her little remaining breath now closed her Book of Chronicles, and was about to take her departure. But her sister detained her a while longer, by inquiring the contents of the huge bandbox, which she was so painfully lugging along with her.

"These are merely a few trifles," replied the Old Year, "which I have picked up in my rambles, and am going to deposit in the receptacle of things past and forgotten. We sisterhood of Years never carry anything really valuable out of the world with us. Here are patterns of most of the fashions which I have brought into vogue, and which have already lived out their allotted term. You will supply their place with others equally ephemeral. Here, put up in little china pots, like rouge, is a considerable lot of beautiful women's bloom, which the disconsolate fair ones owe me a bitter grudge for stealing. I have likewise a quantity of men's dark hair, instead of which, I have left gray locks, or none at all. The tears of widows and other afflicted mortals, who have received comfort during the last twelve months, are preserved in some dozens of essence-bottles, well corked and sealed. Moreover, here is an assortment of many thousand broken promises, and other broken ware, all very light and packed into little space. The heaviest articles in my possession are a large parcel of disappointed hopes, which, a little while ago, were buoyant enough to have inflated a balloon."

"I have a fine lot of hopes here in my basket," remarked the New Year. "They are a sweet-smelling flower——a species of rose."

"They soon lose their perfume," replied the sombre Old Year. "What else have you brought to insure a welcome from the discontented race of mortals?"

"Why, to say the truth, little or nothing else," said her sister, with a smile,——"save a few new Annuals and Almanacs, and some New Year's gifts for the children. But I heartily wish well to poor mortals, and mean to do all I can for their improvement and happiness."

"It is a good resolution," rejoined the Old Year, "and, by the way, I have a plentiful assortment of good resolutions, which have now grown so stale and musty, that I am ashamed to carry them any farther. Many other matters go to make up the contents of my bandbox; but the whole lot would not fetch a single bid, even at an auction of worn-out furniture; and as they are worth nothing either to you or anybody else, I need not trouble you with a longer catalogue."

"And must I also pick up such worthless luggage in my travels?" asked the New Year.

"Most certainly; and well, if you have no heavier load to bear," replied the other. "If these ridiculous people ever see anything tolerable in you, it will be after you are gone forever."

"But I," cried the fresh-hearted New Year,——"I shall try to leave men wiser than I find them. I will offer them freely whatever good gifts Providence permits me to distribute, and will tell them to be thankful for what they have, and humbly hopeful for more; and surely, if they are not absolutely foolish, they will condescend to be happy, and will allow me to be a happy Year. For my happiness must depend on them."

"Alas for you, then, my poor sister!" said the Old Year, sighing, as she uplifted her burden. "We grandchildren of Time are born to trouble. But hark! My task is done."

The clock in the tall church steeple struck twelve; and while the strokes were yet dropping into the air the Old Year either flitted or faded away. As the clock ceased to strike, the maidenly New Year arose from the steps of the City Hall and set out rather timorously on her earthly course.

"A happy New Year!" cried a watchman, eying her figure very

questionably, but without the least suspicion that he was addressing the New Year in person.

"Thank you kindly!" said the New Year; and she gave the watchman one of the roses of hope from her basket. "May this flower keep a sweet smell long after I have bidden you good-by."

Then she stepped on more briskly through the silent streets; and such as were awake at the moment heard her footfall, and said, "The New Year is come!"

(Nathaniel Hawthorne)

译文

姐妹年

前一天夜晚，在十一点到十二点之间，旧年即将迈出最后一个脚步，跨出时间王国的边界。但她发现自己还有一点空余时间，便坐在了——在全世界的所有地方的——新市政大厅的台阶上。带着寒意的月光照耀着她，和地球上其他许多旅人一样，她身躯疲惫，内心凄凉。她身上的衣服，经历了太多恶劣的天气，使用时也没有爱惜，变得十分破旧。她的旅途匆匆忙忙，连短暂的休息都不允许，鞋子已经磨损得不值得再修补。不过，只要再走过一点短暂的距离，旧的一年的旅途就要结束了，可怜的她将会迎来命中注定的、漫长又漫长的睡眠。

我忘记提了，当她在台阶坐下时，还在旁边放置着一个体积庞大的旅行箱，里面装着一大堆珍贵的财物。所有女人出去旅行时都有这个习惯，她也不例外。旅行箱的旁边，是一本对开本的书，就放在她的手下，很像是报纸的年刊。她把它放在双膝上，双手撑着额头，手肘就垫在书上。旧年穿着破旧，身上风尘仆仆，疲惫不堪。她重重地叹了口气，看来，在过去的一年中，她并没有得到任何愉快的回忆。

午夜钟声的敲响，将召唤着她离开，她就要去她那些姐妹们的身边了。这些数不尽的姐妹，就是以往离开的那些年份。她正等着这一刻的到来，这时，自火车站那边的方向，一位少女踮着脚尖，步态轻盈地沿着街道走来。

显然，她是一个陌生人，也许是刚搭着夜班的火车来到镇上。少女美丽的脸颊上洋溢着热情的笑容，说明她非常自信，笃定自己会得到很多人的热情欢迎，而她很快也会跟这些人熟悉起来。她的裙子装饰着飘逸的缎带和其他饰品，看起来太过轻薄，不适合这个季节，轻易就会被猛烈的暴风雨卷走。她以后在多变的路途上继续赶路时，这样的裙子也很容易在毒辣的阳光曝晒下褪去颜色。但是，她的神色看起来依然欢快极了，还带着许多承诺和难以名状的希望。所有人遇见如此的她，都会难以抑制地对她做出期许，想要从她的仁慈中得到一些极其渴望的东西。

这位年轻的少女竟然是一位大人物呢，她就是新年。新年的手臂上挎着一个又小又轻的篮子，里面装着她所有的财物。她热情地和忧郁的旧年打了招呼，在旧年身边的市政厅台阶上坐了下来，等待着那一声信号。这信号会预示着她要出发去漫游世界。她们两人是亲生的姐妹，都是时间的孙女。虽然两人只差了十二个月，旧年看起来却要苍老不少，这不是年龄的缘故，而是因为她饱经艰辛的磨难。

“好吧，我亲爱的姐姐，”在最初的招呼过后，新年说道，“你看上去快要累死了。在这无垠时空的逗留期间，你都在忙些什么呢？”

“哦，我把这些事情记录在了我的年历里，”旧年用沉重的嗓音答道，“里面也没有什么可以取悦你的东西，读起来很无聊。很快，你也会从自己的经历中充分汲取到这样的见识。”

然而，她还是打开了书页，借着月光端详它们。尽管上面记录的事情没有留下愉快的记忆，她还是觉得自己的经历有一股无法抵挡的魅力。

“你为这个城市的发展做了什么吗？”新年问，“根据我目前的一点见闻，这里看起来陈旧又腐朽。”

“我开通了铁路，”旧年说，“每天，你会听见钟声响起六次（这口钟曾被用来召集西班牙修道院的僧侣们进行祈祷仪式），宣告着列车的到来或离开。老教堂现在也面貌一新，比我第一次看到她的时候有活力多了。成百上千的陌生人，同时从波士顿声势浩大地涌来，埃塞克斯大街上充斥着新面孔。火车和公共汽车“咔哒咔哒”地运行在各自的轨道之中，售卖牡蛎的店铺也有了明显的增多，还为那些只短暂停留一日的人建了住处。这个庄严的城镇，正等着发生更重要的变化。社会的运转不再受约束，一些积习已久且陈腐过时的偏见也会随之消失。本地居民那些自身难以察觉的特质，会被外来事物消磨、吞噬，多数会产生喜闻乐见的结果。不论好坏，财富的道德影响在减轻，贵族的统治地位在削弱。从远超我记忆的年代开始，这里就被这两者所主宰统治，比新英格兰的任何其他城市都更为牢固。

旧年说完这些话，几乎已经用尽了她残留的所有气息。她合上年历，准备动身离开，但她的妹妹留了她一会儿，问她费力带在身边的那只大箱子里装了些什么。

“只不过是一些零碎玩意儿，”旧年答道，“都是我在漫游的时候捡的，我准备把它们存放在收纳过往和遗忘的地方。我们姐妹年永远都不会从这世上带走真正宝贵的东西。这是我曾经引领时尚的大部分流行样品，但它们现在已经过时了。你以后也会给这地方带来其他同样转瞬即逝的东西。这些贮藏在小瓷壶里像胭脂一样的东西，是许多美丽女人的青春年华，我偷走了它们，这些闷闷不乐的美人确实该怨恨我。同样的，我也带走了许多男人黑色的头发，并用灰色的取而代之，或者更甚，我什么都不给他们留下。过去的十二个月里，那些遗孀，那些饱受折磨的人，都已经在过去的十二个月里得到抚慰，她们的眼泪被保存在许多个精华瓶里，用塞子塞好封起来。此外，这里是成千上万破碎的承诺和其他破碎之物的混合物，它们都非常轻便，只需一点地方封存。我的东西里，最沉重的要数一大包令人沮丧的失望，在不久之前，这些失望还依然是希望，轻快得能充起气球。”

“我的篮子里有许多很棒的希望，”新年说道，“它们是玫瑰花的一个品种，香气很甜蜜。”

“它们很快就会香消玉殒，”忧郁的旧年说道，“你还带了其他什么东西，能让你确保那些心怀不满的人会欢迎你？”

“嗨，说实在的，少得很，几乎算得上是没有。”她的妹妹笑着说，“就带了一些新的年刊和年历，还有一些给孩子们的新年礼物。但是，我由衷盼着那些穷苦人们好，打算竭尽所能改善他们的生活，让他们变得幸福。”

“这决心很好，”旧年答道，“顺便说一下，我也有过许多美好的决心，现在都已陈旧腐烂，我羞于再带着它们前行。我的箱子里还有许多其他东西，但就算在破旧家具的拍卖会上，也不会有人对这些东西出价。对你和其他人来说，它们一文不值，我也不想列举更长的事物目录来让你费心。”

“我也必须要在旅途中带着这样毫无价值的行李吗？”新年问。

“当然，如果你不需要背负更重的担子的话。”旧年答道，“要是这些愚蠢的人类在你身上看见一些尚可的东西，即使你不在了，它也会永远存在。”

“但是我，”内心依旧新鲜的新年叫道，“我想要人们比我一开始见到他们的时候更聪明。上帝允许的一切好礼，我要自由地分派给他们。我要告诉他们要对所拥有的心怀感激，并在期许更多时保持谦逊。要是他们还没有愚蠢到底，他们一定会放下身段感受快乐，也会让我变成快乐的一年。因为我的幸福全维系在他们身上。”

“我可怜的妹妹，真为你叹息，”旧年一边说一边叹气，她立起了她的箱子，“我们作为时间的孙女，就是生于麻烦之中的。但是谢天谢地！我的任务已经完成了。”

教堂高高的塔尖上，时钟敲击了十二下。钟声还在空气中坠落，旧年就轻飘飘地飞起来，消失了。时钟停止敲击的那一刻，少女模样的新年，自市政厅前的台阶起身，颇为胆怯地开始了她在地球上的旅程。

“一个快乐的新年！”巡夜的人叫道。他不确定地看着新年的身影，但毫无疑问的是，他本人正在对新年说话。

“衷心感谢你！”新年说，从篮子里拿出一枝希望的玫瑰送给巡夜人。“希望这枝花的香气持久，一直维持到我向你说再见的那天。”

然后，她在安静的街道上走得更轻快了。在这个时刻，那些醒着的人听见了她的脚步声，说：“新年到了！”

（纳撒尼尔·霍桑）

作者介绍

1804年，纳撒尼尔·霍桑在马萨诸塞州的塞纳姆市出生。他在这个著名的历史小城以及康科德市度过了大部分的人生。从他还是一个男孩的时候开始，他就习惯以长距离的散步来独自打发很多时间。他的脑中充满了浪漫的想象和精巧的奇思，甚至准备去“发掘黑暗的角落”。他的故事大部分讲述的是新英格兰的生活，充满奇思妙想的魅力和异想天开的幽默。他的《祖父的椅子》描绘了新英格兰的历史，他的《奇妙书》是专门写给孩子们的。在他广为人知的作品中，有《古屋青苔》《凶宅七角楼》《红字》《玉石人像》《莱诺克斯故事集》，还有《重讲一遍的故事》，本文正是出自于后者。霍桑死于1864年，葬于康科德的睡谷墓地。

Water——Some Properties

One of the commonest of common natural objects is water; everybody uses it in one way or another every way; and consequently everybody possesses a store of loose information——of common knowledge——about it. But, in all probability, a great deal of this knowledge has never been attended to by its possessor; and certainly, those who have never tried to learn how much may be known about water, will be ignorant of a great many of its powers and properties and of the laws of nature which it illustrates, and consequently will be unable to account for many things of which the explanation is very easy.

Suppose that we have a tumbler half-full of water. The tumbler is an artificial object; that is to say, certain natural objects have been brought together and heated till they melted into glass, and this glass has been shaped by a workman. The water, on the other hand, is a natural object, which has come from some river, pond, or spring; or it may be from a water butt into which the rain falling on the roof has flowed.

Now the water has a vast number of peculiarities. For example, it is transparent, so that you can see through it; it feels cool; it will quench thirst and dissolve sugar. But these are not the characteristics which it is most convenient to begin with.

The water, we see, fills the cavity of the tumbler over half its height, therefore it occupies that much space, or has that bulk or volume. If you put the closed end of another tumbler of almost the same size into the first, you will find that when it reaches the water, the latter offers a resistance to its going down, and unless some of the water can get out, the end of the second tumbler will not get in. Any one that falls from a height into water will find that he receives a severe shock when he reaches it. Water therefore offers resistance.

If the water is emptied out, the tumbler feels much lighter than it was before; water, therefore, has weight. If you throw the water out of the tumbler at any slightly supported object, the water striking against it would knock it over. That is to say, the water being put in motion is able to transfer that motion to something else.

All these phenomena, are effects of which water, under the conditions mentioned, is the cause, and they may therefore be said to be properties of water. All things that occupy space, offer resistance, possess weight, and transfer motion to other things when they strike against them, are termed material substances or bodies, or simpler matter. Water, therefore, is a kind, or form, of matter.

In the next place, you will observe that, though water occupies space, it has no definite shape, but fits itself exactly to the figure of the vessel that holds it. If the tumbler is cylindrical, the contour of the surface of the water will be circular when the tumbler is held vertically, and will change, without the least break or interruption, to more and more of an oval when the tumbler is inclined; and whatever the shape of the vessel into which you pour it, the sides of the water always exactly fit against the sides of the vessel.

If you put your finger into the water you can move it in all directions with scarcely any feeling of obstacle. If you pull your finger out there is no hole left, the water on all sides rushing together to fill up the space that was occupied by the finger. You cannot take up a handful of water, for it runs away between your fingers, and you cannot raise it into a permanent heap. All this shows that the parts of water move upon one another with great ease. The same fact is illustrated if the tumbler is inclined, so that the level of the surface rises above the edge of the tumbler on one side, and the water is therefore to some extent unsupported by the tumbler at this point. The water then flows over in a stream and falls to the ground, where it spreads out and runs to the lowest accessible place, or gradually soaks up into crevices.

Nevertheless, although the parts of water thus loosely slip and slide on one another, yet they hold together to a certain extent. If the surface of the water is touched with the finger, a little of it will adhere; and if the finger is then slowly and carefully raised, the adjacent water will be raised up into a slender column which acquires a noticeable length before it breaks. So, in the early morning, after heavy dew, you may see the water upon cabbage-leaves and blades of grass in spherical drops, the parts of which similarly hold together.

Material substances, the parts of which are so movable that they fit themselves exactly to the sides of any vessel containing them, and which flow when they are not supported, are called fluids; and fluids the parts of which fly off from one another, but hold together as those of water do, are called liquid.

Water, therefore, is a liquid.

(Thomas Henry Huxley)

译文

水的特性

在我们常见的自然物体中，水是最常见不过的了。每个人都以不同的方式用水，因此，关于水的一些常识性问题，每个人多多少少都有一套又一套的见解。但是，大多数情况下，那些见解十有八九都是不准确的。当然，有些人从没注意过自己到底知道多少关于水的知识，他们会忽略掉许多水的用途、特性和水所揭示的自然规律，所以，他们根本不能解释一些很简单的现象（我们通常把自然界发生的事情称作“现象”）。

假设现在我们有一个玻璃杯，里面装了半杯水。杯子是人造物，也就是说，将某些自然物质混合到一起，再进行加热，直到制成玻璃，最后再由工匠打造出杯子的形状。然而，水却是自然物，可能来自于某条河流、某个池塘或某口泉水，还有可能来自屋檐下收集雨水的大水桶。

由此看来，水有非常多的特性。例如，水是透明的，你可以一眼将它看透；水能给人一种清爽的感觉；水可以解渴，还可以溶解白糖。但是，这些都不是最便于用来开场的特性。

我们可以看到，水装了大半个杯子，因此，水占了很大的空间，也可以说占了很大的容量或体积。如果把一个差不多大小的杯子杯底朝下放入这半杯水里，当这个杯子接触到水面时，你就会发现后者在阻碍它的下沉，除非有一些水被挤出来，否则第二个杯子的杯底根本不能沉入水中。一个人从一定的高度跳入水中时，就会感觉到一种很强烈的震感。这都说明了水是具有阻力的。

如果把杯子里的水倒出来，就会感觉到杯子轻了很多。因此，水是有重量的。如果把杯子里的水抛向任何摇摇欲坠的物体，水击打物体时，可以将它推翻。这也就是说，动态的水可以把这种动能转化为其他的能量。

在上文所提到的情况中，正是因为水的某些特性，才会导致这些现象发生。物质实体、物体或更简单的物质指的是所有占空间、有阻力、有重量又可以在击打的瞬间将动能转化为其他能量的东西。因此，我们可以说水是一种物质，或者说是物质的一种形式。

其次，你会发现，虽然水占据了一定的空间，却没有固定的形状，但可以完全适应容器的形状。若杯子是圆柱形的，当杯子直着放置时，水面的轮廓呈圆形，当杯子斜着放时，不借助任何外力，水面的轮廓就会变成椭圆形。不管你把水倒入什么形状的容器里，水总是能完美贴合容器。

如果你把手指伸入水中，随意地朝着各个方向移动，都几乎感觉不到任何阻碍。如果你把手指抽出水中，不会在水里留下一个洞，因为水会从四面八方汇聚起来，填补到刚刚放手指的地方。你不能用手抓一把水，因为水会从指缝中流出，而且你也不能把水堆到一个固定的高度。这些现象都告诉我们，水的流动性非常强。同样的，如果杯子倾斜，水面的一端也会随之升高，漫过杯口，这也说明了水在一定程度上不受杯子的限制，具有很强的流动性。之后，水就会从杯子里流出来，落到地面上，向四处散开，流向地势最低的地方，或者渐渐渗入裂缝里。

然而，即使水很容易就可以流动，它还是具有一定的内聚力。如果手指轻触水面，就会附上一点点水；如果慢慢把手指小心翼翼地抬起，附着在手指上的水也会随之升起，形成一条细小的水柱，到达一定的高度后，水柱就会破裂。因此，每逢清晨，浓浓的露水过后，你会看到水以圆形水滴的形状附着在卷心菜和青草的叶片上，这同样也是因为水的内聚力的作用。

流动性强到能完全贴合容纳它们的任何容器，且在不受拘束时能自由流动的物质叫作流体。而流动中具有和水相同的内聚力的流体叫作液体。

因此，水是一种液体。

（托马斯·亨利·赫胥黎）

作者介绍

托马斯·亨利·赫胥黎（1825-1895）是英国杰出的科学家。受过医学教育之后，他便成为响尾蛇号的驻舰外科助理医生，这艘军舰隶属于英国皇家海军，被派往澳大利亚大堡礁沿岸进行探勘任务。航行期间，赫胥黎研究了海洋生物，他的重大发现使他在科学界中享誉盛名。赫胥黎毕生致力于科学研究，同时还将毕生所学著文出版，促进了科学教育的发展。

Chapter 4

History | 历史瞬间

Crecy and Calais

It was in the month of July, in the year one thousand three hundred and forty-six, that King Edward III embarked at Southampton for France, with an army of about thirty thousand men in all, attended by the Prince of Wales and by several of the chief nobles. He landed at La Hogue in Normandy. Burning and destroying as he went, according to custom, he advanced up the left bank of the Seine, and fired the small towns even close to Paris; but, being watched from the right bank of the river by the French king and all his army, it came to this at last, that Edward found himself, on Saturday, the twenty-sixth of August, on a rising ground behind the little French village of Crecy, face to face with the French king's force. And, although the French king had an enormous army——in number more than eight times his——Edward there resolved to beat him or be beaten.

The young Prime, assisted by the Earl of Oxford and the Earl of Warwick, led the first division of the English army; two other great earls led the second; and the king, the third. When the morning dawned, the king received the sacrament and heard prayers, and then, mounted on horseback, with a white wand in his hand, rode from company to company, and rank to rank, cheering and encouraging both officers and men. Then the whole army breakfasted, each man sitting on the ground where he had stood; and then they remained quietly on the ground with their weapons ready.

Up came the French king with all his great force. It was dark and angry weather; there was an eclipse of the sun; there was a thunder-storm, accompanied by tremendous rain, the frightened birds flew screaming above the soldiers' heads. A captain in the French army advised the French king, who was by no means cheerful, not to begin the battle until the morrow. The king, taking this advice, gave the word to halt. But, those behind not understanding it, or desiring to be foremost with the rest, came pressing on.

The roads for a great distance were covered with this immense army, and with the common people from the villages, who were flourishing their rude weapons, and making a great noise. Owing to these circumstances, the French army advanced in the greatest confusion ; every French lord doing what he liked with his own men, and putting out the men of every other French lord.

Now, their king relied strongly upon a great body of cross-bowmen from Genoa; and these he ordered to the front to begin the battle. They shouted once, they shouted twice, they shouted three times to alarm the English archers; but the English would have heard them shout three thousand times and would never have moved. At last the cross-bowmen went forward a little, and began to discharge their bolts; upon which the English let fly such a hail of arrows, that the Genoese speedily made off——for their cross-bows, besides being heavy to carry, required to be wound up with a handle, and consequently took time to reload; the English on the other hand, could discharge their arrows almost as fast as the arrows could fly.

When the French king saw the Genoese turning, he cried out to his men to kill those scoundrels, who were doing harm instead of service. This increased the confusion. Meanwhile the English archers, continuing to shoot as fast as ever, shot down great numbers of the French soldiers and knights.

The Prince and his division were at this time so hard pressed, that the Earl of Warwick sent a message to the king, who was overlooking the battle from a windmill, beseeching him to send more aid.

"Is my son killed?" asked the king.

"No, sire, please God," returned the messenger.

"Is he wounded?" said the king.

"No, sire."

"Is he thrown to the ground?" said the king.

"No, sire, not so; but he is very hard-pressed."

"Then," said the king, "go back to those who sent you, and tell them that I shall send no aid; because I set my heart upon my son's proving himself this day a brave knight, and because I am resolved, please God, that the honor of a great victory shall be his."

These bold words, being reported to the Prince and his division so raised their spirits, that they fought better than ever. The king of France charged gallantly with his men many times;but it was of no use. Night closing in, his horse was killed under him by an English arrow, and the knights and nobles who had clustered thick about him early in the day were now completely scattered. At last, some of his few remaining officers led him off the field by force, since he would not retire of himself, and they journeyed away to Amiens.

The victorious English, lighting their watch-fires, made merry on the field, and the king, riding to meet his gallant son, took him in his arms, kissed him, and told him that he had acted nobly, and proved himself worthy of the day and of the crown. While it was yet night, King Edward was hardly aware of the great victory that he had gained; but next day it was discovered that eleven princes, twelve hundred knights, and thirty thousand common men lay dead upon the French side.

Among the dead in the French army was the king of Bohemia, an old blind man; who, having been told that his son was wounded in the battle, and that no force could stand against the Black Prince, called to him two knights, put himself on horseback between them, fastened the three bridles together, and dashed in among the English, where he was presently slain. He bore on his crest three white ostrich feathers, with the motto Ich dien, signifying in English "I serve". The crest and the motto were taken by the Prince of Wales in remembrance of that famous day, and have been borne by the Prince of Wales ever since.

Five days after this great battle, King Edward laid siege to Calais. This siege, ever afterward memorable, lasted nearly a year. In order to starve the inhabitants out, Edward built so many wooden houses for the lodgings of his troops, that, it is said, their quarters looked like a second Calais suddenly sprung around the first. Early in the siege, the governor of the town drove out what he called the useless mouths, to the number of seventeen hundred persons, men and women, young and old.

King Edward allowed them to pass through his lines, and even fed them, and dismissed them with money; but, later in the siege, he was not so merciful——five hundred more, who were afterward driven out, dying of starvation and misery.

The garrison were so bard-pressed at last that they sent a letter to King Philip, telling him that they had eaten all the horses, all the dogs, and all the rats and mice that could be found in the place; and that, if he did not relieve them, they must either surrender to the English or eat one another. Philip made one effort to give them relief; but they were so hemmed in by the English power that he could not succeed, and was fain to leave the place. Upon this they hoisted the English flag, and surrendered to King Edward. "Tell your general," said he to the humble messengers that came out of the town, "that I require to have sent here six of the most distinguished citizens, with ropes about their necks; and let those six men bring with them the keys of the castle and of the town."

When the governor of Calais related this to the people in the market-place, there was great weeping and distress; in the midst of which one worthy citizen, named Eustace de Saint Pierre, rose up and said that if the six men were not sacrificed the whole population would be; therefore he offered himself as the first. Encouraged by this bright example, five other worthy citizens rose up one after another, and offered themselves to save the rest. The governor, who was too badly wounded to be able to walk, mounted a poor old horse, and conducted these good men to the gate while all the people cried and mourned.

Edward received them wrathfully, and ordered the heads of the whole six to be struck off. However, the good Queen Philippa fell upon her knees, and be sought the king to give them up to her. The king replied, "I wish that you had been somewhere else; but I can not refuse you." So she had them properly dressed, made a feast for them, and sent them back with a handsome present, to the great rejoicing of the whole camp.

(Charles Dickens)

译文

英法克雷西及加来之战

1346年7月，英国国王爱德华三世在南安普顿集结了一支总共大约三万人的军队，进攻法国。威尔士亲王和数名主要贵族加入了这次战役。英军在诺曼底的拉霍格登陆，所经之处如往常一样变得火光冲天，废墟成片。他们一路推进到塞纳河左岸，在驻守于塞纳河右岸的法国国王及其军队的眼皮底下放火烧了紧邻巴黎的几个小镇。最终，在8月26日周六这天，在法国小村庄克雷西后面的一个高地，爱德华发现自己正面对上了法国的军队。尽管法国国王拥有一支庞大的队伍，超过英军数量的八倍，但爱德华在那儿下定了决心：要么打败他，要么被他打败。

年轻的亲王在奥克斯福德伯爵和沃里克伯爵的协助下，率领英军第一师，另外两名杰出的伯爵率领第二师，国王自己则率领第三师。破晓时分，将士们在国王面前许下庄严的誓言，同时祈祷战事旗开得胜。随后，国王跨上马背，手里拿着指挥棒，检阅每一个中队每一个行列，激励全体官兵。之后，整个军队开始吃早餐，官兵们在自己的位置席地而坐，吃完后就准备好武器静静留在原地。

法国国王率领他的全部兵力出现了，然而天气险恶，令人沮丧：太阳不见踪影，空中黑云弥漫；雷电交加，暴雨倾盆；受惊的鸟儿哀鸣着从士兵们的头顶飞过。这种情形下，法国国王毫无斗志，他采纳了一名上尉提出的“次日再发动战役”的建议，并命令军队停止前进。但是，那些殿后的官兵也许不理解这一命令，也许渴望和其他人一样成为先锋，他们仍然向前推进。

庞杂的队伍在路上绵延了很远。除了庞大的军队以外，村子里的平民也从四面八方涌来，人声鼎沸地挥舞着他们那简陋的武器。在这种情况下，法国军队行进得非常混乱：领主们各自为政，忙着对自己的人马颐指气使，同时还不忘排挤其他人的部下。

现在，法国国王将战胜的希望寄托在一群来自热那亚的弩手身上，他命令这些弩手赶到前线发起攻击。弩手们大吼了三次以警告英军弓箭手，但就算他们吼上几千次，英军也不会退让半步。最后，弩手们向前推进了一点，开始发射他们的弩箭。当箭镞像冰雹一样砸向英军的时候，热那亚弩手却匆匆逃离了——因为他们的弓弩不但沉重得不便携带，而且需要依靠手柄绷紧弓弦，这自然延迟了重新装箭的速度。恰恰相反，英军的弓箭手能够在一支箭离弦后迅速再次发射。

法国国王看到热那亚弩手转头逃跑，大喊着让人去杀了那些对他有害无益的恶棍。这加剧了法军的混乱。与此同时，英军弓箭手继续飞快地射击，击中了许多法军士兵和骑士。

威尔士亲王和他的师部此时正经受着巨大的压力，沃里克伯爵不得不送信给正从一座磨坊里观望整场战役的国王，恳求他出兵救援。

国王问："我儿子被杀死了吗？"

传令兵回答说："没有，陛下！上帝保佑！"

国王又问："他受伤了吗？"

"没有，陛下！"

国王再问："那他被打倒在地上了吗？"

"没有，陛下，没那回事！但他压力很大。"

国王说："那么，回去告诉派你来的人，我不会出兵救援，因为我决心让我儿子在这一天证明他是一名勇敢的骑士，也因为我认定这场伟大的胜利，如果上帝保佑的话，应是属于他的荣光。"

国王的话被回报给亲王和他的队伍。这些无畏的言语让全体官兵士气大振，他们奋战得比此前更为英勇。法国国王多次鼓舞士兵冲锋，但却毫无效果。傍晚时分，一支英军射来的箭杀死了他胯下的战马，而早先密密聚集在他周围的骑士和贵族们现在完全变得七零八落。最后，由于他自己不肯撤退，一些幸存的军官们强行将他带出战场，向亚眠撤退。

胜利的英军高举火把，在战场上尽情欢乐。而国王则骑着马会见他英勇的儿子，拥抱他，亲吻他，赞扬他高贵的表现证明了自身的价值：无愧于这天，无愧于王冠。由于已是深夜，爱德华国王并没有意识到他获得了一场多么伟大的胜利。但是第二天，他发现英军击毙了法军的十一名领主、一千两百名骑士和三万个平民。

在阵亡的法军中，有这么一名波西米亚国王。有人曾经告诉过他，他的儿子会在这场战争中受伤，而且没有任何力量可以和黑太子爱德华对抗。虽然他是名瞎眼老人，但他把三个马鞍牢牢系在一起，让两名骑士把他夹在马背上，猛然冲到了英军中间，随即就被杀死了。他佩戴的徽章上插了三根白色的鸵鸟毛，上面还刻着“我服务”的座右铭。于是，为了纪念这闻名的一天，威尔士亲王沿用了这个徽章和座右铭。从此以后，他就一直随身佩戴这个徽章。

这场伟大的战争胜利五天后，爱德华国王开始围困加来。这次令后人难忘的围城持续了将近一年。爱德华想要让被困居民饿得受不住，出城投降，因此他为自己的士兵们建造了许多木屋。据说，他们的宿营地看上去就像第二个加来，突然出现在原先的城市周围。在围城早期，加来的地方长官把许多他认为没用的人赶出了城，男女老少总共有一千七百人。爱德华国王让他们通过了他的防线，甚至给他们食物吃，还拿钱遣散了他们。但是在围城后期，爱德华不再这么慈悲，后来被赶出来的五百多人全都在饥饿中悲惨地死去。

最后，加来的守备部队再也扛不住围城的压力，只好送信给菲利普国王求救。信中说，他们已经吃光了所有能找到的马、狗和老鼠，如果国王不去解救他们的话，他们就要向英军投降。菲利普试图带兵救援，但他们深陷于英军的包围之中，结果他没有成功，只好离开了那里。如此一来，他们升起了英国国旗，向爱德华国王投降。爱德华对来自加来的低声下气的送信人说：“告诉你们将军，我要求送六个最受人尊敬的公民过来，他们的脖子要套上绳索，还要带着城堡和城门的钥匙。”

当加来的地方长官把这一消息告知集市上的人们时，泪水和悲痛席卷了一切。这时，人群中一位受人尊敬的名叫尤斯塔斯·圣比埃尔的公民站起来说，如果不牺牲这六个人的话，城里的所有人口都会被杀，所以他自愿当这六个人里的第一个。在榜样的激励下，另外五个受人尊敬的公民一个接一个站了起来，自愿牺牲自己拯救他人。受了重伤的地方长官无法行走，于是他骑上一匹瘦弱的老马，引领着这些好人走向城门口。此时，所有的人都在哭泣，在哀悼。

爱德华怒不可遏地接见了六人，命令砍掉他们所有人的头。然而，善良的王后菲利帕跪下来恳求国王把他们交给她。国王回答说：“我真希望你不在这里，但我没法拒绝你的请求。”于是，她让他们穿上合适的衣服，招待他们吃了一顿宴席，然后让他们带着一件很好的礼物回到了加来城欣喜的人群里。

（查尔斯·狄更斯）

作者介绍

著名的英国小说家查尔斯·狄更斯（1812—1870）出身贫困，父母没有能力让他接受良好教育。他在年少时所获得的知识，来自于在家里零散的阅读和对生活敏锐的观察。他早年当过记者和撰稿人，写的很多文章都署名为“博兹”，这些文章后来被收集在《博兹札记》中。他第一部成功的作品是《匹克威客外传》，其欢快的幽默手法至今无人超越。你们无疑已经很熟悉狄更斯的作品，如《老古玩店》《巴纳比·拉奇》《双城记》《圣诞故事》《董贝父子》《雾都孤儿》等。本文选自《写给孩子看的英国历史》。

练习

1. 数是指代一个或一个以上事物的单词形式或用法。英语语言里有两种数的形式。

(1)单数是指代一个事物的单词形式或用法。例如：year, man, army, he, his, was.

(2)复数形式是指代一个以上事物的单词形式或用法。例如：years, men, armies, they, their, were.

2. 大多数名词的复数形式是在单数形式后面加“s”或“es”。例如：town, towns; bush, bushes.

(1)在本文寻找并列出10个在单数后加“s”构成复数的单词。

(2)在第45、49、50、51页寻找并列出5个在单数后加“es”构成复数的单词。

朗读

In the world's broad field of battle,
In the bivouac of Life,
Be not like dumb, driven cattle!
Be a hero in the strife!

(Henry W. Longfellow)

Loss of the Arctic

It was autumn. Hundreds had wended their way from pilgrimages; from Rome and its treasures of dead art, and its glory of living nature; from the sides of the Switzer's mountains, from the capitals of various nations; all of them saying in their hearts, "We will wait for the September gales to have done with their equinoctial fury, and then we shall embark; we shall slide across the appeased ocean, and, in the gorgeous month of October, we shall greet our longed-for native land, and our heart-loved homes."

And so the throng streamed along from Berlin, from Paris, from the Orient, converging upon London, still hastening toward the welcome ship, and narrowing every day the circle of engagements and preparations. They crowded aboard. Never had the Arctic borne such a host of passengers, nor passengers so nearly related to so many of us.

The hour was come. The signal ball fell at Greenwich. It was noon also at Liverpool. The anchors were weighed; the great hull swayed to the current; the national colors streamed abroad, as if themselves instinct with life and national sympathy. The bell strikes, their heels revolve, the signal-gun beats its echoes in upon every structure along the shore, and the Arctic glides joyfully forth from the Mersey, and turns her prow to the winding channel, and begins her homeward run.

The pilot stood at the wheel, and men saw him. Death sat upon the prow, and no eye beheld him. Whoever stood at the wheel in all the voyage, Death was the pilot that steered the craft, and none knew it. He neither revealed his presence nor whispered his errand. And so hope was effulgent, and lithe gayety disported itself, and joy was with every guest.

Amid all the inconveniences of the voyage, there was still that which hushed every murmur,——home is not far away. And, every morning, it was still one night nearer home! Eight days had passed. They beheld that distant bank of mist that forever haunts the vast shallows of Newfoundland. Boldly they made it, and, plunging in, its pliant wreaths wrapped them about. They shall never emerge. The last sunlight has flashed from that deck. The last voyage is done to ship and passengers.

At noon there came noiselessly stealing from the north that fated instrument of destruction. In that mysterious shroud, that vast atmosphere of mist, both steamers were holding their way with rushing prow and roaring wheels, but invisible. At a league's distance, unconscious, and, at nearer approach, unwarned; within hail, and bearing right toward each other, unseen, unfelt, till, in a moment more, emerging from the gray mists, the ill-omened Vests dealt her deadly stroke to the Arctic.

The death-blow was scarcely felt along the mighty hull. She neither reeled nor shivered. Neither commander nor officers deemed that they had suffered harm. Prompt upon humanity, the brave Luce (let his name be ever spoken with admiration and respect!) ordered away his boat with the first officer, to inquire if the stranger had suffered harm. As Gourley, the first mate of the Arctic, went over the ship's side, oh! That some good angel had called to the brave commander in the words of Paul on a like occasion: "Except these abide in the ship, ye cannot be saved."

They departed, and with them the hope of the ship, for now the waters, gaining upon the hold, and rising up upon the fires, revealed the mortal blow. Oh! Had now that stern, brave mate, Gourley, been on deck, whom the sailors were wont to obey——had he stood to execute efficiently the commander's will——we may believe that we should not have to blush for the cowardice and recreancy of the crew, nor weep for the untimely dead. But apparently each subordinate officer lost all presence of mind, then courage, then honor. In a wild scramble, that ignoble mob of firemen, engineer, waiters, and crew rushed for the boats, and abandoned the helpless women, children, and men to the mercy of the deep! Four hours there were from the catastrophe of the collision to the catastrophe of the sinking!

Oh, what a burial was there! Not as when one is borne from his home, among weeping throngs, and gently carried to the green fields, and laid peacefully beneath the turf and the flowers. No priest stood to pronounce a burial service. It was an ocean grave. The mists alone shrouded the burial-place. No spade prepared the grave, nor sexton filled up the hollowed earth. Down, down they sank, and the quick returning waters smoothed out every ripple, and left the sea as if it had not been.

(Henry Ward Beecher)

译文

消逝的北极号

那是一个秋天。几百人踏上了他们的朝圣之旅：有从罗马来的，带着它旧日文明的珍宝和当代文明的辉煌；有从瑞士群山的另一侧而来的；有从各个国家的首都而来的；他们每一个人都虔诚地说着："我们会等到九月的狂风那昼夜不息的愤怒止息，然后就会起航；我们会穿过沉静安宁的大海，等到了美丽的十月，我们就能见到朝思暮想的祖国，回到心心念念的家园。"

于是，这群人乘船驶过了柏林、驶过了巴黎、驶过了远东，朝着伦敦驶去。这艘备受期待的船朝着目的地急速前进，每一天都陷于航行与准备航行的循环。人们总是挤在甲板上，北极号从未搭载过这么一大群乘客，也从未有那么多乘客与我们这样亲如一家。

终于到了！先是格林威治降下了信号球，然后利物浦也在正午时分降下了信号球。铁锚收起，大船随着水流摇晃。各色人种、各个国家的人蜂拥涌出船舱，仿佛得到了生命的鼓舞和同胞的慰藉。钟声敲响，他们也加快了步伐，信号枪的回声响彻在了海岸的每一个角落，而北极号也满心愉悦地从默西起航，将船身转向弯弯曲曲的航道，开始了返航之旅。

舵手站在舵轮旁，人们看见了他，而死神站在船头，却没有人看见。整个航程中，不论舵轮边站的是谁，操纵这艘船的舵手就是死神，可是这一点却没有人知道。死神从不会露面，也不会泄露他的任务。因此，乘客们依旧满怀希望，喜气洋洋。

尽管航行中有许多不便，但平静缓解了人们的每句怨言，因为家就在前方了。而且，每一天清晨的来临，意味着到家的旅程又过去了一夜。八天过去了，他们看到遥远的海岸边笼着一层雾，这是纽芬兰岛的巨大浅水湾，这里永远都是雾蒙蒙的。很显然他们已经到了那里，驶进了层层雾霭中，多变的雾渐渐包围了他们，再也看不到了。最后一束阳光从甲板上闪过，这艘船连同船上乘客的最后航行也要结束了。

到了中午，命定的毁灭偷偷从北方无声走来。在浓雾的笼罩下，两艘船沿着各自的航道前行，船身急速前冲，舵轮呼啸推进。两艘船之间还有一里格，但谁都没有意识到对方的存在；距离更近了，依然没有人提高警惕；慢慢地，只剩一步之遥，两艘船转向对方的右边，依然什么也看不见，什么也感觉不到；又过了一会儿，浓雾里出现了两艘船，只是，不幸的威斯特号狠狠地撞上了北极号。

这致命一击对这样的大船而言基本没有什么感觉。船既没有打转也没有震颤。无论是船长还是高级船员，都认为他们没有遭受损害。但出于人道的考虑，勇敢的船长卢斯（让我们永远以钦佩与尊敬之心叫出这个名字吧！）以第一长官的身份命令将船驶离，去另一艘船上问问是否有损失。当北极号的大副吉尔利检查船侧的时候，有个好心人已经冲着勇敢的船长大喊保罗在类似场合下说过的话："假如没有船上的人，你们是不可能获救的。"

他们出发了，然而全船的希望也远离了，因为现在海水已经逼近船舱，渐渐上升至锅炉的位置，造成了致命的打击。哦！就在这时，那位坚定勇敢的大副吉尔利来到了甲板，海员们对他已经惯于服从。他的出现，让船长的命令得到了有效的执行。我们也许认为不该因船员们的怯懦胆小羞愧，也不必为过早死去的人们哭泣。但显而易见的是，每一个下级官员都失去了冷静，失去了勇气，最终失去了尊严。在野蛮的争夺中，一群不光彩的司炉工、工程师、服务员、船员冲向救生船，却抛下了无助的妇女、儿童和陷入深海的男人！从相撞到沉船，整整经历了四个小时！

上帝啊！这是一场多么盛大的葬礼！但和平常的葬礼不同，他们并不是在亲友的痛哭中从家里送出，被缓缓地带到绿油油的田野，安详地被埋在草地和花朵之下，更没有牧师在旁主持。这是一个海洋墓场，只有浓雾笼罩着葬地，不需铁锹挖掘，不需司事填土。他们沉向海底，湍急的水流重新抹平海面所有的涟漪，仿佛船没有来过，一切都未曾发生。

（亨利·沃德·比奇）

The Stamp Act in North Carolina

On the 16th day of November, 1765, the people of Wilmington, North Carolina, under the lead of Colonel John Ashe and others, went to Governor Tryon's house and demanded William Houston, who had been appointed stamp-master. Upon Tryon's refusal to surrender him they made preparations to burn the house. Tryon then requested Colonel Ashe to step in and talk with the stamp-master, which he did, and Houston, realizing his danger if he refused the demand made upon him to resign his office, agreed to accompany Colonel Ashe to the street. Escorted thence by a large crowd, they went to the Court House, and there, in the presence of the Mayor and public officers, Houston took and subscribed an oath not to receive or distribute any stamp-paper. Upon the taking and signing of the oath by Houston, the crowd gave three cheers and then dispersed.

Twelve days afterward, the sloop of war Diligence arrived in the Cape Fear river with the stamps, and the welcome which awaited her captain must have astonished him. His name was Phipps, and his vessel was a twenty-gun sloop of war, which was cruising off the coast of Virginia and the Carolinas. He brought the stamp from Virginia whither they had been sent from England, and, doubtless, anticipated no trouble whatever in delivering them to the collector of the port of Brunswick. The idea of resistance of any kind probably never occurred to him, and a suggestion of armed defiance on the part of the people on shore would have seemed the wildest absurdity to a commander of one of His Majesty's war-ships.

Comfortably pacing his deck, as the gallant sloop, with colors flying and all her canvas set, glided curtseying across the bar like a fine lady entering a drawing-room, the Captain was doubtless already enjoying in anticipation the sideboard and table refreshments that awaited him in the hospitable mansions of the Cape Fear planters, and eager to stand, gun in hand, by one of the tall pines of Brunswick and watch the coming of the antlered monarch of the forest before the inspiring music of the hounds.

As the Diligence bowled along "with a bone in her mouth" across the ruffled bosom of the beautiful bay into which the river expands opposite Fort Johnston, a puff of white smoke leaped from her port quarter, followed by a roar of salutation from one of her guns; an answering thunder of welcome came from the fort, and the proud ship walked the waters toward the town of Brunswick, eight miles farther up the river toward Wilmington. An hour later she sighted the town, and a little while afterward, with a graceful sweep and a rushing keel, she gradually put her nose in the wind as if scenting trouble; and then, at the shrill sound of the boatswain's whistle, the growling chains released the anchor from its long suspense, and the Diligence rested opposite the Custom House of Brunswick, with her grinning port-holes open and all her guns exposed. Then her rigging blocks chuckled as she lowered and clewed her sails, and she rode at her moorings beneath the flag of the Mistress of the Seas.

The Captain at once observed that the little town seemed to be unusually lively and expectant. He soon discovered the cause. A considerable body of armed men occupied the streets and lined the shore. Presently he was informed that Colonel Hugh Waddell, an experienced soldier, who had been on the lookout for the Diligence with the militia of Brunswick County, had notified Colonel Ashe of New Hanover of his movements. These two gentlemen, with the armed militia of both counties, confronted him and informed him that they would resist the landing of the stamps and would fire on anyone attempting it. Here was one of His Majesty's twenty-gun sloops of war openly defied and threatened by British subjects armed and drawn up in battle array! Here was treason, open, flagrant and in the broad light of day——treason armed and led by the most distinguished soldier of the Province and Speaker of the Assembly!

The Captain of the Diligence prudently concluded that it would be folly to attempt to land the stamps in the face of such a threat, backed by such force, and promised a compliance with the demands of the people. The "Son of Liberty", as they were afterward called, then seized one of the boats of the Diligence, and, leaving a guard at Brunswick, marched with it mounted on a cart to Wilmington, where there was a triumphal procession through the streets, and at night a general illumination of the town.

And this was more than ten years before the Declaration of Independence, and more than nine before the battle of Lexington, and nearly eight years before the Boston "Tea Party".

(Alfred Moore Waddeli)

译文

北卡罗来纳州的印花税法案

1765年11月16日，北卡罗来纳州威尔明顿的人民在约翰·阿什上校和其他人的带领下，来到了特赖恩州长的官邸跟前，要求传唤被任命为印花税负责官的威廉·休斯敦。当特赖恩拒绝后，他们便打算烧了整个官邸。特赖恩只好请求阿什上校进屋来与印花税官员进行交涉。上校这么做了，休斯敦意识到如果他拒绝人们要他辞职的要求，自己的人身安全就会受到威胁，便同意陪同阿什上校一起走上大街，于是他们在大量群众的护送下来到了法院。在市长和公职人员在场的情况下，休斯敦做出了不再接受并派发印花税的宣言并签了字。他做出并签下誓言后，人们三次高声欢呼，随后便散去了。

十二天后，单桅风帆战舰“勤奋号”载着印花税票抵达了开普菲尔河，而等候船长的欢迎仪式肯定会让他大吃一惊。船长名叫菲普斯，他的战舰是一艘在弗吉尼亚州和卡罗来纳州海岸巡航的，具有二十门大炮的单桅风帆战舰。他带着英国派发的印花税票从弗吉尼亚州出发，按他的预期，将它们送交不伦瑞克港征收者的过程中肯定不会遇上任何麻烦。他可能从来没有想过会受到任何形式的抵抗，而对于一名国王陛下的战舰的指挥官来说，遭遇岸上人民的武装抵抗更是一件天方夜谭般的事。

他悠闲地在那张满风帆、绚丽多彩的华丽帆船的甲板上踱着步，并且有如一名进入客厅的优雅的女士那般，屈膝轻轻走过酒吧间。毫无疑问，船长的心思已经飞进了开普菲尔种植园主那款待周到的公馆里，期待着那正等候他的餐柜和桌上的点心。他热切地盼望着持枪站在不伦瑞克高大的松树旁，在激动人心的猎犬吠鸣中注视着头戴鹿角的森林之主向他走来。

“勤奋号”在美丽的海湾那波澜起伏的怀抱中破浪前进，来到了约翰斯顿堡对面的河流入海口。一缕白烟从左舷船尾方向腾空升起，紧随着的是一声问候性的火炮低鸣。从堡垒处传来了一声轰鸣作为回应后，这艘得意的军舰便向威尔明顿方向，河流上游十三千米处的不伦瑞克驶去。一小时后它发现了城镇，又过了不久，随着优雅而又迅速的前行，它开始仔细地观察着周围的情况以确定是否有麻烦。然后，响起了水手们尖锐的哨声，悬挂着的船锚随着“隆隆”作响的锁链被放了下来，“勤奋号”在不伦瑞克海关对面停下了。它的舱盖打开着，所有的火炮都露在外面。随后索具开始“咯咯”地运转，船帆被降下并收拢了，整条船便停在了泊位里，船上悬挂着英国的旗帜。

船长立刻发现小镇看上去异常的热闹，人们都翘首以盼着什么。他马上发现了原因，一大群武装人员占据了大街，并在岸边列好了队形。此时他接到了通报，经验丰富的休·沃德尔上校正在和不伦瑞克郡的民兵们一起警戒着“勤奋号”的动向，并已经向新汉诺威的阿什上校通报了他的行动。这两位先生带领着两个县的民兵和他对抗，表明了他们反对把印花税票卸下来，并会朝任何企图这样做的人开火。一艘国王陛下的二十门炮单桅风帆战舰居然受到那些武装起来、进入战斗队列的英国臣民们公然的藐视和威胁！这简直是一种光天化日之下公开的反叛行为——由这个州最杰出的战士和下院议长带领的武装叛乱！

“勤奋号”的船长明智地认为在这种武力威胁下卸下印花税票是一种愚蠢的行为，便按着人民的要求作了妥协。后来被称作“自由之子”的组织夺取了“勤奋号”的一艘小划船，在不伦瑞克留下一个护卫队后，就将小船装上运货马车向威尔明顿驶去。那天晚上整个小镇一片灯火通明，街道上还举行了一个凯旋仪式。

这已是独立宣言十多年前的事情了，它发生在列克星敦战役九年多前，也就是波士顿倾茶事件八年前左右。

（阿尔弗雷德·摩尔·沃德尔）

Webster Defending His Alma Mater

[The charter of Dartmouth College was granted by the British crown in 1769. It was under the government of twelve trustees and was virtually a private institution. In 1816 the legislature of New Hampshire amended this charter, making the college a public institution governed by officials appointed by the state. The case was appealed to the Supreme Court of the United States, where Daniel Webster made the principal argument in favor of the old charter being retained, and won the case.]

Mr. Webster went on for more than four hours with a statement so luminous, and a chain of reasoning so easy to be understood, and yet approaching so nearly to absolute demonstration, that he seemed to carry with him every man of his audience without the slightest effort or uneasiness on either side. A single circumstance will show you the clearness and absorbing power of his argument.

I observed that Judge Story, at the opening of the case, had prepared himself, pen in hand, as if to take copious minutes. Hour after hour I saw him fixed in the same attitude, but, so far as I could perceive, with not a note on his paper. The argument closed, and I could not discover that he had taken a single note. Others around me remarked the same thing, and it was among the on dits [They say's] of Washington, that a friend spoke to him of the fact with surprise, when the Judge remarked, "Everything was so clear, and so easy to remember, that not a note seemed necessary, and, in fact, I thought little or nothing about my notes."

The argument ended, Mr. Webster stood for some moments silent before the court, while every eye was fixed intently upon him. At length, addressing the Chief Justice, he proceeded thus, "This, Sir, is my case. It is the case not merely of that humble institution, it is the case of every college in the land. It is more. It is the case of every eleemosynary institution throughout our country,——of all those great charities founded by the piety of our ancestors, to alleviate human misery, and scatter blessings along the pathway of life.

"It is more! It is, in some sense, the case of every man among us who has property of which he may be stripped; for the question is merely this: Shall our State Legislatures be allowed to take that which is not their own, to turn it from its original use, and apply it to such ends or purposes as they in their discretion shall see fit?

"Sir, you may destroy this little institution; it is weak; it is in your hands! I know that it is one of the lesser lights in the literary horizon of our country. You may put it out. But, if you do so, you must carry through your work! You must extinguish, one after another, all those greater lights of science which, for more than a century, have thrown their radiance over our land! It is, Sir, as I have said, a small college. And yet there are those who love it——"

Here, the feelings, which he had thus far succeeded in keeping down, broke forth. His lips quivered; his firm cheeks trembled with emotion; his eyes were filled with tears, his voice choked, and he seemed struggling to the utmost simply to gain that mastery over himself which might save him from a burst of feeling. I shall not attempt to give you the few broken words of tenderness in which he went on to speak of his attachment to the college. The whole seemed to be mingled throughout with the recollections of father, mother, brother, and all the privations and trials through which he had made his way into life. Every one saw that it was entirely unpremeditated, a pressure on his heart, which sought relief in words and tears.

The court-room during these two or three minutes presented an extraordinary spectacle. Chief Justice Marshall, with his tall and gaunt figure bent over, as if to catch the slightest whisper, the deep furrows of his cheeks expanded with emotion, and his eyes suffused with tears; Mr. Justice Washington at his side, leaning forward with an eager, troubled look; and the remainder of the court at the two extremities, pressing, as it were, toward a single point, while the audience below were wrapping themselves round in closer folds beneath the bench, to catch each look and every movement of the speaker.

If a painter could give us the scene on canvas,——those forms and countenances, and Daniel Webster as he stood there in the midst,——it would be one of the most touching pictures in the history of eloquence. One thing it taught me, that the Pathetic depends not merely on the words uttered, but still more on the estimate we put upon him who utters them. There was not one among the strong-minded men of that assembly who could think it unmanly to weep, when he saw standing before him the man, who had made such an argument, melted into the tenderness of a child.

He sat down. There was a death-like stillness throughout the room for some moments; every one seemed to be slowly recovering himself, and coming gradually back to his ordinary range of thoughts and feeling.

(Chauncey Allen Goodrich)

译文

守护母校的韦伯斯特

[达特茅斯学院的特许状是在1769年由英国王室敕发的，它基本上是一个由十二名理事管理的私立机构。1816年，新罕布什尔州议会修改了这个特许状，使学院成了一个公立机构，并由国家任命的官员来进行管理。这个案件上诉到了美国联邦最高法院，丹尼尔·韦伯斯特作了支持保留旧特许状的重要辩护并赢得了这场官司。]

韦伯斯特先生的发言持续了四个多小时，他的陈述简单明了，推理平易浅显，但论证能力非常强大。他似乎没有给任何一名两方的听众带来哪怕是最轻微的压力和不安。一个单独的场景就能够向你展现出他那明晰而又带有迷人力量的辩论。

我看到斯托里法官在案子开始时已经拿着笔做好准备，似乎要做大量的记录。几个小时过去了，我看到他还是保持着那个姿势，但就我所知，他没有在纸上做过一点笔记。辩论结束了，我发现他没有记过一笔。我周围的人们也注意到了同样的事，这在关于华盛顿的传闻中也出现过，一位朋友曾惊讶地向他谈及此事，那位法官说道："每件事都很明白了，也很容易记住。

看来是不必记笔记了，事实上我认为我记的笔记基本没什么用。”

辩论结束了，韦伯斯特先生在法庭前静静地站了一会儿，所有眼睛都专注地盯着他。终于，他对首席法官如此说道：“先生，这是我的案子，这案子不只关乎那个卑微的机构，它和这片土地上每一个大学都有关。不仅如此，它还是我国每一个接受捐赠的机构的案子——所有那些出于我们祖先的虔诚而建立的慈善组织，它们缓解了人类的苦难并在生活道路上散播了祝福。

“不仅如此！在某种意义上，所有拥有财产而又可能会被剥夺这些财产的人，都与这个案件有关。问题仅在于此：我们的州议会能被允许占有本不属于他们的东西吗？他们可以改变一样东西原有的用途，在经过考虑后觉得合适就把它用于别的目的吗？

“先生，你会毁了这个小机构；它很弱小；它听凭你的处置！我知道，它是我国文学地平线上的小灯塔之一。你可能会熄灭它。但是，如果你这么做，你的做法必将会贯彻下去。你必定会一座接一座地消灭那些伟大的科学灯塔，那些一个多世纪内在我们这片土地上播撒光芒的灯塔。先生，正如我所说的，它是一所小学院，但是还是有人深爱着它——”

说到这里，他一直控制住的感情爆发了出来。他的嘴唇抖动着，坚毅的脸颊激动地颤抖着，双眼充满了泪水，声音也哽咽了。他似乎正极力控制住自己不让感情爆发出来。我不打算凭借寥寥几个表达温柔的词语来描述他接下来谈到的对学院的依恋之情。他所说的这一切自始至终同以下的回忆混杂在了一起：关于父亲、关于母亲、关于兄弟，以及关于这一路走来所遇到的一切贫困和患难。每个人都可以看出这完全不是事先准备好的。被压迫的心灵正通过言辞和眼泪来寻找慰藉。

这两三分钟内，审判室呈现出了一种非凡的景象。首席大法官马歇尔那高瘦的身躯弯曲着，似乎想要听清哪怕是最轻微的低语，他脸颊上的皱纹因为激动而伸展开来，眼中含满了泪水；华盛顿法官在他身边，身子关切地前倾着，并露出了不安的表情；法庭两头其余的人都挤向一边。而底下的观众们则围绕着法官席下方近处的护栏，以便看清发言者的每一个表情和动作。

如果一名画家能将这个场景展现在画布上——画下那一个个的形体和面容，而最中间站着的是丹尼尔·韦伯斯特——它将会成为辩论历史上最动人的画作之一。它教会了我一个道理，同情的产生不仅仅是依靠说出的话语，而更取决于我们对于那个说话人的评价。当看到站在眼前的男子刚做完这样的辩论，又流露了孩子般的温柔时，任何一名铁石心肠的与会者都不会认为哭泣是一种怯懦的行为。

他坐了下来，房间里好一会儿一片死寂。每个人似乎慢慢地清醒过来，渐渐地回到了正常的思索和感觉中。

（昌西·艾伦·古德里奇）

作者介绍

昌西·艾伦·古德里奇是一名出生于康涅狄格州纽黑文的美国学者。他毕业于耶鲁大学，后来在那里担任修辞学和神学教授。他将个人和学院利益紧密地联系在一起，这使得他非常欣赏韦伯斯特为了守护母校而进行的热情辩护。

Mount Mitchell

预习

Mystick Krewe 狂欢节国王的保镖

Ceres 谷物女神

float /floʊt/ 浮现

scaled /skeɪld/ 成比例的

Before we were half-way up the ascent, we realized the folly of attempting it on horseback, but then to go on seemed as easy as to go back. The way also was exceedingly steep in places, and what with roots, and logs, and slippery rocks and stones, it was a desperate climb for the horses.

What a magnificent forest! Oaks, chestnuts, poplars, hemlocks, the cucumber (magnolia), and all sorts of northern and southern growths meeting here in splendid array. And this gigantic forest, with little diminution in size of trees, continues two thirds of the way up. Half-way up, Big Tom, our guide, showed us his favorite, the biggest tree he knew. It was a poplar, or tulip. It stands more like a column than a tree, rising high into the air, with scarcely a perceptible taper, perhaps sixty, more likely a hundred, feet before it puts out a limb. Its girth six feet from the ground is thirty-two feet! It stood here, of course, a giant, when Columbus sailed from Spain.

As we approached the top, Big Tom pointed out the direction, a half mile away, of a small pond, a little mountain tarn, overlooked by a ledge of rock, where Professor Mitchell lost his life. Big Tom was the guide that found the body. That day, as we sat on the summit, he gave in great detail the story, the general outline of which we already knew.

The first effort to measure the height of the Black Mountains was made in 1835, by Professor Elisha Mitchell, professor of mathematics and chemistry in the University of North Carolina at Chapel Hill. Mr. Mitchell was a native of Connecticut, graduated at Yale; and became a professor at Chapel Hill in 1818.

He first ascertained and published the fact that the Black Mountains are the highest land east of the Rocky Mountains. In 1844 he visited the locality again. Measurements were subsequently made by Professor Guyot and by Senator Clingmen. One of the peaks is named for the senator, and a dispute arose as to whether Mitchell had really visited and measured the highest peak.

The estimates of altitudes made by the three explorers named differed considerably. The height now fixed for Mt. Mitchell is 6,711 feet; that of Mt. Washington is 6,285 feet. There are twelve peaks in this range higher than Mt. Washington, and if we add those in the Great Smoky Mountains, which overtop it, there are some twenty in North Carolina higher than the granite giant of New Hampshire. In order to verify his statement, Professor Mitchell made a third ascent in June, 1857. He was alone, and went up from the Swannanoa side. He did not return. No anxiety was felt for two or three days, as he was a good mountaineer, and it was supposed that he had crossed the mountain and made his way out by the Caney River.

But when several days passed without tidings of him a search party was formed. Big Tom Wilson was with it. They explored the mountains in all directions unsuccessfully. At length Big Tom separated himself from his companions and took a course in accordance with his notion of that which would be pursued by a man lost in the clouds or the darkness. He soon struck the trail of the wanderer, and following it, discovered Mitchell's body lying in a pool at the foot of a rocky precipice some thirty feet high. It was evident that Professor Mitchell, making his way along the ridge in darkness or fog, had fallen off.

There was some talk of burying him on the mountain, but the friends decided otherwise, and the remains, with much difficulty, were taken down to Asheville and there interred. Some years afterwards, I believe at the instance of a society of scientists, it was resolved to transport the body to the summit of Mount Mitchell. The task was not easy. A road had to be cut, and the hardy mountaineers who undertook the removal, were three days in reaching the summit with their burden.

The remains were accompanied by a considerable concourse, and the last rites on the top were participated in by a hundred or more scientists and prominent men from different parts of the State. Such a strange cortège had never before broken the silence of this lonely wilderness, nor was ever burial more impressive than this wild interment above the clouds.

After a struggle of five hours, we emerged from the balsams and brier into a lovely open meadow, of lush clover, timothy, and blue grass. The meadow sloped up to a belt of balsams and firs, a steep rocky knob, and climbing that on foot we stood upon the summit of Mitchell at one o'clock.

There, in the center of the stony plot on the summit, lie the remains of Mitchell. To dig a grave in the rock was impracticable, but the loose stones were scooped away to the depth of a foot or so, the body was deposited, and the stones were replaced over it. It was the original intention to erect a monument, but the enterprise of the projectors of this royal entombment failed at that point.

The grave is surrounded by a low wall of loose stone, to which each visitor adds one, and in the course of ages the cairn may grow to a good size. The explorer lies there without name or headstone to mark his awful resting-place.

The mountain is his monument. He is alone with its majesty. He is there in the clouds, in the tempests, where the lightnings play, and thunders leap, amid the elemental tumult, in the occasional great calm and silence and the pale sunlight. It is the most majestic, the most lonesome grave on earth tarn, a mountain lake or pool.

(Charles Dudley Warner)

译文

米切尔峰

在爬到半山腰之前，我们意识到骑马攀峰是一种愚蠢的尝试，但是继续爬上去的难度和折返的难度似乎看起来一样。四处的山路陡峭险峻，遍布树根和砍伐下来的原木，还有松动的大小石块，对于马儿们来说，是难以攀爬的绝境。

真是广阔秀美的森林！有橡树、栗树、美国白杨、铁杉、美国黄玉兰（木兰科）等，所有的北国植物和南国植物在此交汇，生长得丰美茂盛。在这片广袤的森林里，树木被稍作砍伐，开拓出三分之二的攀爬路线。半路上，我们的向导大汤姆给我们指他最爱的树，也是他所见过的最高大的树——一棵美国鹅掌楸，人们也称之为美国白杨。它伫立在那里，高耸入云。它只有一根主干，越往上变得越细，大约到二十米，实则更可能是四十米的高度，才伸出一根枝干。它看起来不像一棵树，更像一根圆柱子。在离地一米多高的地方，它的躯干周长竟达五米多！自哥伦布从西班牙航行而来，它便如同巨人一般矗立在此。

我们到达了山顶，站在一块突起的石头上俯瞰，大汤姆给我们指了指去往一个小湖的方向。这个山中小湖在八百米之外，米切尔教授就丧命于此。对于此事，我们已经知道大致经过。大汤姆是发现其遗体的向导，我们坐在山顶的时候，他给我们补充了很多细节。

人类第一次尝试测量布拉克山脉是在1835年，由北卡罗来纳大学数学与化学系的以利沙·米切尔教授主持。米切尔教授毕业于耶鲁大学，是土生土长的康涅狄格州人。自1818年起，他作为教授受聘于教堂山。

他是第一个确认并公布布拉克山脉是落基山脉东部最高山的人。1844年，他重访该地。其后，又有盖约特教授和议员克林曼进行了一系列测量，人们还以该议员的名字命名了一座山峰。争议也由此而起，米切尔所攀上及测量的真是最高峰吗？

由三位探险家命名的山峰，测量出来的海拔高度差异很大。米切尔峰如今确定的海拔高度为两千零四十五米。华盛顿山位于新罕布什尔州，是一座满布花岗岩的巨大山峰，海拔为一千九百一十五米。这里附近的十二座山峰比华盛顿山还要高。如果再算上比它更高的大雾山脉，在北卡来罗纳州就有二十多座山峰比华盛顿山要高了。1857年6月，米切尔教授为了核实自己的结论，进行了第三次攀登。他独自前行，从斯旺纳诺河一侧攀爬而上，再也没有回来。由于米切尔教授是一个优秀的登山家，过了两三天，人们也没有感到焦急，只是猜测他已跨越了整座山峰，从凯尼河那一侧出来了。

过了数天，他依然杳无音讯，一支搜救队才出动了，大汤姆·威尔逊就在其中。他们从各个方向搜寻整个山脉，都一无所获。最后，大汤姆和队友分开，他依照自己的判断，选择了一条在云雾中或在黑暗中迷路的人会走的路。他很快就找到了米切尔教授留下的踪迹，并沿着它前行，最终在一座湖里找到了米切尔的遗体。这个小湖就处在一块岩石悬崖脚下，很显然，在黑暗或是在迷雾之中，米切尔教授沿着山脊前行，在这块九米多高的岩石上失足跌落。

有人提议在山上直接把他埋葬，但朋友们做出了另外的选择，也是难度很高的选择。他们把他的遗体和遗物带下山，在阿什维尔下葬。几年后，应一群科学家的要求，他的遗体被重新带回到米切尔峰的山顶，我想这是一个非常有决心的决定。这任务可不简单，需要开辟出一条道路，登山者也需要坚忍的意志去做搬运工作，再加上身上的负重，他们得花三天时间才能到达山顶。

陪伴着遗体上山的人有很多，参与了山顶上最后的告别仪式的，有一百多名科学家和杰出人士，他们来自全国各地。从未有如此陌生的人群打破过这处山地的孤寂，也没有哪个葬礼比这个云端上举行的野外葬礼更令人印象深刻。

艰难跋涉了五小时，我们从一堆凤仙花和野蔷薇丛中挤了出来，来到了一个开阔的秀美草地。苜蓿、梯牧草和早熟禾在这里茂盛生长。草地斜向上是凤仙花和冷杉的植被带，还有一块陡峭的突起来的岩石。我们徒步走上去，站在了米切尔峰的山巅，此时已是一点整。

山顶上的一块石头地中央，就躺着米切尔教授的遗体。在石头上挖一个坟墓是不可行的，人们只好把松动的石块挖走，形成一个约三十厘米深的坑。遗体被安放进去，再把刚才移走的石块放上去。原本的打算是在这里立一个碑，但这个盛大葬礼的谋划者们最终还是放弃了这个想法。

每个参观者来到这里，都会下放一块石头，在坟墓四周围起一堵松散的石头矮墙。随着时间的流逝，它的体积也许会越来越大。米切尔教授就躺在这里，他的安息之处令人敬畏，没有墓碑，也没有署名用以标记。

整座山峰实则就是米切尔教授的纪念碑。他独自在这里，与威严的山体做伴。时而云雾掠过，时而暴风雨带着电闪雷鸣袭来，时而苍白的阳光洒落，他身处于大自然的喧嚣之中，同时又体验着巨大的宁静与安寂。这是高山湖泊旁边最为庄严、最为寂寥的墓。

（查尔斯·达德利·沃纳）

A Cavalry Charge

The introduction of gunpowder and bullets and of long-range repeating rifles has, in modern warfare, greatly lessened the effectiveness of cavalry in general battle with infantry, and deprived that great arm of the service of the terror which its charges once inspired. In wars of the early centuries, the swift horseman rode down the comparatively helpless infantry and trampled its ranks under the horses' feet. For ages after the dismemberment of the Roman Empire, it was the vast bodies of cavalry that checked and changed the currents of battles and settled the fate of armies and empires. This is not true now——can never be true again; but a cavalry charge, met by a counter-charge of cavalry is still, perhaps, the most terrible spectacle witnessed in war. If the reader has never seen such a charge, he can form little conception of its awe-inspiring fury.

Imagine yourself looking down from Gettysburg heights upon the open, wide-spreading plain below, where five thousand horses are marshaled in battle line. Standing beside them are five thousand riders, armed, booted and spurred, and ready to mount. The bugles sound the "Mount!" and instantly five thousand plumes rise above the horses as the riders spring into their saddles. In front of the respective squadrons the daring leaders take their places. The fluttering pennants or streaming guidons, ten to each regiment, mark the left of the companies. On the opposite slope of the same plain are five thousand hostile horsemen clad in different uniforms, ready to meet these in counter-charge.

Under those ten thousand horses are their hoofs, iron-shod and pitiless, beneath whose furious tread the plain is soon to quiver. Again on each slope of the open field the bugles sound. Ten thousand sabers leap from scabbards and glisten in the sun. The trained horses chafe their restraining bits, and, as the bugle notes sound the charge, their nostrils dilate and their flanks swell in sympathy with their dashing riders. "Forward!" shouts the commander. Down the lines and through the columns in quick succession ring the echoing commands, "Forward,

forward!" As this order thrills through eager ears, sabers flash, and spurs are planted in palpitating flanks. The madly flying horses thunder across the trembling field, filling the air with clouds of dust and whizzing pebbles.

Their iron-rimmed hoofs in remorseless tread crush the stones to powder and crash through the flesh and bones of hapless riders who chance to fall. As front against front these furious riders plunge, their sweeping sabers slashing edge against edge, cutting a way through opposing ranks, gashing faces, breaking arms, and splitting heads, it is a scene of the wildest war, a whirling tempest of battle, short-lived but terrible.

(John Brown Gordon)

译文

一场骑兵对战

在现代战争中，火药和子弹以及远距离连发步枪的引入，大大削减了骑兵在与步兵的普通战斗中的优势效果，并使得这一重要兵种丧失了曾经能带来的威慑作用。之前几个世纪的战争中，迅猛的骑士能飞快地赶上相对弱小的步兵，用马蹄将他们的队伍踏平。罗马帝国解体后的很长一段时间里，众多的骑兵是决定或扭转战局的关键，维系着军队和帝国的命运。现在不是如此了——也不可能再是如此了；但是一场骑兵冲锋，对上一场骑兵反攻，可能仍会是战争中最惨绝的壮观景象。如果读者从未见识过这样一场对战，恐怕很难构想出那令人惊叹、敬畏的狂怒画面。

想象一下你正身处于葛底斯堡之上，眼下是一片开阔、广袤的平原，五千匹马整齐地排列在战线上，旁边站着五千骑兵，全副武装、穿着马靴、带着踢马刺，准备着随时上马。军号发出“上马”的号令，顷刻间，骑手们就登上了马鞍，马具上的五千根羽毛也高高扬起。勇敢的指挥们在各自的队伍前面准备就绪。每个团有十个连，连队的左侧以翻飞的三角旗或者流动的队旗作为标记。而同一片平原上，对面的斜坡上就是敌军五千骑兵，穿着不同的制服，准备着反击。

这一万马匹之下，就是它们的马蹄，钉着马蹄铁，冰冷冷的，平原几乎都要在它们狂躁的足下颤抖起来。旷野两边的山坡上，军号声再度响起。霎时万柄军刀出鞘，在阳光下熠熠发光。训练有素的马匹摩擦着束缚它们的缰绳，然后，随着号角发出信号宣告对战开始，它们的鼻孔扩张、肋腹隆起和雄赳赳的骑士们一道共赴生死。“前进！”指挥官喊道。命令的回应声沿着纵横的队列陆续响起：“前进！前进！”命令穿透士兵们热切的耳朵激起一阵振奋，军刀闪光而出，脚下的马刺也深深刺入发抖的马腹。发狂般飞奔的马匹如雷劈入颤动的战场，空气中弥漫着尘土和呼啸而过的砂石。

它们镶着铁边的蹄子无情地将石头踏为齑粉，碾过不幸落马的血肉身躯。这面对面硬碰的决战使这些激烈的骑兵们摔下马背，他们横扫的军刀以刃对刃彼此冲击，在敌对的军队、伤痕累累的面颊、破碎的甲胄和断裂的头颅中砍出一条血路，这就是最原始残酷的战争中的景象，一场眩晕的风暴战，短暂而可怖。

（约翰·布朗·戈登）

作者介绍

约翰·布朗·戈登出生于乔治州，并在州立大学接受教育，毕业后从事法律行业。1861年美国南北内战打响时，他作为步兵团首领加入了同盟军。之后他晋升到中将军衔，并在李将军投降后指挥了阿波马托克斯驻军的一支侧翼队伍。他曾多年担任美国参议院议员的职位，1887—1990年间担任乔治亚州的州长。他还曾是同盟军退伍军人的总司令。《一场骑兵对战》选自他的《内战回忆录》，该书由斯克里布纳之子公司出版。

The Man Without a Country

"Sir: You will receive from Lieutenant Neale the person of Philip Nolan, late a Lieutenant in the United States Army.

"This person on his trial by court martial expressed with an oath the wish that he might 'never hear of the United States again'.

"The court sentenced him to have his wish fulfilled.

"For the present, the execution of the order is intrusted by the President to this department.

"You will provide him with such quarters, rations, and clothing as would be proper for an officer of his late rank, if he were a passenger on your vessel on the business of his government.

"The gentlemen on board will make any arrangements agreeable to themselves regarding his society. He is to be exposed to no indignity of any kind, nor is he ever unnecessarily to be reminded that he is a prisoner.

"But under no circumstances is he ever to hear of his country or to see any information regarding it; and you will specially caution all the officers under your command to take care that in the various indulgences which may be granted this rule, in which his punishment is involved, shall not be broken.

"It is the intention of the government that he shall never again see his country, which he has disowned. Before the end of your cruise, you will receive orders which will give effect to this intention.

"Respectfully yours,

"W. Southard, for the

"Secretary of the Navy."

If I had only preserved the whole of this paper, there would be no break in the beginning of my sketch of this story. For Captain Shaw, if it was he, handed it to his successor in the charge, and he to his, and I suppose that the commander of the Levant has it to-day as his authority for keeping this man in this mild custody.

The rule adopted on board the ships on which I have met "the man without a country" was, I think, transmitted from the beginning. No mess liked to have him permanently, because his presence cut off all talk of home or of the prospect of return, of politics or letters, of peace or of war——cut off more than half the talk men like to have at sea. But it was always thought too hard that he should never meet the rest of us, except to touch hats, and we finally sank into one system.

He was not permitted to talk with the men, unless an officer was by. With officers he had unrestrained intercourse, as far as they and he chose. But he grew shy, though he had favorites. Then the captain always asked him to dinner on Monday. Every mess in succession took up the invitation in its turn. According to the size of the ship, you had him at your mess more or less often at dinner. His breakfast he ate in his own stateroom——he always had a stateroom, which was where a sentinel or somebody on the watch could see the door. And whatever else he ate or drank, he ate or drank alone.

Sometimes, when the marines or sailors had any special jollification, they were permitted to invite "Plain-Buttons", as they called him. Then Nolan was sent with some officer, and the men were forbidden to speak of home while he was there. I believe that the theory was, that the sight of his punishment did them good. They called him "Plain-Buttons" because, while he always chose to wear a regulation army uniform, he was not permitted to wear the army button, for the reason that it bore either the initials or the insignia of the country that he had disowned.

I remember, soon after I joined the navy, I was on shore with some of the older officers from our ship and from the Brandywine, which we had met at Alexandria. We had left to have a party, and go up to Cairo and the Pyramids. As we jogged along (we went on donkeys then), some of the gentlemen fell to talking about Nolan, and some one told the system which was adopted from the first about his books and other reading.

As he was almost never permitted to go on shore, even though the vessel lay in port for months, the time, at the best, hung heavy; and everybody was permitted to lend him books, if they were not published in

America, and made no allusion to it. These were common enough in the old days, when people in the other hemisphere talked of the United States as little as we do of Paraguay. He had almost all the foreign papers that came into the ship, sooner or later; only somebody must go over them first, and cut out any advertisement or stray paragraph that alluded to America.

This was a little cruel sometimes, when the back of what was cut out might be as innocent as Hesiod. Right in the midst of one of Napoleon's battles, or one of Canning's speeches, poor Nolan would find a great hole, because on the back of the page of that paper there had been an advertisement of a packet for New York, or a scrap of the President's message. I say this was the first time I ever heard of this plan, which afterward I had enough, and more than enough, to do with. I remember it, because poor Phillips, who was of the party, as soon as the allusion to reading was made, told a story of something that happened at the Cape of Good Hope on Nolan's first voyage; and it is the only thing I ever knew of that voyage.

They had touched at the Cape, and had done the civil thing with the English Admiral and the fleet, and then, leaving for a long cruise up the Indian Ocean, Phillips had borrowed a lot of English books from an officer, which, in those days, was quite a windfall. Among them was the "Lay of the Last Minstrel", which all of them had heard of, but which most of them had never seen. I think it could not have been published long.

Well, nobody thought there could be any risk of anything national in that, so Nolan was permitted to join the circle one afternoon when a lot of them sat on deck, smoking and reading aloud. It so happened that in his turn Nolan took the book and read to the others; and he read very well, as I know. Nobody in the circle knew a line of the poem, only it was all magic and Border chivalry, and was ten thousand years ago. Poor Nolan read steadily through the fifth canto, stopped a minute and drank something, and then began without a thought of what was coming.

Breathes there a man with soul so dead,
Who never to himself hath said——

It seems impossible to us that anybody ever heard this for the first time; but all these fellows did then, and poor Nolan himself went on, still unconsciously or mechanically,——

This is my own, my native land!

Then they all say something was to pay; but he, expecting to get through, I suppose, turned a little pale, but plunged on,——

Whose heart hath ne'er within him burned,
As home his footsteps he hath turned
From wandering on a foreign strand.
If such there be, go, mark him well.

By this time the men were all beside themselves, wishing there was any way to make him turn over two pages, but he had not quite presence of mind for that; he coughed a little, colored crimson, and staggered on,——

For him no minstrel raptures swell;
High though his titles, proud his name,
Boundless his wealth as wish can claim,
Despite these titles, power, and pelf,
The wretch, concentred all in self——

And here the poor fellow choked, and could not go on, but started up, swung the book into the sea, vanished into his stateroom, "And," said Phillips, "we did not see him again for two months."

That story shows about the time when Nolan's braggadocio must have broken down. At first, they said, he took a very high tone, considered his imprisonment a mere farce, affected to enjoy the voyage, and all that; but Phillips said that after he came out of his stateroom he was never the same man again. He never read aloud again unless it was the Bible or Shakespeare, or something else he was sure of. But it was not merely that. He never entered in with the other young men exactly as a companion again. He was always shy afterward when I knew him——very seldom spoke unless he was spoken to, except to a very few friends.

(Edward Everett Hale)

译文

没有国家的人

“阁下：兹有前美军上尉菲利普·诺兰，自尼尔上尉处前往你处。

“此人在军事法庭审判中发誓，希望‘永不再听到美国的消息’。

“法庭如其所愿下达判决。

“目前，总统委托你部门执行该判决。

“你处须依其前军衔标准提供住处、口粮和衣物，将其当成一名因国家事务而出差的乘客。

“船上的人应尽可能与此人和谐相处，不得轻慢侮辱，如非必要，不得提醒其囚犯身份。

“任何情况下，不得让此人听到或看到任何有关美国的消息。你方须特别提醒执行命令的全体军官注意，在可能泄密的各种娱乐场合，在涉及他的处罚的场合，都不得违反此项规定。

“政府决定，此人既已与美国脱离关系，便不得再看见美国。你方将于航行结束前收到相关指令。

“海军部长W. 索瑟德敬上”

倘若我手中有这封信的全文，这个故事的开头就不会这么断断续续了。这封信可能是由肖船长交给下一任船长，下一任又交给下下一任，我猜眼下持有这封信的是黎凡特号船长，因为现在是由他负责软禁那位菲利普·诺兰。

我是在该规定被执行的船甲板上遇到那个“没有国家的人”的。我想，有关他的这项规定应该是从一开始就传下来的。没有哪艘船愿意一直留着诺兰，因为有他在场就不能谈论家乡和归程，不能谈论政治和信件，也不能谈论和平与战争——海上航行的人喜欢聊的话题，多半都不能提了。但一直有人觉得，不让他跟我们其他人交流，只能见面打个招呼，这样太让人为难，但最终我们都只遵循了一种规定。

诺兰只有在军官陪同时才能与其他人交谈，跟军官则可以自由交往，交往程度由他们自行决定。然而他虽有朋友，却很羞涩。船长总会邀请他参加周一的晚宴，接收他的船都延续着这个传统。根据船舰的大小，有的船上人多，有的船上人少，或多或少你总会在晚宴上碰到他几次。早餐他在舱室里吃——他有自己的舱室，设在卫兵或者其他监视他的人看得见的地方。除了晚宴之外，不管吃什么、喝什么，他都是一个人。

有时候士兵和水手们举办什么特别的庆祝活动，也可以邀请“没扣子”——他们这样称呼诺兰。他会与某位军官同来，有他在场时不得谈论家乡。我觉得他们邀请他，是为了看他受罚取乐。之所以叫他“没扣子”，是因为他总穿着军装，却禁止佩戴军服纽扣；因为扣子上有祖国的首字母或徽章，而他已经与祖国断绝了关系。

我记得自己加入海军没多久的时候，有一次在埃及的亚历山大港认识的几个布兰迪万的老军官，跟我们船上几个年纪大点儿的军官一起上了岸。我们聚在一起，要去开罗的金字塔。我们骑着驴子走在路上，有人提起诺兰，说到了在他身上一直沿用的有关读书的规定。

他几乎不能上岸，哪怕船在港口停泊几个月都不行，这段日子很是难熬，不过大家可以借书给他，只要书不是在美国出版的，里面也没有提到美国就可以。以前这样的书很多，地球那一边的人们极少提及美国，就像我们不怎么说巴拉圭的事一样。他几乎得到了带上船的所有外国书，但必须有人要先翻过一遍，把提到美国的广告和段落裁掉。

这种事情难免有些残酷，有时候被裁掉的那些文字背面的内容简直像赫西奥德一样无辜。可怜的诺兰，可能会在描写拿破仑战役的文字或者坎宁的一篇演讲中间，赫然看到一个大洞，因为这一页背面是给纽约寄包裹的广告，抑或是美国总统的一点消息。这是我第一次听说这个规定，后来则了解得越来越多。之所以记得这样清楚，是因为当时一提到这个，与我们同行的菲利普斯就讲起了发生在好望角的一段往事。那是诺兰的第一段旅途，而关于那段旅途，我只知道这么一件事情。

他们在好望角接了诺兰，跟英国上将和舰队交涉完毕，启程去往印度洋。那是一段漫长的旅程，菲利普斯向一个军官借到了许多英文书——在那时候，这可是意外之喜。其中有一本《最后一个吟游诗人的歌》，这本书大家都听说过，却没几个人见过，我想应该是刚出版没多久。

没人觉得这本书里会有什么涉及国家的东西，于是一天下午，很多人坐在甲板上抽着烟大声读书的时候，诺兰也获准参与进来。恰巧轮到他拿到了那本书，朗读给其他人听。据我所知，他读得非常好。这些人并不熟悉这首诗，只知道是好几百年前写的有关魔法和骑士的故事。可怜的诺兰，他一口气读完第五章，停下来喝了些东西，接着读第六章，并不知道接下来的内容是什么。

有这样一个无情之人，

他从未对自己说过——

我们现在好像觉得不可能有人以前从来没读过这首诗，但当时在场的所有人的确都是第一次接触这些文字。可怜的诺兰接着往后读，尚未察觉不妥，抑或是没有考虑那么多——

这就是我的，我的祖国！

大家都开始觉得不妙了。诺兰的脸色有点儿发白，但他自己大概是以为这段读完就没事了。然而读下去更糟糕——

他从异乡的土地

辗转回归故园，

心头并无火焰。

若有这样的人，请记住他。

这时所有人都慌了，希望能想个什么办法让诺兰翻过两页去，但他自己并没有多么在意。他轻轻咳嗽，涨红了脸，艰难地继续往下读——

因为诗人不会为他吟唱；

纵然他地位崇高、声名显赫，

纵使他手中金银用之不尽，

纵使这冷血之人，

钱财权势集于一身——

读到这里，可怜的诺兰读不下去了。他跳起来，把书扔进海里，消失在自己的舱室。“然后，”菲利普斯说，“我们足有两个月没看到他。”

经过这件事情，诺兰的自负必定已经崩毁。他们说，起先他十分高傲，觉得自己的刑罚完全是一场闹剧，若无其事地享受着旅途。然而据菲利普斯说，那次他从舱室出来，就像彻底换了个人似的。他不再朗读，除非是《圣经》或者莎士比亚剧本之类他知道内容的书。不只如此，他也不再跟其他年轻人为伴。我认识他的时候，他已经变得很内向，极少主动开口与人交谈，除非是他为数不多的几个朋友。

（爱德华·埃弗里特·黑尔）

背景知识

西奥德，古希腊诗人，据说一生安分守己，却无辜被人杀死，抛入海中。

乔治·坎宁，英国政治家、演说家。

《最后一个吟游诗人的歌》(一译《末代行吟诗人之歌》)是英国诗人司各特的第一部长篇叙事诗，展示了16世纪英格兰和苏格兰之间的一次边境纠纷。

Chapter 5

Stories | 趣味故事

The High Society of Inquiry

It must have been three weeks or a month after I entered Mr. Bird's school that, on a rainy holiday, as I was walking through one of the halls alone, I was met by two boys, who ordered me peremptorily, to "halt". Both had staves in their hands, taller than themselves, and one of them addressed me with words:

"Arthur Bonnicastle, you are arrested in the name of The High Society of Inquiry, and ordered to appear before that august tribunal, to answer for your sins and misdemeanors. Right about face!"

Marching between the two officials, I was led directly to my own room, which I was surprised to find quite full of boys, all of whom were grave and silent.

"We have secured the offender," said one of my captors, "and now have the satisfaction of presenting him before this honorable Society."

"The prisoner will stand in the middle of the room, and look at me." said the presiding officer, in a tone of dignified severity. I was accordingly marched to the middle of the room and left alone, where I stood with folded arms, as became the grand occasion.

"Arthur Bonnicastle," said the officer before mentioned, "you are brought before The High Society of Inquiry on a charge of telling so many lies that no dependence can be placed upon your words. What have you to reply to this charge? Are you guilty or not guilty?"

"I am not guilty. Who says I am?" I exclaimed indignantly.

"Henry Hulm, advance!" said the officer.

Henry rose, and, walking by me, took a position near the officer, at the head of the room.

"Henry Hulm, you will look upon the prisoner and tell the Society whether you know him."

"I know him well. He is my chum," replied Henry.

"What is his general character?"

"He is bright and very amiable."

"Do you consider him a boy of truth and veracity?"

"I do not."

"What is the character of his falsehoods?"

"He tells," replied Henry, "stunning stories about himself. Great things are always happening to him, and he is always performing the most wonderful deeds."

I now began, with great shame and confusion, to realize that I was to be exposed to ridicule. The tears came into my eyes and dropped from my cheeks, but I would not yield to the impulse, either to cry, or to attempt to fly.

"Will you give us some specimens of his stories?" said the officer.

"I will," responded Henry, "but I can do it best by asking him questions."

"Very well," said the officer, with a polite bow, "pursue the course you think best."

"Arthur," said Henry, addressing me directly, "did you ever tell me that, when you and your father were on the way to this school, your horse went so fast that he ran down a black fox in the middle of the road, and cut off his tail with the wheel of the chaise, and that you sent that tail home to one of your sisters to wear in her winter hat?"

"Yes, I did," I responded, my face flaming and painful with shame.

"Did your said horse really run down said fox in the middle of said road, and cut off said tail; and did you send home said tail to said sister to be worn in said hat?" inquired the judge, with a low, gruff voice. "The prisoner will answer so that all can hear."

"No," I replied; and, looking for some justification of my story, I added, "but I did see a black fox——a real black fox as plain as day."

"Oh! Oh! Oh!" ran around the room in chorus. "He did see a black fox, a real black fox, as plain as day!"

"The witness will pursue his inquiries," said the officer.

"Arthur," Henry continued, "did you tell me that when on the way to this school, you overtook Mr. and Mrs. Bird in their wagon, that you were invited into the wagon by Mrs. Bird, and that one of Mr. Bird's horses chased a calf on the road, caught it by the ear, tossed it over the fence, and broke its leg?"

"I suppose I did," I said, growing desperate.

"Did said horse really chase said calf, and catch him by said ear, and toss him over said fence, and break said leg?" inquired the officer.

"He didn't catch him by the ear," I replied doggedly, "but he really did chase a calf."

"Oh! Oh! Oh!" chimed in the chorus again. "He didn't catch him by the ear, but he really did chase a calf."

"Witness," said the officer, "you will pursue your inquiries."

"Arthur, did you, or did you not tell me," Henry continued, "that you have an old friend who is soon to go to sea, and that he has promised to bring you a male and female monkey, a male and female bird-of-paradise, a barrel of pine-apples, and a Shetland pony?"

"It doesn't seem as if I told you exactly that," I replied.

"Did you, or did you not tell him so?" said the officer, severely.

"Perhaps I did," I responded.

"Did said friend, who is soon to go to sea, really promise to bring you said monkeys, said birds-of-paradise, said pine-apples, and said pony?"

"No," I replied, "but I really have an old friend who is going to sea, and he'll bring me anything I wish."

"Oh! Oh! Oh!" swept around the room again, "he really has an old friend who is going to sea, and he'll bring him anything he wishes."

"Did you, or did you not," said Henry, turning to me again, "tell me one day, when dining at your Aunt's, you saw a magic portrait of a boy, upon the wall, that came and went, and came and went, like a shadow or a ghost?"

"Yes," I responded, "and it looked just like you. Oh! It did, it did, it did! There——turn your head a little more that way——so! It was a perfect picture of you, Henry. You never could imagine such a likeness."

"You are a little 'blower'," volunteered Jack Linton, from a corner.

"Order! Order! Order!" swept around the room.

At this moment a strange silence seized the assembly. All eyes were directed toward the door, upon which my back was turned. I wheeled around to find the cause of the interruption. There, in the door-way, towering above us all, and looking questioningly down upon the little assembly, stood Mr. Bird.

"What does this mean?" inquired the master.

I flew to his side and took his hand. The officer who had presided, being the largest boy, explained that they had been trying to break Arthur Bonnicastle of lying, and that they were about to order him to report to the master for confession and correction.

Then Mr. Bird took a chair, and patiently heard the whole story. Without a reproach, further that saying that he thought me much too young for experiments of the kind they had instituted in the case, he explained to them and to me the nature of my misdemeanors.

"The boy has a great deal of imagination," he said, "and a strong love of approbation. Somebody has probably flattered his power of invention, and to secure admiration, he has exercised it, until he has acquired the habit of exaggeration. I am glad if he has learned, even by the severe means used, that, if he wishes to be loved and admired, he must always tell the exact truth, neither more nor less. If you had come to me, I could have told you all about the lad, and instituted a better mode of dealing with him. But I venture to say that he is cured. Aren't you, Arthur?" And he stooped and lifted me to his face and looked into my eyes.

"I don't think I shall do it any more," I said.

Bidding the boys disperse, he carried me down stairs into his own room, and charged me with kind counsel. I went out from the interview, humbled, and without a revengeful thought in my heart toward the boys who had brought me to my trial. I saw that they were my friends, and I was determined to prove myself worthy of their friendship.

Jack Linton was waiting for me on the piazza, and wished to explain to me that he hadn't anything against me. "I went in with the rest of them, because they wanted me to," said Jack, "and because I wanted to see what it would be like; but, really, now, I don't object so much to 'blowing' myself."

I told him that I wasn't going to "blow" any more, and that I had arranged it all with Mr. Bird. He shook hands with me, and then stooped down and whispered, "You don't catch me trying any High old Society of Inquiries on a chap of your size, again."

(Josiah Gilbert Holland)

译文

最高调查协会

我在伯德先生的学校待了一段时间——少则有三周，多则有一个月了。记得那是个假日，下着雨，我独自踏入了一间大厅，结果碰到了两个男孩，他俩见了我就断然命令道："站住！"这两个男孩每人手里拿了一根比自己还高的棍子，其中一个郑重其事地跟我说道：

"亚瑟·博尼卡斯尔，我们以最高调查协会的名义逮捕你，你的案子将于八月开庭，届时你必须出席，对自己犯下的错误负责。向后转！"

两个裁判员押着我，直接把我带到了我的房间，不过，让我惊讶的是，房间里全是男孩子，可是每一个人都一本正经的，谁也不说话。

"我们已经抓住犯人了，"其中一个说道，"我们非常荣幸能把他带到这神圣的法庭来。"

"让这个囚犯站在屋子正中央。好了，现在抬头看我。"审裁官严厉地说道。

按审裁官的要求，我被押到了房间正中，然后留我独自两手交叉地站着，像是有什么大事发生。

"亚瑟·博尼卡斯尔，"审裁官说道，"你因诈欺嫌疑而在最高审讯协会开庭前被带来这里。现在，你对诈欺起诉还有什么话要说？你是否承认自己有罪？"

"我是无辜的。是谁说我诈欺的？"我激动地大叫道。

"是亨利·休姆起诉的。"审判员面无表情地说。

亨利从座位上起身，从我旁边走过去，然后在审判员旁边找了个位子坐了下来——在屋里的上座坐了下来。

"亨利·休姆，你看看这个囚犯，告诉调查协会你认不认识他。"

"我和他很熟。他可是我的密友！"亨利答道。

"他性格大概怎样？"

"他很聪明，又非常平易近人，待人很和善。"

"那你觉得他诚实吗？"

"他并不诚实。"

"他说了什么谎吗？"

"他讲了很多令人难以置信的事情，"亨利答道，"一些关于他自己的事。按他的说法，他总能碰到一些不可思议的事情，而他自己永远都是最棒的那个。"

在羞愧和惶惑中，我开始意识到自己将会成为众人的笑柄。眼泪夺眶而出，慢慢滑到了我的脸颊，但我绝不能屈服，不能冲动行事，不能喊叫，更不能想方设地逃跑。

"你能给我们举一些例子吗？关于他说的那些话。"审判员说道。

"可以，"亨利回答说，"但我觉得如果能问他一些问题，效果会更好。"

"很好，"审判员礼貌地鞠了一躬，说道，"按你觉得最好的方式来吧。"

"亚瑟，"亨利直接喊我的名字，"你是否有对我说过，曾经有一次，你父亲送你去上学的路上，你们的马跑得飞快，结果撞到了路中央的一直黑狐狸，还用马车的轮子碾断了黑狐狸的尾巴，然后你把黑狐狸的尾巴送给了你的一个妹妹，让她在冬天当帽子戴？"

"是的，我说过。"我回答说，而我的脸早已因羞愧烧得通红。

"你真的有说过，马把路中央的狐狸给撞了，还把它的尾巴给碾断了？你是否说过，你把狐狸尾巴带回家送给了一个妹妹，还让她冬天的时候当帽子戴？"法官用低沉的嗓音问道，"囚犯，请你用所有人都能听到的声音回答。"

"没有，我没说过，"我大声地说，然后迅速回想我之前说过的事情，想从中找到点为自己辩解的理由，"但是我真的看到了一只黑狐狸——看得真真切切。"

"天啊！天啊！天啊！"屋子里顿时充满了惊叹声，"他真的看到了一只黑狐狸，一只真正的黑狐狸，还真真切切地看到了！"

“证人，请继续你的提问。”审判员说道

“亚瑟，”亨利继续问道，“你是否有跟我说过，有一次在上学的路上，你正好赶上伯德夫妇的马车，伯德太太邀请你搭乘他们的马车，结果他们的一匹马在路上追起了一头小牛犊，追上后，咬住小牛犊的耳朵叼起了它，还把小牛直接扔到了栅栏那头，把小牛的腿都给摔断了。”

“我好像是有这么说过。”我慢慢地说，不断升腾的绝望感却像是要把我淹没了。

“你是否说过，马追捕牛，还咬住牛的耳朵把牛叼起来，并把牛扔到栅栏外，结果把牛的腿摔断了？”这次提问的是审判员。

“马没有叼小牛的耳朵，”我坚持说道，“但那匹马真的在追一头小牛。”

“天啊！天啊！天啊！”惊叹声再次响彻满堂，“马没有叼牛的耳朵，但马真的有追着小牛跑。”

“证人，”审判员打断议论声，说道，“你可以继续提问。”

“亚瑟，”亨利继续说，“你是否有跟我说过，你有一个朋友准备去海边，他答应给你带一公一母两只猴子、一公一母两只极乐鸟、一桶菠萝和一匹雪特兰矮种马？”

“我好像不是那么说的。”我回答道。

“你是否有对他说这些话？”审判员再次严肃地问道。

“或许我有说过。”我答道。

“你是否有说过，你有一个准备去海边的朋友，他是否真的答应给你带猴子、极乐鸟、菠萝和矮种马？”

“不是，”我回答说，“但我以前确实有一个朋友准备去海边，他答应过会给我带我想要的任何东西。”

“天啊！天啊！天啊！”满堂又是阵阵惊叹，“他真的有一个要去海边的朋友，他那个朋友会给他带他想要的任何东西。”

“你有没有对我说过，”亨利再次朝向我，问道，“有一次你在你阿姨家吃饭时，看到墙上有一个男孩的脸，来来去去，若隐若现的，像一个影子，又有点像一个幽灵？”

“我说过，”我回答道，“那个男孩看着很像你。哎呀，真的很像你，真的很像！这样——你把头往那边再转一点过去——就是了！那个脸简直就是你，亨利。你绝对想象不到有多像。”

“你好像蛮喜欢吹牛啊。”角落里的杰克·林顿插嘴说。

“判决！判决！判决！”满堂的呼喊声。

就在这时，大堂里忽然安静了下来。所有人的眼睛直直盯着门的方向——我背对的地方。我赶紧转过身，想看看究竟是什么原因，让所有人瞬间安静下来。原来，门口有个人，高大的他倒像是在俯视我们所有人——是满脸诧异的伯德先生。

“这是在干什么？”伯德先生问道。

我飞奔去他旁边，拉住了他的手。而此次审判的主席也走到伯德先生身边，向他解释了一番，他说他们正在想办法揭露亚瑟·博尼卡斯尔的谎言，还说他们准备让我自己向伯德先生坦诚自己的错误并及时改正。

然后伯德先生找了个椅子坐了下来，耐心地听完事情的前因后果。听完后，他非但没有责罚我，还说他觉得我年纪还太轻，不能按他们的规定处置。他还向所有人解释了我这种不当行径的本质。

“这孩子的想象力很丰富，”他说，“同时，他很希望能得到大家的认可和赞美。或许以前有人夸赞过他的创造力，而他为了能一直听到这种赞美，便不断锻炼自己的创造力，结果一不小心，就养成了夸夸其谈的习惯。虽然他用了不当的方式，但我还是很高兴能看到他对爱和赞美的期待。当然，他多少得实话实说，这一点是必须的。如果你们早点来问我，我可以告诉你们这个小伙儿的所有事，然后给你们提一个更好的解决办法。但冒昧说一句，他已经改了。是不是，亚瑟？”伯德先生停下来，转身面向我，对着我的眼睛问道。

“我再也不会那样了。”我说道。

伯德先生命周围的人都散开，然后带我下楼，来到他自己的房间，说了许多劝解的话，并给我提了一些善意的建议。结束谈话后，我慢慢地走了出来，心里满是谦卑。而对之前抓我的那两个人，一点仇恨之心都没有。我明白他们都是真心待我的朋友，我决定向他们证明，我不会辜负他们的友情。

杰克·林顿正在走廊等我，他想向我解释，他对我并没有任何恶意。“我只是加入了他们，因为他们希望我那么做，”杰克说道，“当然也是因为我想看看事情会如何发展。但说真的，现在我已经没那么反对吹嘘自己了。”

我跟他说我以后再也不会吹嘘任何东西，这一点我已经向伯德先生保证过了。他跟我握了握手后准备走，但又突然停了下来，然后在我耳边轻轻说道："你可不要把我抓去，想再来一遍你那样的最高协会审判啊。"

作者简介

乔西亚·吉尔伯特·霍兰，美国诗人、作家。他出生于马萨诸塞州的一个小镇。他的写作生涯从一份小杂志开始。数年后他成了闻名的记者。他的代表作《蒂莫西·蒂特科姆写给青年人的信》最早刊登于《斯普林菲尔德文摘报》，当时霍兰是这家报纸的编辑。同时，他还是《斯克里布纳杂志》(现已改名为《世纪》杂志)的创办人之一，之后又担任了这家杂志社的主编。他的很多小说最早都是刊登在这本杂志上的。本文选自《亚瑟·博尼卡斯尔》，由查尔斯·斯克里布纳兄弟出版公司许可授权。

练习

名词：表示人、事物、地点或事物的名称。

专有名词：表示人、地点或事物等特有的名词。例如：乔赛亚、马萨诸塞州、世纪。

普通名词：表示某一类人、某一类事物的名词。例如：儿子、河流。

从上文中找出十个专有名词和十个普通名词。

How I Became a Writer

预习

to send packing 毫不客气地打发走。

buffet-stool 用于碗柜或是餐柜的一种有三或四条脚架的小工具。

My mother was a great reader, and with ten minutes to spare before the starch was ready, would begin the "Decline and Fall"——and finish it, too, that winter. Foreign words in the text annoyed her and made her bemoan her want of classical education,——she had attended only a Dame's school during some easy months,——but she never passed the foreign words by until their meaning was explained to her, and when next she and they met it was as acquaintances.

Biography and exploration were her favorite reading; for choice, the biography of men who had been good to their mothers, and she liked the explorers to be alive so that she could shudder at the thought of their venturing forth again, but though she expressed a hope that they would have the sense to stay at home henceforth, she gleamed with admiration when they disappointed her.

In later years I had a friend that was an African explorer, and she was in two minds about him; he was one of the most engrossing of mortals to her, she admired him prodigiously, pictured him at the head of his caravan, now attacked by savages, now by wild beasts, and adored him for the uneasy hours he gave her, but she was also afraid that he wanted to take me with him, and then she thought that he should be put down by law.

Explorers' mothers also interested her very much; the books might tell her nothing about them, but she could create them for herself and wring her hands in sympathy with them when they had got no news of their sons for six months. Yet there were times when she grudged the explorer to his mother——as the day when he returned victorious. Then what was before her eyes was not the son coming marching home again, but an old woman peering for him round the window curtain and trying not to look uplifted. The newspaper reports would be about the son, but my mother's comment was, "She's a proud woman this night."

We read many books together when I was a boy, "Robinson Crusoe" being the first (and the second), and the "Arabian Nights" should have been the next, for we got it out of the library (a penny for three days), but on discovering that they were "nights" when we had paid for "knights", we sent that volume packing, and I have curled my lips at it ever since.

"The Pilgrim's Progress" we had in the house, and so enamoured of it was I that I turned our garden into Sloughs of Despond, with pea-sticks to represent Christian on his travels and a buffet-stool for his burden, but when I dragged my mother out to see my handiwork she was scared, and I felt for days with a certain elation, that I had been a dark character.

Besides reading every book we could hire or borrow, I also bought one now and again, and while buying (it was the occupation of weeks) I read, standing at the counter, most of the other books in the shop, which is perhaps the most exquisite way of reading. And I took in a magazine called "Sunshine", the most delicious periodical, I am sure, of any day.

I know not whether it was owing to the loitering of this magazine on the way one month to an extent flesh and blood could not bear, or because we had exhausted the penny library, but on a day I conceived a glorious idea, or it was put into my head by my mother, then desirous of making progress with her new rug.

The notion was nothing short of this, why should I not write the tales myself? I did write them——in the garret——but they by no means helped her to get on with her work, for when I finished a chapter I bounded down stairs to read it to her, and so short were the chapters, so ready was the pen, that I was back with new manuscript before another clout had been added to the rug. They were tales of adventure, no characters were allowed within if I knew their like in the flesh, the scene lay in unknown parts, desert islands, enchanted gardens, with knights (none of your nights) on black chargers.

At twelve or thereabout I put the literary calling to bed for a time, having gone to a school where cricket and football were more esteemed, but during the year before I went to the university, it woke up, and I wrote a great part of a three-volume novel. The publisher replied that the sum for which he would print it was a hundred and——however, that was not the important point: where he wounded us both was in writing that he considered me a "clever lady". I replied stiffly that I was a gentleman, and since then I have kept that manuscript concealed.

At last my opportunity came, and I was rashly engaged as a leader-writer on an English provincial paper. At the moment I was as uplifted as the others, and was to receive what we all regarded as a prodigious salary, but I was wanted in the beginning of the week, and it suddenly struck me that the leaders were the one thing that I had always skipped.

Leaders! How were they written? My mother was already sitting triumphant among my socks, and I durst not let her see me quaking. I retired to ponder, and presently she came tome with the daily paper. Which were the leaders? She wanted to bow, so evidently I could get no help from her. Had she any more newspapers? I asked, and after rummaging she produced a few with which her boxes had been lined. Others, very dusty, came from beneath carpets, and lastly a sooty bundle dragged down the chimney. Surrounded by these I sat down, and studied how to become a journalist.

(Sir James Matthew Barrie)

译文

作家养成记

母亲十分热爱阅读，就算在等淀粉浆做好的十分钟里，她也会读一读《罗马帝国衰亡史》——一个冬天的时间就能看完这本书。她常常为文章中的外语头疼不已，惋惜自己没有受过正统教育，只上了几个月的圣母院学校。但她从来不会放过这些外语，直到弄懂它们的意思，等下次再碰到这些词的时候，她和这些词就像老朋友一般了。

母亲最喜欢阅读传记类和探险类的书籍。在传记类书籍当中，她偏好孝顺母亲的人物，而在探险类书籍当中，她希望这些探险家都能安然无恙，因此一想到他们的探险经历，母亲就不寒而栗。虽然她很希望这些探险家都从此待在家里别出门，但令她失望的是他们从未如此，不过她对那些冒险家们仍怀着深深的崇敬之情。

之后的几年，我认识了一位朋友，他是个非洲探险家，母亲对他的看法摇摆不定。一方面，母亲对他最着迷，十分崇拜他，认为他是探险队中的佼佼者，母亲沉浸于他的探险经历中，时而遭野人袭击，时而遭野兽攻击，让她惊心动魄；但另一方面，母亲担心他把我给带上，一起去探险，还想过用法律制止他这样的行为。

她对探险家的母亲也很感兴趣，即使书里并没有提及这些内容，但她也能自己想象出来，在这些母亲六个月都没有收到儿子的消息时，她会难过地用力绞扭自己的双手，十分同情她们。然而在这些探险家凯旋时，她又会嫉妒那些母亲。这个时候，她能看到的不是探险家一路赶回家的画面，而是他们的母亲透过家里的窗帘，对即将归家的儿子望眼欲穿，还掩饰着内心的激动。尽管报纸报道的是她们的儿子，但是母亲的评论却是“今晚，那些母亲一定很得意”。

小时候，我和母亲一起看了很多的书，《鲁滨逊漂流记》是第一本，之后又看了一遍，接下来是从图书馆借来的《一千零一夜》，花一便士可以借三天，但是当我们发现这本书讲的不是骑士（knights）的故事，而是黑夜（nights）的故事，便毫不客气地把它还回去了。我从此对这本书嗤之以鼻。

我们家里有《天路历程》这本书，我对这本书如走火入魔一般，把家里的花园弄得像书中的绝境，用豌豆的枝条表示基督徒的朝圣之路，用餐桌的凳子当他身上的重担，当我带母亲来欣赏我亲手布置的花园时，把她给吓到了。虽然我的性格向来忧郁沉闷，但那些天里我却感觉兴高采烈。

我除了看借来和租来的书，有时还买新书。我一边买书（可以连续逛几个星期的书店），一边看书，挨着柜台，把店里其他的书几乎都看了个遍，这也许是种最惬意的阅读方式。我还订阅了一本名为《阳光》的杂志，这绝对是我这辈子读过的最好的杂志。

我不知道是不是因为这本杂志要磨蹭一个月才出一本，超过了常人所能忍受的范围，还是因为借不起图书馆的书，但是有一天，我有了一个很好的想法，这个想法来源于我的母亲，那时她正在奋力缝着她的新毯子。

这个念头在我脑中只是电光一闪，为什么我不自己写故事呢？于是，我在阁楼上写了一些文章，每当完成一个章节，我就立刻跑下楼，给母亲读我写的文字。这并没有让她的缝纫工作变得更加顺利。因为章节比较短，钢笔又备在身旁，所以在母亲缝上另一块布片之前，我又完成了一篇文章。我写的是冒险故事，没有一个角色在生活中有原型，故事发生在一些不知名的地方，一些荒岛上，一些迷人的花园里，其中还有一些骑着黑色战马的骑士（我才不要看什么黑夜的故事呢）。

大约零点的时候，我带着创作欲望进入梦乡，梦见我来到了一所学校，板球和足球运动在那里比较受到人们的认可，但是在梦见我快要考入大学的时候，我就醒了，于是开始奋笔疾书，完成了一本三卷的小说。出版社回复说，他们会印一百本，但重点是，他们在信中认为我是个“聪颖的女性”，这让我们双方都很受伤。我气冲冲地告诉他们我是个男人，并且从此对那份手稿只字不提。

我的机遇终于来了，我很快成了英国一份地方性报纸的主笔。那一刻，我和其他人一样欣喜若狂，而且将要拿到一份大家都觉得很可观的薪水，但是在我上班的头一个星期的前几天，我才猛然发现，我过去一直漏读了报纸的头条。

头条！头条是怎样写成的？母亲得意洋洋地看着我写的那些幽默短文，我不敢让她看到我落魄的样子。我默默回到房间里，开始沉思冥想，母亲给我带来一份日报。哪些是头条？母亲想要低下头看看时，我清醒地意识到她也不了解这些东西。母亲有更多的报纸吗？我问道。在四处翻找后，她找到了几份垫在盒子里的报纸，还有一些是在地毯下找到的，布满了灰尘，最后还在烟囱里拽下一捆黑乎乎的报纸。我坐下来，研究这些年代久远的报纸，学习如何做一名新闻撰稿人。

（詹姆斯·马修·巴里）

作者介绍

詹姆斯·马修·巴里出生于苏格兰的一个小镇，是一名小说家和剧作家。从爱丁堡大学毕业后，做了一名记者——他在这篇选自《玛格丽特·奥格维》的小品文里讲述了是如何成为记者的。《玛格丽特·奥格维》是他为母亲写的传记，广受大众欢迎。巴里写的故事几乎都围绕苏格兰人民的日常家庭生活展开，富于同情心和幽默感。他的著作有《窗锁珠帘》《小牧师》《忧伤的汤米》及其续集《汤米与格丽泽尔》和《小白鸟》，广受欢迎的彼得潘的故事就出自于《小白鸟》。

The Runaway Cannon

预习

prophet's vision 以利沙看见伊利亚（希伯来先知）的景象。见《列王记》，第十一章

mizzen-mast 三桅杆船只上的最后一根桅杆

hand spike 棍子或是杠杆，通常为木制

breach /briːtʃ/ 裂口

breech /briːtʃ/ 后膛

carriage /ˈkærɪdʒ/ 四轮马车

inaccessible /ˌɪnækˈsesəbl/ 难接近的

larboard /ˈlɑːˌbəd/ 左舷

livid /ˈlɪvɪd/ 苍白的；暴怒的

summary /ˈsʌməri/ 摘要

A terrible thing had happened. One of the short cannons of the battery, a twenty-four pounder, had got loose. This is perhaps the most formidable of ocean accidents. Nothing more terrible can happen to a vessel in open sea and under full sail.

A gun that breaks its moorings becomes suddenly a monster. This mass turns upon its wheels, has the rapid movements of a billiard-ball, rolls with the rolling, pitches with the pitching, goes, comes, pauses, seems to meditate, resumes its course, rushes like an arrow from end to end of the ship, circles about, rears, breaks, kills. The mad mass has the bounds of a panther, the weight of an elephant, the agility of a mouse, the obstinacy of an ass, the unexpectedness of the surge, the rapidity of lightning, the deafness of the tomb. It weighs ten thousand pounds, and it rebounds like a child's ball. What is to be done? How to end this?

A tempest ceases, a wind falls, a leak is stopped, a fire dies out; but how to control this brute of bronze? In what way can one attack it? How to foresee its comings and goings, its re-turns, its stops, its shocks? One has to deal with a projectile which thinks, which seems to possess ideas, and which changes its direction each instant. The horrible cannon flings itself about, advances, recoils, strikes to the right, strikes to the left, flees, passes, breaks down obstacles, crushes men like flies.

The fault was the chief gunner's. He had neglected to fasten the gun securely in place. As a heavy wave struck the port, the carronade, weakly attached, recoiled, burst its chain, and began to rush wildly about.

At the moment when the lashings gave way, the gunners were in the battery, some in groups, others standing alone, occupied with such duties as sailors perform when expecting the command to clear for action. The cannon, hurled forward by the pitching, dashed into this knot of men and crushed four at the first blow; then flung back and shot out anew by the rolling, it cut in two a fifth poor fellow, glanced off to the larboard side and struck a piece of the battery with such force as to unship it.

Then arose the cry of distress. The men rushed to the ladder; the gun deck emptied in the twinkling of an eye. The enormous cannon was left alone. She was her own mistress, and mistress of the vessel. She could do what she willed with both. The whole crew, accustomed to laugh in battle, trembled now.

The captain and lieutenant, although both brave men, stopped at the head of the stairs, and remained mute, pale, hesitating, looking down on the deck. Someone pushed them aside with his elbow and descended. It was their passenger, the peasant, ——the man of whom they had been speaking the moment before. When he reached the foot of the ladder he stood still.

The cannon came and went along the deck. One might have fancied it the living chariot of the prophet's vision. The marine lanterns swinging from the ceiling added a dizzying whirl of lights and shadows. The shape of the cannon could not be distinguished, so rapid was its course. The whole ship was filled with the awful tumult.

The captain promptly recovered his composure, and at his order the sailors threw down into the deck everything which could deaden and check the mad rush of the gun,——mattresses, hammocks, spare-sails. But what could these rags avail? No one dare descend to arrange them in any needful fashion, and in a few instants they were mere heaps of lint.

There was just enough sea to render an accident as complete as possible. A tempest would have been desirable; it might have thrown the gun upside down, and the four wheels once in the air, the monster could have been captured. But the destruction increased. The mizzenmast was cracked, and the mainmast itself was injured, under the convulsive blows of the gun. The battery was being destroyed. Ten pieces out of thirty were disabled; the breaches multiplied in the side, and the ship began to take water.

The old passenger, who had descended to the gun-deck, looked like a form of stone. He stood motionless, gazing sternly about. Indeed, it seemed impossible to take a single step forward.

Each bound of the cannon menaced the destruction of the vessel. A few minutes more, and shipwreck must come. They must perish or put a summary end to the disaster; a decision must be made; but how? They must check this mad monster. They must seize this flash of lightning. They must overthrow this thunderbolt.

"Do you believe in God, chevalier?" said the captain to the lieutenant.

"Yes. No. Sometimes," was the reply.

"In a tempest?"

"Yes; and in moments like this."

"Only God can aid us here," said the captain.

All were silent. Only the cannon kept up its horrible din. The waves heat against the ship; their blows from without responded to the strokes of the cannon. It was like two hammers alternating.

Suddenly, into the midst of this inaccessible circus, there sprang a man with an iron bar in his hand. It was the author of the accident, the gunner whose negligence caused it——the captain of the gun. Having been the means of bringing about the misfortune, he desired to repair it. He had caught up a handspike in one fist, a tiller-rope with a slipping noose in the other, and jumped down into the gun-deck.

Then a strange combat began——the struggle of the gun against the gunner, a battle between matter and intelligence. Livid, calm, tragic, rooted as it were in the planks, he waited. He waited for the cannon to pass near him. He began to address it as he might have done his dog.

"Come!" said he.

Perhaps he loved it. He seemed to wish it would turn toward him. But to come toward him would be to spring upon him. Then he would be lost. All stared in terrified silence. No one breathed freely, except, perchance, the old man, who stood, a stern second, in his place at the foot of the ladder. He might himself be crushed by the piece. He did not stir. Beneath them the blind sea directed the battle.

At the instant when, accepting this awful hand-to-hand contest, the gunner came near to challenge the cannon, some chance movement of the waves kept it for a moment still, as if stupefied.

"Come on!" the man said to it. It seemed to listen. Suddenly it darted upon him. He avoided the shock. The struggle began——struggle unheard of; the thing of flesh attacking the brazen mute; on the one side blind force, on the other a soul. A soul; but you would have said that the cannon had one also——a soul filled with rage and hatred. The monster seemed to be watching the man.

There was—one might have fancied so at least——cunning in the mass. It became a gigantic insect of metal, having, or seeming to have, the will of a demon. Sometimes it struck the low ceiling of the gun-deck, then, falling back on its four wheels like a tiger upon its four claws, it darted anew on the man. He——supple, agile, adroit——would glide like a snake from the reach of these lightning-like movements. He avoided the blows; but they fell upon the vessel with continued destruction.

An end of broken chain remained attached to the gun. This chain had twisted itself——one could not tell how——about the screw of the breech button. One end of the chain was fastened to the carriage. The other, hanging loose, whirled wildly about the gun.

Nevertheless the man fought. Sometimes even it was the man who attacked the cannon. He crept along the side, bar and rope in hand, and the cannon had the air of understanding, and fled as if it saw the snare. The man pursued. Such a duel could not last long. The gun seemed suddenly to say to itself, "Come, we must make an end," and it paused. One felt the approach of a crisis.

It sprang unexpectedly upon the gunner. He jumped aside and cried out, with a laugh, "Try again!" The gun, as if in a fury, broke a cannon to larboard, then seized anew by the invisible sling which held it, was flung to starboard toward the man, who escaped. Three cannon gave way under the blows of the gun; then, as if blind, and no longer conscious of what it was doing, it turned back on the man, rolling from the stern to the bow, bruising the stern and making a breach in the planking of the prow.

The gunner had taken refuge at the foot of the stairs, a few steps from the old man, who was watching. The gunner held his handspike in rest. The cannon seemed to perceive him, and without taking the trouble to turn itself, backed upon him with the quickness of an axe-stroke. The gunner, if driven back against the side, was lost. The crew uttered a cry.

But the old passenger, until now motionless, made a spring more rapid than all those wild whirls. He seized a bale of false assignats, and, at the risk of being crushed, succeeded in flinging it between the wheels of the cannon. The bale had the effect of a plug. A pebble may stop a log, a tree-branch turn an avalanche.

The cannon stumbled. The gunner, in his turn, seizing this terrible chance, plunged his iron bar between the spokes of one of the bind wheels. The cannon was stopped. It staggered. The man, using the bar as a lever, rocked it to and fro. The heavy mass turned over with a clang like a falling bell, and the gunner, dripping with sweat, rushed forward headlong and passed the slipping noose about the bronze neck of an overthrown monster.

It was ended. The man had conquered. The pygmy had taken the thunder-bolt prisoner. The whole crew hurried down with cables and chains, and in an instant the cannon was securely lashed.

(Victor Hugo, from *"Ninety Three"*)

译文

失控的大炮

可怖的事情发生了。炮台上的一尊短炮，一个六十多千克的巨物，松动了。这恐怕是最难应付的海上事故；对于在无边的海上满帆航行的船舶来说，情况不能更糟糕了。

一门大炮在挣脱它的枷锁之后猛然变成了一只怪兽。这只巨兽随着轮子转动，像台球一样撞来撞去，随着船的摇晃而摇晃，随着船的倾斜而倾斜，它来来回回，跑跑停停，仿佛在沉思，假想它的攻击路线，它像一支箭从船的这头刺向另一头，回旋、后退、破坏、杀戮。这愤怒的庞然大物弹跳力好似豹子，重量好似大象，敏捷好似老鼠，像蠢货般顽固，像巨浪般不可预料，像闪电般迅速，像坟墓般听不见。它似千斤重，却像小孩子的皮球一样弹跳不停。该怎么办？怎样才能结束这场噩梦？

暴雨会停歇，狂风会平息，漏水的洞可以补上，起火可以扑灭；但是要怎样才能控制这头铜制的残暴野兽？要采用何种方式来出手？如何预见它的来去，它的回旋，它的停顿和冲击？我们要对付的是一个能思考的大炮，一个看起来还拥有思想，能随时改变它的方向的大炮。这个恐怖的大炮跳来跳去，前进又弹回，一下攻击右边，一下子又撞到左边，它会迅速逃跑，从身旁经过，然后摧毁一切障碍，将人如蝼蚁一般碾碎。

这一切都是那个炮长的过失。他玩忽职守，没有把火炮安全地系紧在固定的位置。当巨浪打上船舱，那松散连接着的短重炮，反冲出去，挣断了铁链，然后开始疯狂肆虐。

当捆绑物断裂的那一刻，炮手们还在炮位里，有的三五成群，有的则独自站着，都在忙于等待行动的准确命令尽到水手的职责。那门大炮，随着船只倾斜被用力投掷出去，冲入这一群人之中，一下就压死了四个人；然后又猛地转回来，随着颠簸再次射出去，把第五个可怜的家伙切成了两半，掠过船的左舷，撞上一个炮位，力量之强，几乎是要将它大卸八块。

于是悲痛的哭喊声响起。人们跑向梯子。一眨眼炮甲板就空无一人，只剩下这座庞大的火炮；它现在是自己的主人，也是这艘船的主人了。它可以为所欲为。所有早已习惯在硝烟战场上谈笑风生的船员们，此刻颤抖了。

船长和他的副官，两个很勇敢的男人，也在楼梯口站住了，沉默着，脸色苍白，踌躇不前，俯看着甲板。有人用手肘将他们推到了一旁然后走了下去。那是他们的乘客，那个农民——之前他们还在谈论的男人。当他走到楼梯底部的时候站住不动了。

大炮在甲板上来回跑动，人人都以为它就是先知眼里的有生命的战车（译注：世界末日的恐怖景象）。悬挂在天花板上的航海灯增添了一分光影交错、使人头晕目眩的感觉。大炮的速度太快，以至于它的形状都有些模糊不清了。整个船舱都被笼罩在可怕的混乱中。

船长迅速恢复镇定。在他的命令下，船员们把所有能减缓或阻止这门疯狂暴走的大炮的东西都扔到了甲板上——床垫、吊床、备用船帆。然而这些玩意儿能有什么用呢？没人敢下去把这些东西排成应有的样子，不过几分钟，它们就被碾成了碎片。

就是海上的几种状况凑在一起造成了这场事故。要是能下一场暴风雨该多好，它能将这大炮打翻在地，一旦它四个轮子朝天，人们就能抓住这怪兽了。然而破坏还在继续，在大炮不断地撞击下，后桅已经裂开，主桅杆也已被损伤。炮台正在被摧毁，三十座中的十座已经无法使用；舷侧的破洞越来越多，而船内也开始进水了。

那个下到炮台甲板的老乘客，看上去像石像一样。他纹丝不动，目光严峻地注视着这些。显然，再往前迈一步都不可能。

火炮的每一次弹跳落下都是对船体的威胁。要不了多久，船舶就会遇难。他们要么死亡，要么就给这场灾难做个了结，必须做出选择。但是如何了结？他们必须制止这发疯的怪物，必须抓住这闪电的光亮，必须打倒这霹雳雷电。

“你相信上帝吗，斗士？”船长问向副官。

“信，也不信。有时候信。”他回答。

“起风暴的时候？”

“是的；还有这种时候。”

“现在只有上帝能救我们了。”船长说。

所有人都在沉默，只有火炮继续发出可怕的喧闹声。风浪拍打着船舶，和火炮的撞击相互回应，就像两只锤子轮流敲打着船只。

突然，在这个难以接近的战场中间，出现了一个手持铁棒的男人。他就是炮长，这个事故的肇事者，由于疏忽造成这一切的炮手，造成了这场悲剧的他希望能弥补过错。他一手拿起一个绞盘棒，另一只手拿着打活结的操舵索，然后跳到了炮台甲板上。

一场诡异的搏斗就此展开——大炮对抗炮手，物体对垒智力。他面色铁青，冷静而悲壮，一动不动地等待着，等着大炮与他擦身而过。他开始像对自己养的狗一样对它说话。

“过来！”他说。

也许他很爱护它。他似乎希望那门炮转向他，但是转向他就是碾过他。那样他就死定了。压抑的静默中，所有人都盯着他屏住呼吸，可能除了那个老头。这个坚定的第二号勇者，就站在楼梯脚下，也可能被碾成碎片。他没有一点颤动。在他们下面，鲁莽的大海指挥着这场战斗。

这一刻，炮手接受了这残酷的赤手空拳的搏斗，他走近向大炮发出挑战。碰巧海浪的波动让它此刻静止，仿佛是被吓愣了一般。

“来啊！”男人对它说。它似乎听到了。突然，它向他扑过去，他躲开了攻击。较量开始了——闻所未闻的较量：血肉之躯向无耻的黄铜默兽发起进攻；一边是盲目的蛮力，另一边是灵魂。灵魂；可你会说这炮也有灵魂——由狂怒和仇恨构成的灵魂。这个怪兽似乎在看着男人。

这个巨物确实有——至少有人会想象它有——狡猾的一面。它变成巨型铁虫，有或者看起来像有魔鬼的意识。它不时撞击炮台低矮的天花板，接着以它的四个轮子撤退，如同老虎用四只爪子着地，再冲向那个男人。他——柔韧、敏捷、灵活——能在闪电般快速的攻击下像蛇一样滑动躲开。他避开了撞击，但那些撞击都落在了船体上，并不断造成破坏。

一小截断掉的铁链仍连在火炮上。它——不知怎么搞的——缠到了炮闩纽的螺钉上。铁链一端被固定在炮架上，另一端松垮的悬着，在火炮周围疯狂地旋转。

不过那个男人还在战斗。有时候甚至去进攻大炮。他从一侧爬过去，手中拿着绳和棍子，然而大炮明白过来，仿佛看穿了这陷阱一样偷跑了。男人追击上去。这样的决斗不会持续很长时间。那门大炮似乎突然对自己说："来吧，我们来做个了断吧。"它暂时停住了。人们感觉到危机的来临。

它出其不意地弹起来攻向炮手。他跳开了，爆发出一声大笑："再来啊！"怒火中烧的大炮撞坏了左舷的短炮，然后像是被无形的吊索拉回来，甩向站在右舷的男人，他躲开了。三门短炮被大炮的撞击摧毁。之后，大炮就像失明了，不知道自己在干什么一样，它背对着男人，从船尾晃到船首，挫坏了船尾，在船头的船壳板上弄出了一条裂痕。

炮手在楼梯底下闪躲，距离观战的老人只有几步之遥。炮手举起了手中的铁棍。大炮仿佛察觉到他的意图，不打算费力掉头，就像劈出的斧子一样迅速后退过来。要是那炮手被逼到船边就必死无疑了！人群发出惊呼声。

但是此时，一直站着不动的老乘客突然跳了上去，比那些疯狂的旋回更加迅猛。他抓起一包伪造的指券（译注：流通于1789至1796年法国大革命期间的纸券），冒着被压死的风险，成功地投掷到大炮的轮子之间。那包东西起到了阻塞的作用。就像一颗卵石能阻挡一棵原木、一根树枝能避免一场雪崩一样。

大炮被绊了一下。现在轮到炮手了，他抓住这个宝贵的时机，把铁棒插到固定轮子的辐条间。大炮被制服了，它摇摇晃晃。而男人，用棍子像杠杆一样来回摇动它。这庞然大物"哐当"一声翻倒在地，如同钟鼓坠地。汗流浃背的炮手一头冲上去，将活结套系在这被掀翻的铜兽的脖颈上。

终于结束了。这个男人取得了胜利。矮人放倒了雷霆般的囚犯。全体船员都带着缆线和链条跑下来，不一会，大炮就被牢牢地绑住了。

（维克多·雨果，选自《九三年》）

练习

1. 绝大多数以f、ff或fe结尾的词，都是规律的复数形式。如：grief, griefs.

少数以f结尾的名词，变复数时会改f为v加es。如：half, halves.

写出以下单词的复数形式：

beef, fife, loaf, sheaf, thief,

calf, knife, reef, shelf, wharf,

cliff, leaf, scarf, skiff, wife,

elf, life, self, strife, wolf.

2. 还有少数的名词，单复数都是同一个的结构。如:cannon, cod, deer, mackerel, sheep, swine, trout等。

Patrasche

预习

essay /ˈeseɪ/ 散文

gaunt /gɔːnt/ 憔悴的；荒凉的

guise /gaɪz/ 伪装

pharmacy /ˈfɑːrməsi/ 药剂学

respective /rɪˈspektɪv/ 各自的

sluggish /ˈslʌgɪʃ/ 懒惰的

upshot /ˈʌpʃɑːt/ 结果

vanquish /ˈvæŋkwɪʃ/ 征服

In a little hut on the edge of a village near Antwerp dwelt Nello and Patrasche. It was the hut of a very old man, of a very poor man, of old Jehan Daas, who in his time had been a soldier. When he had reached the age of full eighty, his daughter had died, and had left him her little son two years old. The old man could ill contrive to support himself, but he took up the additional burden uncomplainingly, and it soon became welcome and precious to him. Little Nello, which was the pet name for Nicholas, throve with him, and the old man and the little child lived in the poor little hut contentedly.

It was a very humble little mud hut, indeed, but it was clean and white as a sea-shell, and stood in a small plot of ground, which yielded beans and herbs and pumpkins. They were very poor, terribly poor, many a day they had nothing at all to eat. But the old man was gentle and good to the boy, and the boy was a beautiful, innocent, truthful, tender-natured creature; and they were happy on a crust and a few leaves of cabbage, and asked no more of earth or Heaven; save, indeed, that Patrasche should be always with them, since without Patrasche where would they have been?

For Patrasche was their treasury and their granary; their store of gold and wand of wealth; their only friend and comforter. Patrasche dead or gone from them, they must have laid themselves down and died likewise. Patrasche was body, brains, hands, head, and feet to both of them: Patrasche was their very life, their very soul. For Jehan Daas was old and a cripple, and Nello was but a child; and Patrasche was their dog.

A dog of Flanders——yellow of hide, large of head and limb, with wolf-like ears that stood erect, and legs bowed and feet widened by many generations of hard service. Patrasche came of a race which had toiled hard and cruelly-slaves of slaves, dogs of the people, beasts of the shafts and the harness. Before he was fully grown Patrasche had known the bitter gall of the cart and the collar. Before he had entered his thirteenth month he had become the property of a hardware dealer, who was accustomed to wandering over the land north and south, from the blue sea to the green mountains. They sold him for a small price because he was so young.

This man was a drunkard and a brute. The life of Patrasche was hard and cruel. His purchaser heaped his cart full of pots and pans and flagons and buckets, and other wares of crockery and brass arid tin, and left Patrasche to, draw the load as best he might, while he himself lounged idly by the side in fat and sluggish ease, smoking his black pipe, and stopping at every wine shop on the road.

Happily for Patrasche——or unhappily——he was very strong; he came of an iron race, long born and bred to cruel work; so that he did not die, but managed to drag on a wretched existence under the brutal burdens, the lashes, the hunger, the thirst, the blows, the curses, and the exhaustion; which were the only wages his hard master paid him.

One day after two years of this service, Patrasche was going on as usual along one of the straight, dusty, unlovely roads leading to Antwerp. It was full midsummer, and very warm. His cart was heavy, piled high with goods in metal and earthenware. His owner sauntered on without noticing him otherwise than by the crack of the whip as it curled round his body. The man had paused to drink beer himself at every wayside house, but he had forbidden Patrasche to stop a moment for a draught from the canal. Going along thus, in the full sun, on a scorching highway, having eaten nothing for twenty-four hours, and, what was far worse for him, not having tasted water for nearly twelve, blind with dust, sore with blows, and stupefied with the merciless weight of his burden; Patrasche, for once, staggered, foamed a little at the mouth, and fell.

He was sick unto death, and motionless. His master gave him the only medicine in his pharmacy-kicks and blows. After a while, deeming life gone in him, the heartless man dragged the dog aside in the grass, and then pushed the cart lazily off up the hill.

Patrasche lay there, flung in the grass. It was a busy road that day, and hundreds of people, on foot and on mules, in wagons and in carts, went by, tramping quickly and joyously on to the city. Some saw him, most did not even look; all passed on. A dead dog more or less-it was nothing to them.

After a time, there came a little old man, who was bent and lame and very feeble. He was in no guise for feasting, he was poorly clad, and dragged his silent way slowly through the dust among the pleasure-seekers. He looked at Patrasche, passed, wondered, turned aside, then kneeled down in the grass and weeds, and surveyed the dog with kindly eyes of pity. There was with him a little rosy, fair-haired, dark-eyed child, a few years old, who pattered in amidst the bushes, and gazed upon the poor, great, quiet beast. Thus it was that these two first met the little Nello and the big Patrasche.

The upshot of that day was, that old Jehan Daas, with much laborious effort, drew the sufferer homeward to his own little hut, and there tended him with so much care, that his sickness, which had been a brain seizure, brought on by heat and thirst and exhaustion, passed away with time and shade and rest. Health and strength returned, and Patrasche staggered up on his four stout, tawny legs.

Now for many weeks he had been useless, powerless, sore, near to death; but all this time he had heard no rough word, had felt no harsh touch; but only the pitying murmurs of the little child's voice, and the soothing caress of the old man's hand.

In his sickness they had grown to care for him, this lonely old man and the little happy child. He had a corner of the hut, with a heap of dry grass for his bed; and they had learned to listen eagerly for his breathing in the dark night, to tell them that he lived; and when he first was well enough to essay a loud, hollow, broken bay, they laughed aloud, and almost wept together for joy at such a sign of his sure restoration; and little Nello, in delighted glee, hung chains of daisies round the dog's rugged neck, and kissed him with fresh ruddy lips.

So then, when Patrasche arose, himself again, strong, big, gaunt, powerful, his great wistful eyes had a gentle astonishment in them that there were no curses to rouse him and no blows to drive him; and his heart awakened to a mighty love, which never wavered once in its fidelity while life abode with him.

But Patrasche, being a dog, was grateful. Patrasche lay pondering long with grave, tender, musing brown eyes, watching the movements of his friends.

The old soldier, Jehan Daas, could do nothing for his living but limp about a little with a small cart, with which he carried daily into Antwerp the milk-cans of those happier neighbors who owned cows. The villagers gave him the employment a little out of charity,——more because it suited them well to send their milk into the town by so honest a carrier, and bide at home themselves to look after their gardens, their cows, their poultry, or their little fields. But it was becoming hard work for the old man. He was eighty-three, and Antwerp was a good League off, or more.

Patrasche watched the milk-cans come and go that one day when he had got well and was lying in the sun with the wreaths of daisies round his tawny neck.

The next morning, before the old man had touched the cart, Patrasche arose and walked to it and placed himself between its handles, and testified as plainly as dumb show could do his desire and his ability to work in return for the bread of charity which he had eaten. Jehan Daas resisted long, for the old man was one of those who thought it was a shame to bind dogs to labor for which nature never formed them. But Patrasche would not be gainsaid: finding that they did not harness him, he tried to draw the cart onward with his teeth.

At length Jehan Daas gave way, vanquished by the persistence and the gratitude of this creature whom he had succored. He fashioned his cart so that Patrasche could run in it, and this the faithful dog did every morning of his life thenceforward.

When the winter came, Jehan Daas thanked the blessed fortune that had brought him to the dying dog. The old man became feebler with each year, and he would ill have known how to pull his load of milk-cans over the snow and through the ruts, if it had not been for the strength and industry of the animal he had befriended. As for Patrasche, his home seemed Heaven to him. After the frightful burdens that his old master had compelled him to strain under, at the call of the whip at every step, it seemed nothing to him but amusement to walk out with this little light green cart, by the side of the gentle old man, who always paid him with a tender caress and with a kindly word. Besides his work was over by four in the day, and after that time he was free to do as he would, to stretch himself, to sleep in the sun, to wander in the fields, to romp with Nello, or to play with other dogs. Patrasche was very happy.

A few years later, old Jehan Daas, who had always been a cripple, became so paralyzed with rheumatism that it was impossible for him to go out with the cart any more. Then little Nello, now six years old, and knowing the town well from having accompanied his grandfather so many times, took his place beside the Bart, sold the milk, received the coins in exchange, and brought them back to their respective owners with a pretty grace and seriousness charming to all who beheld him.

Nello and Patrasche did the work so well and so joyfully together that Jehan Daas himself, when the summer came and he was better again, had no need to stir out, but could sit in the doorway in the sun and see them go forth through the garden wicket, and then doze and dream and pray a little, and then wake again as the clock tolled three and watch for their return. On their return Patrasche would shake himself free of his harness with a bay of glee, and Nello would recount with pride the doings of the day. Then they would all go in together to their meal of rye bread and milk or soup, and would see the shadows lengthen over the great plain, and see the twilight veil the fair cathedral spire; and then they would lie down together to sleep peacefully while the old man said a prayer. And so the days and the years went on.

(Louise De La Rame)

译文

忠犬帕奇

在安特卫普大教堂附近有一个小村落，尼洛和帕奇就住在这个村落边上的小屋里。小屋里住着一个又老又穷的老头，老头名叫杰罕·达斯，年轻时当过兵。杰罕·达斯满八十岁的那一年，他的女儿去世了，留下了她两岁大的儿子。老头的生活虽然艰难，但还是毫无怨言地接下了这个包袱，没过多久，小家伙就变得越来越讨人喜爱，成为老头最珍视的宝贝。小尼洛——这只是小家伙的昵称，他的大名叫尼古拉斯——渐渐地长大了，一老一少在破旧的小屋里心满意足地生活着。

小屋非常简陋，只不过是个小窝棚，却被拾掇得像贝壳一样干净洁白。屋外有一个小菜园，里面种有蚕豆、香草和南瓜。他们很穷，简直穷到了极点，有时甚至一连很多天一丁点儿东西都吃不到。尽管如此，老头对小男孩始终很好，关爱着小家伙的成长，而小家伙漂亮又纯真，是个诚实善良的小孩儿。对他们而言，只要有一片干面包和几片卷心菜叶，生活就很幸福了，再也不需要向土地或上天要求什么了。当然，帕奇得每天都跟他们在一起，因为没了帕奇，他们又要怎么活下去呢?

因为帕奇就是他们的全部，他是他们的宝库、粮仓，是他们的金库和最大的财富，是他们唯一的朋友与仅有的安慰。假如帕奇死掉或者离开了，他们也一定会被生活压垮，随他一同死去。帕奇就等于他们的躯干、大脑、头颅和四肢，帕奇是他们的生命之源、灵魂之本。因为杰罕·达斯只是个跛脚老头，尼洛也不过是个小孩子，而帕奇，则是他们唯一能依靠的爱犬。

帕奇是条佛兰德斯犬，一身金色的皮毛，硕大的头颅和四肢，如狼耳一般高耸的双耳，四腿如弓，脚掌宽阔，肌肉发达——这是世代苦工磨练出来的结果。帕奇出身于勤劳的种族，他们祖祖辈辈都在做苦工，世世代代都为人类所奴役，总是被车辕牢牢拴住，只能不停干活。小帕奇还没长大，就已经尝够了货车和颈圈带来的苦痛。还没满十三个月，他就已经归一个五金经销商所有了，跟着主人，从蔚蓝的海洋，到绿树青山，过惯了走南闯北的生活。但他们以极低的价格卖掉了它，因为它过于年幼。

之后的主人是一个酒鬼、一个野兽。从此，帕奇的生活就只剩下了艰难与折磨。新主人在手推车上放满了罐子、盘子、酒壶和水桶，还有各种陶器、铜器和锡器，让帕奇独自拼命拉车，自己却懒洋洋地在旁边溜达着，嘴里叼着黑烟斗，缓缓挪动肥胖的身躯，每逢在路边碰见小酒馆，都要停下来进去喝一杯。

万幸，或者说不幸的是，帕奇非常坚强，毕竟他属于铁打的品种，生长于极其苦难的环境之中，所以他非但没有被苦难击倒，还努力在残酷的重压之下苦捱下去，忍受皮鞭、饥渴、殴打、辱骂和筋疲力尽，而这些是他从残忍的主人那里获得的唯一酬劳。

两年后的一天，帕奇像往常一样，走在一条笔直却灰尘满天飞的路上，这条路通向安特卫普大教堂。当时正值盛夏，天气炎热。帕奇的拖车非常沉重，车上的金属制品和陶器堆积如山，他的主人却在一旁闲逛，不但对帕奇的痛苦无动于衷，反而还“噼噼啪啪”鞭打颤抖的帕奇。每次在路边经过小酒馆，主人就要停下来进去喝几杯啤酒，但帕奇却连停下来歇息片刻、去河边喝几口水都不行。一整天都饿着肚子的他只能顶着火辣辣的毒日头，拖着疲惫的身躯走在被烈日炙烤的大道上，更要命的是他已经将近十二小时滴水未进了，尘土迷了他的双眼，殴打摧残着他的身躯，背上沉重的负担让他渐渐失去知觉。这一次，可怜的帕奇终于不堪重负，踉踉跄跄地站不住脚，口边吐出一股白沫，最终跌倒了。

他就这么一动不动地躺着，快要病死了；而他的主人却把踢打和咒骂当作万金油送给帕奇。没多久，主人觉得帕奇已经死了，这个狠心的家伙便把帕奇拖到了草丛间丢掉，然后懒洋洋地把货车推上了山坡。

被主人抛弃的帕奇，一动不动地躺在草丛里。那天，这条路格外繁忙，成百上千的行人从那里经过，他们有的步行，有的骑骡子，有的乘马车，也有的推手推车，一个个喜气洋洋地朝城市的方向疾驰。他们当中有一些看到了帕奇，但更多的却连看都没看一眼，所有人都只顾着匆匆赶路，对他们而言，一条死狗又算得了什么呢？

又过了一会儿，人群中出现了一位驼背跛脚、瘦骨嶙峋的老头。他压根不像是要去享乐，衣衫褴褛的他，吃力地穿过寻欢作乐者扬起的灰尘，默默向前走去。忽然，他看到了帕奇，盯了他一会儿，继续赶路，又迟疑了一会儿，终是转过身走到了帕奇身边，跪坐在杂草丛间，怜惜地细细端详着这条狗。老头身旁跟着一个几岁大的小男孩，生着一张玫瑰色的小脸、一头金色的头发、一双乌黑的眼睛。小家伙快速穿过齐胸高的灌木丛，来到帕奇身旁，呆呆地凝视着这条安静却可怜的大狗。小尼洛和帕奇初次见面的情形就是这样。

老杰罕·达斯费了九牛二虎之力，终于在那天傍晚，把重病的帕奇拖回他的小茅屋，并精心地照顾着这条可怜的狗。其实，帕奇只是因酷热、饥渴和过度劳累而折磨得昏死过去，在阴凉处休息一段时间，就能恢复过来。终于，帕奇的身体渐渐恢复了，力气也渐渐恢复，还能靠着四条粗壮的大黄腿，摇摇晃晃地站起来了。

接下来的几个星期，帕奇依旧什么活儿也不能干，全身酸痛无力，感觉就快死了；但在这段时间，他没有听到一句咒骂，也没有遭受任何毒打，耳边只有小男孩同情的低语，身上只能感觉老人抚慰他的双手。

在帕奇生病期间，这个孤独的老头和快乐的小男孩，对他的感情日益加深。他们在小屋的角落里用干草为帕奇铺了一张床，他们也已经习惯在深夜听到帕奇的呼吸声，因为这说明他还活着；而当帕奇刚刚痊愈，并第一次尝试用低沉的嗓音大叫时，老头和小男孩都大笑起来，甚至幸福地流下了眼泪，因为这声音说明帕奇已经彻底恢复健康了。小尼洛简直高兴坏了，做了雏菊花环套在帕奇粗壮的脖子上，用红润的嘴唇亲吻着他。

就这样，当帕奇重新站起来、恢复到从前强壮有力的状态时，他那双忧郁的大眼睛里闪过一丝讶异的目光，因为他们既没用咒骂恐吓他，也没用殴打驱赶他，他的心终于被这种强大的爱的力量唤醒了，从此，他的心不再摇摆，永远忠于爷孙俩。

尽管只是一条狗，帕奇却懂得感恩。躺在地上的他，总是陷入久久的沉思，并用棕色的双眼，深情地凝视着两个朋友的一举一动。

因为跛了脚，老杰罕·达斯干不了什么活，只能每天推着一辆小推车，替那些养了奶牛的幸福邻居，往安特卫普运牛奶。村民让他做这份工作，并不是因为好心帮他，主要还是因为他是村里最合适的人选，他是个非常诚实的搬运工，会把牛奶完好无损地运到城里，而他们正好也能安心在家照料自家的菜园、奶牛、家禽或是小农田。可是这份工作对老达斯而言越来越艰难了，他已经八十三岁了，而安特卫普离他的家少说也有四五千米，说不定还要更远些。

一天，已经恢复健康的帕奇边晒太阳，边望着搬进搬出的牛奶罐发呆，他那褐色的脖子上还挂着雏菊花环。

第二天一大早，没等老头来到拖车跟前，帕奇就已经站起来走到拖车前，站在了拖车的两个把手间，无声却又直截了当地表达了要拉车的愿望和能力，想以此回报他们对自己的照顾。老杰罕·达斯却一直不肯同意，因为他觉得，把狗拴在车上做苦工是违反狗的天性的无耻行径。但帕奇却想这么做，他看爷孙俩都不肯为他拴上挽具，便试着用牙齿拉动推车。

最终，老杰罕·达斯还是让步了，他被帕奇的执着打动了，对自己曾经救下的这条狗充满了感激。于是，他把小推车稍稍改装了一番，好方便帕奇使用。从这一天起，忠犬帕奇便开始了每天早上都要拉车的生活。

每到冬天，老杰罕·达斯都很感激上天对他的眷顾——让他遇见了那条垂死的狗。老头一年比一年衰弱，如果没有勤劳强壮的帕奇的帮助，他都不知道要如何拉着装满牛奶罐的推车翻过积雪，走过泥泞。而对帕奇来说，他现在的家简直就是个天堂。在经历了从前被主人逼迫着拉沉重的货物、每走一步都要遭受毒打的生活后，现在拉着轻便的小车行走，旁边还有个和蔼的老头，时不时跟他说说话，温柔地爱抚他，这样的生活简直就是种享受。他每天只需工作三四个小时，其余时间他可以想做什么就做什么，比如伸伸懒腰，在太阳底下睡大觉，去田间散步，和尼洛嬉闹，和同伴一起玩耍，等等。总之，帕奇觉得生活幸福极了。

又过了几年，一直跛脚的老杰罕·达斯终因风湿病而瘫倒在床上，再也不能拖着推车进城送牛奶了。而这时的小尼洛虽刚满六岁，却对小城镇早已非常熟悉。因为他经常陪着姥爷进城，帮姥爷推车、卖牛奶、收硬币，再把空奶罐带回来，认真又有礼貌地还给它们的主人。

尼洛和帕奇接下了这个活，并且做得很出色，加之有彼此做伴，他们觉得过得很快乐。至于老杰罕·达斯，夏天到来的时候，他的病又好起来了，虽然还不能出门，但能坐在门口，晒着太阳，注视着尼洛和帕奇从菜园小门离去的身影，然后打个盹儿，做个梦，祈祷会儿，等钟敲响三声时再睁开眼睛，等他们归来。他们回来的时候，帕奇总是快乐地吠叫着挣脱挽具，而尼洛则会自豪地讲起当天发生的事情。然后，他们会一起进屋，吃一顿由黑面包、牛奶或者菜汤构成的晚餐。他们也会看到，长长的影子蔓延到原野上，而黄昏会为美丽的教堂披上一层朦胧的面纱，尼洛和帕奇就会一起躺下来，在老头的晚祷声中沉沉睡去。日子就这样一天又一天、一年又一年地过去了。

（路易斯·德拉·雷姆）

作者简介

路易斯·德拉·雷姆出生于英格兰，但她的父亲有法国血统。一般，大家对她的笔名“奥维达”会更熟悉，这个名字源于她小时候对路易斯的发音。《忠犬帕奇》选自她的《佛罗德斯的狗》，这本书是她众多有趣的儿童文学里的一本。

练习

抽象名词：表示品质、感觉、某人的状态或者物品的抽象概念。

例如：凄凉、悠闲、怜悯、疾病、忠诚。

从本篇最后三段中找出十个以上的抽象名词。

Odysseus and Polyphemos

I

When the blue hills of the Lotos-land had faded away in the far distance, the ships of Odysseus went on merrily with a fresh breeze: and the men thought that they would soon come to rocky Ithaca, where their homes were. But Athene was angry with Odysseus, and she asked Poseidon, the lord of the sea, to send a great storm and scatter his ships. So the wind arose, and the waters of the sea began to heave and swell, and the sky was black with clouds and rain.

Many days and many nights the storm raged fiercely; and when it was over, Odysseus could see only four or five of all the ships which had sailed with him from Troy. The ships were drenched with the waves which had broken over them and the men were wet and cold and tired; and they were glad indeed when they saw an island far away. So they sat down on the benches, and took the great oars and rowed the ships towards the shore; and as they came near, they saw that the island was very beautiful with cliffs and rocks, and bays for ships to take shelter from the sea.

Then they rowed into one of these quiet bays, where the water was always calm, and where there was no need to let down an anchor, or to tie the ship by ropes to the sea shore, for the ship lay there quite still of itself. At the head of the bay a stream of fresh water trickled down from the cliffs, and ran close to the opening of a large cave, and near the cave some willow trees drooped their branches over the stream which ran down towards the sea.

So they made haste to go on shore; and when they had landed, they saw fine large plains on which the corn might grow, but no one had taken the trouble to sow the seed; and sloping hills for the grapes to ripen on the vines, but none were planted on them. And Odysseus marveled at the people who lived there, because they had no corn and no vines, and he could see no houses, but only sheep and goats feeding on the hill-sides. So he took his bows and arrows, and shot many of the goats, and he and his men lay down on the ground and had a merry meal, and drank the rich red wine which they had brought with them from the ship. And when they had finished eating and drinking they fell asleep, and did not wake up till the morning showed its rosy light in the eastern sky.

Then Odysseus said that he would take some of his men and go to see who lived on the island, while the others remained in the ship close to the sea-shore. So they set out, and at last they came to the mouth of a great cave, where many sheep and goats were penned up in large folds; but they could see no one in the cave or anywhere near it; and they waited a long while, but no one came. So they lit a fire, and made themselves merry, as they ate the cheese and drank the milk which was stored up round the sides of the cave.

Presently they heard a great noise of heavy feet stamping on the ground, and they were so frightened that they ran inside the cave, and crouched down at the end of it. Nearer and nearer came the Cyclops, and his tread almost made the earth shake. At last in he came, with many dry logs of wood on his back ; and in came all the sheep, which he milked every evening;but the rams and the goats stayed outside.

But if Odysseus and his men were afraid when they saw Polyphemos the Cyclops come in: they were much more afraid when he took up a great stone, which was almost as big as the mouth of the cave, and set it up against it for a door. Then the men whispered to Odysseus and said, "Did we not beg and pray you not to come into the cave? but you would not listen to us; and now how are we to get out again? Why, two-and-twenty wagons would not be able to take away that huge stone from the mouth of the cave." But they were shut in now, and there was no use in thinking of their folly for coming in.

So there they lay, crouching in the corner of the cave, and trembling with fear lest Polyphemos should see them. But the Cyclops went on milking all the sheep, and then he put the milk into the bowls around the sides of the cave, and lit the fire to cook his meal. As the flames shot up from the burning wood to the roof of the cave, it showed him the forms of Odysseus and his companions, where they lay huddled together in the corner; and he cried out to them with a loud voice, "Who are you that dare to come into the cave of Polyphemos? Are you come to rob me of my sheep, or my cheese and milk that I keep here?"

Then Odysseus said, "No; we are not come to do you harm: we are Achaians who have been fighting at Troy to bring back Helen, whom Paris stole away from Sparta, and we went there with the great king Agamemnon, whom everybody knows. We are on our way home to Ithaca; but Poseidon sent a great storm, because Athene was angry with me; and almost all our ships have been sunk in the sea, or broken to pieces on the rocks."

When he had finished speaking, Polyphemos frowned savagely and said, "I know nothing of Agamemnon, or Paris, or Helen." And he seized two of the men, and broke their heads against the stones, and cooked them for his dinner. That day Polyphemos ate a huge meal, and drank several bowls full of milk; and after that he fell fast asleep. Then as he lay there snoring in his heavy sleep, Odysseus thought how easy it would be to plunge the sword into his breast, and kill him; and he was just going to do it, when he thought of the great stone which Polyphemos had placed at the mouth of the cave; and he knew that if Polyphemos were killed no one else could move away the stone, and so they would all die shut up in that dismal place.

So the hours of the night went wearily on, but neither Odysseus nor his friends could sleep, for they thought of the men whom Polyphemos had eaten, and how they would very likely be eaten up themselves. At last they could tell from the dim light which came in between the top of the stone and the roof of the cave, that the morning was come; and soon Polyphemos awoke and milked all the sheep again; and when he had done this, he went to the end of the cave, and took up two more men and killed and ate them. Then he took down the great stone from the mouth of the cave, and drove all the cattle out to graze on the soft grass on the hills;

and Odysseus began to hope that they might be able to get away before Polyphemos came back. But the Cyclops was not so silly as to let them go, for, as soon as the cattle were gone out, he took up the huge stone again as easily as if it had been a pebble, and put it up against the mouth of the cave; and there were Odysseus and his friends shut up again as fast as ever.

Then Odysseus began to think more and more how they were to get away, for if they stayed there they would soon be all killed, if Polyphemos went on eating four of them every day. At last, near the sheep-fold, he saw a club which Polyphemos was going to use as a walking-stick. It was the whole trunk of an olive-tree, fresh and green, for he had only just cut it and left it to dry, that he might carry it about when it was fit for use. There it lay like the mast of a ship, which twenty men could hardly have lifted; and Odysseus cut off a bit from the end, as much as a man could carry, and told the men to bring it to a very sharp point; and when they had done this he hardened it in the fire, and then hid it away till Polyphemos should come home.

II

By and by, when the sun was sinking down, they heard the terrible tramp of his feet, and felt the earth shake beneath his tread. Then the great stone was taken away from the mouth of the cave, and in he came, driving the sheep and goats and the rams also before him, for this time he let nothing stay outside. So he milked the sheep and the goats, as he had done the day before; and then he killed two more men, and began to eat them for his supper. Then Odysseus went towards him with a bottle full of wine, and said, "Drink this wine, Polyphemos; it will make your supper taste much nicer; I have brought it to you because I want you to do me some kindness in return."

So the Cyclops stretched out his hand to take the wine, and he drank it off greedily and asked for more. "Give me more of this honey-sweet wine," he said, "Surely no grapes on this earth could ever give such wine as this: tell me your name, for I should like to do you a kindness for giving me such wine as this." Then Odysseus said, "O Cyclops, I hope you will not forget to give me what you have promised : my name is Nobody." And Polyphemos said, "Very well, I shall eat up Nobody last of all, when I have eaten up all his companions; and this is the kindness which I mean to do for him."

But by this time he was so stupid with all he had been eating and drinking, that he could say no more, but fell on his back fast asleep; and his heavy snoring sounded through the whole of the cave. Then Odysseus cried to his friends, "Now is the time; come and help me, and we will punish this Cyclops for all that he has done." So he took the piece of the olive-tree, which had been made sharp, and put it into the fire, till it almost burst into a flame, and then he and two of his men went and stood over Polyphemos, and pushed the burning wood into his great eye as hard and as far down as they could.

It was a terrible sight to see; but the Cyclops was so stupid and heavy in sleep that at first he could scarcely stir. Presently he gave a great groan, so that Odysseus and his people started back in a fright, and crouched down at the end of the cave: and then the Cyclops put out his hand and drew the burning wood from his eye, and threw it from him in a rage, and roared out for help to his friends, who lived on the hills round about. His roar was as deep and loud as the roar of twenty lions; and the other Cyclopes wondered when they heard him shouting out so loud, and they said, "What can be the matter with Polyphemos? we never heard him make such a noise before: let us go and see if he wants any help."

So they went to the cave, and stood outside the great stone which shut it in, listening to his terrible bellowings; and when they did not stop they shouted to him, and asked him what was the matter. "Why have you waked us up in the middle of the night with all this noise, when we were sleeping comfortably? Is any one taking away your sheep and goats, or killing you by craft and force?" And Polyphemos said, "Nobody, my friends, is killing me by craft and force." When the others heard this they were angry, and said, "Well, then, if nobody is killing you, why do you roar so? If you are ill, you must bear it as best you can, and ask our father Poseidonto make you well again." And then they walked off to their beds, and left Polyphemos to make as much noise as he pleased.

It was of no use that he went on shouting. No one came to him any more; and Odysseus laughed because he had tricked him so cunningly by calling himself Nobody. So Polyphemos got up at last, moaning and groaning with the dreadful pain, and groped his way with his hands against the sides of the cave until he came to the door. Then he took down the great stone, and sat with his arms stretched out wide; and he said to himself, "Now I shall be sure to catch them, for no one can get out without passing me."

But Odysseus was too clever for him yet; for he went quietly and fastened the great rams of Polyphemos together with long bands of willow. He tied them together by threes, and under the stomach of the middle one he tied one of his men, until he had fastened them all up safely. Then he went and caught hold of the largest ram of all, and clung on with his hands to the thick wool underneath his stomach; and so they waited in a great fright, lest after all the giant might catch and kill them. At last the pale light of the morning came into the eastern sky, and very soon the sheep and the goats began to go out of the cave. Then Polyphemos passed his hands over the backs of all the sheep as they went by but he did not feel the willow bands, because their wool was long and thick, and he never thought that any one would be tied up underneath their stomachs.

Last of all came the great ram to which Odysseus was clinging; and when Polyphemos passed his hand over his back, he stroked him gently and said, "Is there something the matter with you, too, as there is with your master? You were always the first to go out of the cave, and now today for the first time you are the last. I am sure that that horrible Nobody is at the bottom of all this. Ah, old ram, perhaps it is that you are sorry for your master, whose eye Nobody has put out. I wish you could speak like a man, and tell me where he is. If I could but catch him,

I would take care that he never got away again, and then I should have some comfort for all the evil which Nobody has done me."

So he sent the ram on; and when he had gone a little way from the cave, Odysseus got up from under the ram, and went and untied all his friends, and very glad they were to be free once more, although they could not help grieving, when they thought of the men whom Polyphemos had killed. But Odysseus told them to make haste and drive as many of the sheep and goats as they could to the ships. So they drove them down to the shore and hurried them into the ships, and began to row away; and soon they would have been out of the reach of the Cyclops, if Odysseus could only have held his tongue. But he was so angry himself, that he thought he would like to make Polyphemos also still more angry; so he shouted to him, and said. "Cruel Cyclops, did you think that you would not be punished for eating up my friends? Is this the way in which you receive strangers, who have been tossed about by many storms upon the sea?"

Then Polyphemos was more furious than ever, and he broke off a great rock from the mountain, and hurled it at Odysseus. On it came whizzing through the air, and fell just in front of his ship, and the water was dashed up all over it; and there was a great heaving of the sea, which almost carried them back to the land. Then they began to row again with all their might; but still, when they had got about twice as far as they were before, Odysseus could not help shouting out a few more words to Polyphemos. So he said,"If any one asks you how you lost your eye, remember, mighty Cyclops, to say that you were made blind by Odysseus, the plunderer of cities, the son of Laertes, who lives in Ithaca."

Terrible indeed was the fury of Polyphemos when he heard this, and he said, "Now I remember how the wise Telemos used to tell me that a man would come here named Odysseus, who would put my eye out. But I thought he would have been some great strong man, almost as big as myself; and this is a miserable little wretch, whom I could almost hold in my hand if l caught him. But stay, Odysseus, and I will show you how I thank you for your kindness, and I will ask my father Poseidon to send you a pleasant storm to toss you about upon the dark sea."

Then Polyphemos took up a bigger rock than ever, and hurled it high into the air with all his might. But this time it fell just behind the ship of Odysseus: up rose the water and drenched Odysseus and all his people, and almost sank the ship under the sea. But it only sent them further out of the reach of the Cyclops; and though he hurled more rocks after them, they now fell far behind in the sea, and did them no harm. But even when they had rowed a long way, they could still see Polyphemos standing on the high cliff, and shaking his hands at them in rage and pain. But no one came to help him for all his shouting, because he had told his friends that Nobody was doing him harm.

(Homer)

译文

奥德修斯和波吕斐摩斯

I

忘忧之乡的蓝色山峰逐渐消失在遥远的天际，奥德修斯的船队在清新的微风吹拂下欢快地航行。不久，他们就要回到岩石遍布的家乡伊塔卡岛了。但是雅典娜非常恼恨奥德修斯，她请求海神波塞冬刮起暴风吹散他的船队。于是海上狂风大作，水面波涛汹涌，天空乌云密布、暴雨倾盆。

猛烈的风暴刮了许多个日夜。当暴风停下之时，奥德修斯发现和他一起从特洛伊起航的船队只剩下四五艘船了，它们浸透在那曾吞没过它们的波涛里。船上的人浑身湿淋淋的，个个又冷又累。因此，当远方的岛屿出现在视野中时，他们由衷地感到高兴，坐在长凳上奋力划桨，让船朝着岸边驶去。随着他们的靠近，岛屿越发显得美丽：峭壁林立，岩石遍地。海上船只可以在海湾躲避风雨。

他们把船划进了一个平静的海湾，那里风平浪静，船只静静浮在水面，完全不需要下锚或是用绳索固定在海岸。海湾前方，一条淡水小溪从峭壁上缓缓流淌下来，向着海洋流去。途中流经一个巨大的洞穴附近，那里有几棵柳树在溪水上方低垂着枝条。

于是，他们匆忙上了岸，这才看清眼前的景象：广阔的平原土地肥沃，本可用来种植玉米，但却没人愿意费心劳力去播种；高高的山坡本可用来种植葡萄，然后挂在藤上等待成熟，却空空如也，什么都没有。奥德修斯对生活在这里的人们感到惊奇，因为这里没有玉米，没有葡萄树，也看不到房子，只有绵羊和山羊在山坡上悠闲进食。于是他带上弓和箭，射杀了许多的山羊。他和手下们躺在地上休息了一会儿，然后愉快地大吃了一顿，还喝了从船上带来的醇厚的红葡萄酒。吃喝结束后，他们全都睡着了，直到东边的天空亮起玫瑰色的晨光才醒来。

奥德修斯让一些人留在海边的船里，然后带着另一些人去探访生活在岛上的居民。他们很快出发了，并且最后来到了一个巨大的洞穴口。那里有许多大围栏，里面关着很多绵羊和山羊，而洞穴和附近的地方却都没有一个人影。他们在那里等了很长时间，但还是没人来。于是，他们升起火堆，纵情欢乐，一边吃着奶酪一边喝着奶，这些原本都是储存在洞穴里四周围的。

不久，他们听到一声声沉重的脚从地上踏过的轰隆巨响，心里害怕极了，于是跑进了洞穴尽头蜷曲着躲起来。独眼巨人越走越近，他的踩踏几乎让整个大地都摇晃起来。最后他终于进入了洞穴，背上背着许多干燥的大树干。所有的绵羊也进来了——他每天晚上都要给它们挤奶，但公羊和山羊都留在洞穴外面。

如果说奥德修斯一行人看见独眼巨人波吕斐摩斯进来的时候感到害怕的话，那么当他们看到波吕斐摩斯举起一块几乎和洞口一样大的石头，并把它当成一扇门塞到洞口的时候，他们更加害怕了。大伙儿悄悄地跟奥德修斯耳语，说："难道我们没有再三请求你不要进入洞穴吗？但你却根本听不进我们的话。现在，我们要怎么出去呢？唉，二十二辆马车都没法把那块巨石从洞口拉走。"然而，如今他们已经被关在洞里了，再去想他们之前钻进洞穴这个愚蠢的行为也于事无补。

于是他们只有蜷曲在洞穴角落里，浑身发抖，满心恐惧，唯恐波吕斐摩斯看见他们。独眼巨人仍旧在给绵羊们挤奶，然后他把羊奶放进洞穴四周的碗里，生起一堆火准备做饭。火苗从燃烧着的木头上窜起，舔舐着洞穴顶部，照出了奥德修斯和同伴们在角落里挤作一团的身形，他顿时声如雷鸣般地吼道："你们是谁，竟然胆敢走进波吕斐摩斯的洞穴里？你们要抢我的羊，还是要抢我存在这儿的奶酪和羊奶？"

奥德修斯回答说："不，我们不是来害你的。我们是阿凯亚人，曾经跟随着人人皆知的伟大国王阿伽门农在特洛伊之战中夺回了海伦，她曾被帕里斯从斯巴达抢走。我们本来航行在通往家乡伊塔卡的海上，但是因为雅典娜恼恨于我，所以波塞冬刮起了一场暴风，导致我们的船几乎要么沉到了海里，要么撞到岩石上摔成了碎片。"

他说完话后，波吕斐摩斯却猛皱着眉头，不满地说："我一点都不知道什么阿伽门农，也不知道帕里斯和海伦。"他抓起他们中的两个人，在石头上撞碎了他们的脑袋，接着把他们做成了晚餐。那天波吕斐摩斯吃了一顿丰富的大餐，喝了满满几碗羊奶，然后很快睡着了。当他躺在那儿打着呼噜酣睡的时候，奥德修斯心里则想着：趁这时候将剑插入他的胸膛杀死他是多么容易的事啊。他正准备动手的时候，想起了波吕斐摩斯放在洞口的那块巨石。如果杀了波吕斐摩斯的话，就没有人能移开石头，那么他们就会被一直关在这个阴暗的地方直到死去。

那个晚上非常漫长，奥德修斯和他的朋友们没有人睡得着，因为他们都想着那两个被波吕斐摩斯吃掉的人，想着他们自己很可能会被全部吃光。最终，他们发现时间已经是第二天早上了，他们能从巨石顶部和洞穴顶部的缝隙里辨别出微弱的光线。很快，波吕斐摩斯就醒了，他再一次挤了羊奶，完事后走向洞穴尽头，又抓了两个人杀了当早餐吃掉。然后，他从洞口移走了巨石，把所有的牛都赶出去，好让它们到山上柔软的草地上进食。奥德修斯开始燃起希望，也许他们能在波吕斐摩斯回来之前逃出去。但是独眼巨人并没有愚蠢到要让他们离开，因为牛群一出去，他就像拿着一颗鹅卵石一样轻松地拿起了巨石，重新把它放回洞口。于是，奥德修斯和他的朋友们再次被关在了洞穴里。

如果波吕斐摩斯每天吃掉四个人的话，他们留在这里就很快会被杀光了。因此，奥德修斯开始寻求逃出去的办法。终于，他在靠近绵羊围栏的地方看见了一根波吕斐摩斯准备拿来当手杖用的棍子。那是一棵橄榄树的整个树干，还是新嫩的绿色，因为他刚刚把它砍下来，想等这根树干变得干燥好用并可以随身携带。它像一艘船的桅杆一样躺在那儿，即使二十个人也很难举起它。奥德修斯从它的一端砍了一片下来，砍下来的部分一个人就能拿得动。他吩咐手下把它弄得十分尖锐，随后自己把它放在火里煅烧，令其变得更硬。在波吕斐摩斯回来之前，他们做完了一切，并把这尖尖的木片藏了起来。

II

终于，在太阳下山的时候，他们听见了那可怕的脚步声，感觉到地面在踩踏下震颤摇晃。很快，洞口的巨石就被移走了，波吕斐摩斯赶着绵羊走了进来。这次他把山羊和公羊也赶了进来，没让它们留在洞外。接下来，他像前一天一样，先给绵羊和山羊挤奶，然后杀了两个人当作晚餐。奥德修斯拿着整整一瓶葡萄酒向他走去，说："波吕斐摩斯，喝点儿这酒，它能让你的晚餐尝起来更美味。我把它送给你，希望你能给我一点仁慈作为回报。"

于是，独眼巨人伸出手接过葡萄酒，贪婪地喝光了它，并且还想要更多。"给我更多的这种甜蜜的葡萄酒。"他说，"我确定这块土地上没有葡萄能酿出这样的葡萄酒。告诉我你的名字，你送给我这么好喝的葡萄酒，我很乐意帮你一个忙。"奥德修斯说："独眼巨人啊，我希望你不要忘记你的承诺。我的名字叫'没有人'。"波吕斐摩斯说："很好，我会先吃光'没有人'的所有同伴，最后再吃'没有人'。这是我赐予他的仁慈。"

但这次他做了蠢事。大吃大喝之后，他再也说不出更多的话了，倒在地上瞬间陷入沉睡，浓重的呼噜声响彻整个洞穴。奥德修斯立即对他的朋友们大喊说："现在是时候了！来帮我，我们要为这个独眼巨人所做的一切而惩罚他！"他拿出之前被弄得十分尖锐的那根橄榄树木片，放入火中直到它几乎变成一道火舌。接着，他和两个手下走向波吕斐摩斯，站到他身上，将燃烧着的木头竭尽全力地深深插进他的巨眼之中。

这真是一个可怕的场景。但独眼巨人太笨了，他睡得如此之沉以至于一开始几乎醒不过来，随即他发出一声巨大的呻吟，于是奥德修斯和他的手下惊恐地向后退去，蹲伏在洞穴尽头。独眼巨人伸手把燃烧的木头从他的眼睛里抽出来，怒气冲冲把它扔得老远，吼叫着向居住在周围山上的朋友求救。他的咆哮声像二十头狮子齐声吼叫，轰然作响，远远传了出去。当其他独眼巨人听见这惊天动地的叫声时都感觉非常诧异，然后他们说："波吕斐摩斯出了什么事？我们以前从来没听到他弄出这么大的声音。让我们去看看他是否需要帮助。”

于是他们走向洞穴，站在堵住洞口的巨石外面，听着他发出可怕的吼叫，而叫声一直没有停下。他们大喊着问他发生了什么事：“为什么你要在半夜我们睡得正舒服的时候，发出这样的声音吵醒我们？是有人抢走了你的绵羊和山羊，还是有人在用诡计和武力谋杀你？”波吕斐摩斯说：“我的朋友，‘没有人’正在用诡计和武力谋杀我。”当其他独眼巨人听到这个回答，他们非常生气，说：“那么好吧，如果没有人在谋杀你，为什么你咆哮成这样？如果你生病了，你必须尽力忍受它，并且请求我们的父亲波塞冬让你再次好起来。”然后他们离开了洞外，回到了他们的床上，留下波吕斐摩斯，任其大吼大叫。

他再怎么吼叫也没用了，没有一个人会再来帮他。奥德修斯笑了，因为他说自己叫“没有人”，非常狡猾地欺骗和戏弄了波吕斐摩斯。所以，波吕斐摩斯最后站了起来，剧痛让他止不住地呻吟抱怨。他用手摸索着洞穴四周，走到门口，取下巨石，张大双臂坐下来，自言自语道：“现在我肯定能抓到他们，因为没有人能不经过我就逃出去。”

但奥德修斯的聪明才智足够对付波吕斐摩斯。他悄悄走过去，用长长的柳枝把波吕斐摩斯的大公羊绑在一起。他把它们三只三只绑在一起，在中间那只羊的肚子下绑上一个人，直到所有的人都安全地被绑在羊肚子下，接着他捉住最大的一只公羊，紧紧用手抓住羊肚子下厚厚的羊毛。然后他们忐忑不安地等待着，生怕最终巨人会抓到他们，杀了他们。终于，东方的天空亮起了微弱的晨光，绵羊和山羊很快就开始往洞外走去。每一只绵羊经过的时候，波吕斐摩斯都会用手摸遍它的背，但是由于羊毛太厚太长了，他完全感觉不到柳枝，而且他从来没想过有人会被绑在羊肚子下面。

奥德修斯攀附着的大公羊是最后一个出来的。当波吕斐摩斯摸索它的背时，他温柔地抚摸着它说：“你也出了什么事吗，就像你的主人一样？你以前总是第一个走出洞穴，但今天你第一次成了最后一个。我肯定这一切都是那个可怕的‘没有人’搞的鬼。啊，老公羊，也许你是在为你这个眼睛被‘没有人’戳瞎的主人感到难过。我真希望你能像人一样会说话，然后告诉我他在哪儿。如果我能抓住他，我会小心不让他再次逃走，这样才能补偿‘没有人’对我所做的一切恶行，让我从中得到些许安慰。”

他把大公羊放出了洞穴。当它离开洞穴一段距离后，奥德修斯从羊肚子下站起来，去给他所有的朋友松绑。他们既高兴又伤心，高兴的是他们再次获得了自由，伤心的是波吕斐摩斯杀死了好几个人。但奥德修斯吩咐他们尽快且尽可能多地驱赶绵羊和山羊回到船上。于是，他们把羊群赶向海岸，迅速把它们赶进船里，然后开始划船离开。如果奥德修斯能闭上他的嘴巴的话，他们本可以很快就离开独眼巨人的势力范围。但他自己很生气，所以也想让波吕斐摩斯更生气。于是他对他大吼说："残忍的独眼巨人，你以为你不会因为吃了我的朋友而遭受惩罚吗？难道这就是你接待曾多次被海上风暴折腾过的陌生人的方式吗？"

波吕斐摩斯空前地愤怒，他从山上掰下一块巨石，猛力把它投向奥德修斯。巨石"飕"的一声从空中飞过，恰恰落在他船的前面。刹那间，水面疯狂涌动吞没了巨石，海水起伏翻腾，几乎要把他们带回陆地。他们重新开始拼命划船，但当他们划得比上一次远了一倍的距离时，奥德修斯又一次忍不住向波吕斐摩斯喊叫，他说："嚣张的独眼巨人，如果有人问你，你是怎么失去眼睛的，记得说是城市的掠夺者拉埃尔特斯的儿子奥德修斯弄瞎了你的眼睛，他居住在伊塔卡。"

波吕斐摩斯听到这些，简直是暴怒无比，他说："现在我知道特里莫斯是多么明智了。他曾经告诉我说，一个名字叫奥德修斯的人会来到这里弄瞎我的眼睛。但我本以为他会是一个和我一样高大强壮的人，结果却是个一旦被我抓住就能握在手心里的可怜虫。但是，停下来，奥德修斯！我会让你看见我是如何感谢你的好意的，我会请求我的父亲波塞冬刮起一场可爱的风暴，让你在黑暗的大海上翻滚。"

然后波吕斐摩斯举起了一块比之前那块更大的石头，用尽全力将它高高投向空中，但这次它正好落在了奥德修斯的船的后方，溅起巨大的水花，浇湿了奥德修斯和他的所有手下，差点让船沉到海里。不过，它掀起的波浪只会帮他们离开独眼巨人更远，虽然他在他们身后投掷了更多的石头，但它们都远远掉在了海里，对他们不造成任何危害。他们划了很长一段距离后，仍然能看见波吕斐摩斯站在高高的悬崖上，愤怒而痛苦地朝着他们挥舞双手。但是他那些痛苦的咆哮并没有引来任何一个帮忙的人，因为他曾告诉他的朋友说"没有人"在伤害他。

（荷马）

练习

1. 以“y”结尾的名词，构成复数的形式是在其后加“s”或者“ies”。

(1) 当单数名词以元音字母加“y”结尾时，构成复数的形式是按常规方法在后面加“s”。例如：volley，volleys.

(2) 当单数名词以辅音字母加“y”结尾时，构成复数的形式是把“y”变成“i”再加“es”。例如：berry，berries.

2. 在《拿破仑·波拿巴》一文中寻找并列出十个以上以“y”结尾的名词，将它们改成复数形式。

3. 写出以下名词的复数形式：gallery，enemy，valley，lily，journey，pulley，city，monkey，country，pansy.

A Fable

A wealthy ploughman drawing near his end,
Called in his sons apart from every friend,
And said, "When of your sire bereft,
The heritage our fathers left
Guard well, nor sell a single field.
A treasure in it is concealed:
The place, precisely, I don't know,
But industry will serve to show.
The harvest past, Time's forelock take,
And search with plough, and spade, and rake;
Turn over every inch of sod,
Nor leave unsearched a single clod."
The father died. The sons——and not in vain——
Turned over the soil, and over again;
That year their acres bore
More grain than ever before.
Though hidden money found they none,
Yet had their father wisely done,
To show by such a measure,
That toil itself is treasure.

(Jean de la Fontaine)

译文

寓言一则

富有的庄稼汉临终之时，
在众亲朋好友面前，将他的儿子们叫到跟前，
说："在我死后，

祖先留下的遗产
请一定守护好，不要变卖任何一块土地。
因为宝藏就藏于其中。
但准确的位置，我也不知道，
不过只要勤奋耕耘，就会有所收获。
秋收过后，抓紧时机，辛勤劳作，
用锄犁、铁铲和耙子仔细搜寻；
翻遍每一寸土地，
不要落下任何地方。”
说罢，父亲便辞世了。儿子们不负父亲的托付，
翻遍了每一寸土地，一遍又一遍；
那一年，他们的土地收获了
比往年更多的庄稼。
虽然他们丝毫未见宝藏的踪影，
但却明白了父亲这样做的深意，
通过这种方式，
父亲想告诉他们劳作本身就是宝藏。

Men to Be Honored

Two men I honor, and no third: first, the toil-worn crafts-man, that with earth-made implement, laboriously conquers the earth, and makes her man's. Venerable to me is the hard hand; crooked, coarse——wherein, notwithstanding, lies a cunning virtue, indefeasibly royal, as of the scepter of this planet.

Venerable, too, is the rugged face, all weather-tanned, be-soiled, with its rude intelligence! for it is the face of a man living man-like. Oh, but the more venerable for thy rudeness, and even because we must pity as well as love thee! Hardly laboring brother! Hardly entreated brother! For us was thy back so bent, for us were thy straight limbs and fingers so deformed.

Thou were our conscript, on whom the lot fell, and fighting our battles wert so marred. For in thee, too, lay a God-created form, but it was not to be unfolded; encrusted must it stand with the thick adhesions and defacements of labor; and thy body, like thy soul, was not to know freedom. Yet toil on, toil on; thou art in thy duty, be out of it who may; thou toilest for the altogether indispensable, for daily bread.

A second man I honor, and still more highly: him who is seen toiling for the spiritually indispensable; not daily bread, but the bread of life.

Highest of all is he when his outward and inward behavior are one; when we can name him artist; not earthly craftsman only, but inspired thinker. If the poor and humble toil that we have food, must not the high and glorious toil in return, that we have light and guidance, freedom, immortality?

Unspeakably touching is it, however, when I find both dignities united; and he that must toil outwardly for the lowest of man's wants, is also toiling inwardly for the highest. Sublimer in this world I know nothing than a peasant saint. Such a one will take thee back to Nazareth itself; thou wilt see the splendor of heaven spring forth from the humblest depths of earth, like a light shining in great darkness.

It is not because of his toils that I lament for the poor. We must all toil or steal, which is worse. No faithful workman finds his task a pastime. The poor is hungry and athirst, but for him also there is food and drink; he is heavy laden and weary, but for him also the heavens send sleep, and of the deepest. In his smoky cribs, a clear, dewy heaven of rest envelops him, and fitful glimmerings of cloud-skirted dreams.

(Thomas Carlyle)

译文

值得尊敬的人

我尊敬两类人，没有第三类：一类是因辛勤工作而憔悴不堪的工匠，他们用产自地球的工具艰苦地征服地球，使她成为人类的家园。我尊敬那努力的手：弯曲的，粗糙的——尽管如此，其中具备的却是熟练灵巧的美德，它无可置疑是高贵的，如同这个星球的权杖。

我也尊敬那粗犷的脸，因为那是一张人之所以为人的脸，它饱经风霜，历尽沧桑，充满鲁莽的智慧！哦，但更值得尊敬的是你的鲁莽，即使我们必须一边爱你一边怜惜你！艰辛劳作的兄弟！努力谋生的兄弟！为了我们，你挺直的背部变得佝偻；为了我们，你挺直的四肢和手指变得畸形。

你是我们征召的士兵，命运选中了你，但为我们而战给你带来了如此的伤害。因为你的内心也住着一个上帝创造的形象，但它没有被展现出来，而一定是包裹着一层硬壳——它很厚，满是劳作带来的粘连和损伤。你的肉体和你的灵魂一样，注定不懂得自由。你辛勤苦干，专注于你的责任。谁会不去完成它呢？你为了必需的一切，为了每天的面包而艰辛劳苦。

我尊敬的第二类人，依旧是很高尚的：他为了精神上的必需品而艰苦努力，不是每日的面包，而是人生的食粮。

当他的外在表现和内在表现相同时，他就是最高尚的人。我们可以称他为大师，他不再是世俗的工匠，而是激励人心的思想家。如果是贫乏低下的苦工让我们拥有食物，那么作为回报，难道不是高尚光荣的劳作让我们拥有光芒、指引、自由和不朽?

然而，当我发现这两种高尚融为一体时，那种感动无法用语言形容。于外，他必须为了人类的最低需求而劳作；于内，他也必须为了人类的最高需求而努力。这个世界的崇高之人，除了圣人般的农夫外，我不知道其他。他是这样一个人，会把你带回上帝的家园；你会看见天堂的辉煌，它从最卑微的大地深处蓬勃而出，就像漆黑中闪烁着的一点光芒。

我并不是为了穷人的劳苦而悲伤。我们所有人都必须辛勤工作，否则只能盗窃，这更加糟糕。忠实的工人不会把他的工作当成一种消遣。穷人又饥又渴，但他也有食物和饮水；他处在生活的重压之下，疲惫不堪，但他也有上天赠与的最深的睡眠。在那满是烟雾的木屋里，一个明亮的、带着露水的宁静天堂包围着他，包围着云遮雾绕的梦境里那时而闪烁的微光。

（托马斯·卡莱尔）

作者简介

托马斯·卡莱尔出生于苏格兰一个叫作埃克尔费亨的小村庄，他在那里就读普通学校，然后进入了爱丁堡大学。从孩童时代起，他就极其喜爱读书，他在故事中透露出的读书总量简直让人难以置信。因此，他能成为著名的“学者”也并不奇怪了——“学者”就是知识渊博的人。作为历史学家和随笔作家，很少有作者在风格的出色上能和他相提并论。“这是卡莱尔的特殊天赋——让呆板的物和死去的人真正变得充满活力，让过去在当下重现，让我们了解男人和女人作为真正有血有肉的人在生活舞台上的表现。”他最伟大的作品包括《衣裳哲学》《过去与现在》《腓特烈大帝史》《法国革命》和《英雄及英雄崇拜》。

Choosing a Class of People to Be Exterminated

预习

Great Panjandrum 由英国剧作家塞缪尔·富特创造的虚构人物，这里用来表示重要的人

sic 拉丁语，经常用于一个词句后以引起对其准确性存疑的注意

alacrity /əˈlækrəti/ 敏捷

benignly /bɪˈnaɪnli/ 亲切地

gratuitous /grəˈtuːɪtəs/ 无缘无故的

inanity /ɪˈnænəti/ 空虚

venomous /ˈvenəməs/ 恶意的

In the midst of a queer higglety-pigglety dream last night, I thought the Great Panjandrum appeared to me with the kind offer to have someone class of my fellow beings immediately exterminated; provided I could, without taking too much of his valuable time, decide which particular class it should be. Just seven minutes were given in which to make and announce the decision.

Of course I accepted with alacrity, and at once hastened to run over in my mind such of the obnoxious varieties of human nature as could most speedily be recalled. At first I thought that I would select the people who do not answer letters; but I reflected that sometimes we write letters in haste, which had better be answered at leisure, or even not at all, on the principle that the least said, soonest mended.

Then I dallied for a moment with the idea that it should be those who, hearing us say things in joke, straightway report them as things said in earnest. Surely, thought I to myself, we can't go amiss in having this venomous species obliterated! But as the genial destroyer looked at his watch a little impatiently, I hurriedly recollected other deserving candidates. There were those who always allow for everybody else's being late at appointments, and so afflict the punctual soul with a quarter of an hour of painful fidgets.

Then there were those who send us lukewarm verses, with a request for an introduction to the favorable notice of the editors of the great magazines; and those who borrow tennis-rackets and sheet-music; and the book-store attendants who tag us around with recommendation of the latest inanities; and the brotherhood [sic] of locomotive engineers who agonize the ear at night with gratuitous shrieks as of whistling fiends; and the literary ladies who follow up our plainest observation with praise of how nicely, or prettily, or nobly, or something, it was said.

"Six minutes and three quarters," whispered the Great Panjandrum, punching at me with his scepter, and knocking his little round button at top against the ceiling, as he hastily rose. I made one more rapid snatch among my recollection of people who are with difficulty to be endured, and cried, "Take those who carry a perpetual countenance of cold displeasure, and contrive to make each member of the household, or the company, feel that he is at all times the special object of it!" The departing monster nodded benignly over his shoulder and winked, as who should say, "You have chosen well!"

(Edward Rowland Sill)

译文

选择消灭一类人

昨晚我做了一个奇特而又颠三倒四的梦，梦里一位大人物向我善意地提供了一个可以瞬间消灭一类人的机会，并让我决定消灭哪一类特定的人，但不能占用他太多的宝贵时间。七分钟内我必须告诉他我的决定。

我当然是欣然答应了，随即便在脑海中急忙浏览我能尽快想到的人类劣根性。我起初打算选择那种不回信的人，但又考虑到人们常常会非常草率地写信，对于此类信件还是慢慢回复，甚至干脆不回为好，这大概就是通常所说的少说为妙。

随后我的思绪在另一类人身上耽搁了一会儿，那种人总是把别人的玩笑话当成真话传播开来。当然，我认为从世上抹去这样讨厌的人肯定不会有错！但那和善的毁灭者已经有点不耐烦地看着表了，我便又匆匆忙忙地去回想其他该受到报应的候选者，比如有些人总是纵容别人在约会中迟到，如此做法会让那些准时到场的人经受一刻钟的焦躁折磨。

接着我又想到了以下人群：那些给我寄来不温不火的诗歌、请求我推荐给著名杂志编辑以获得好评的人；那些老是借网球拍和乐谱的人；那些围着我们推荐新出的无聊玩意儿的书店店员；那些机车技师的“好哥儿们”，他们会在晚上像吹口哨的恶魔那样无故地鸣响尖锐的汽笛声来折磨我们的耳朵；还有那些文艺腔的女士，她们会用“多么美妙”“多么华丽”“多么崇高”之类的称赞对我们最普通的言论穷追不舍。

“已经六分四十五秒了。”大人物轻声说道，用权杖戳了戳我，迅速站了起来，使得那权杖上部的小圆头撞上了天花板。我再次快速地在记忆中搜寻那种难以忍受的人，最后叫道：“就是那种人了，他们永远带着冷漠不快的表情，想方设法地要让家中或公司里的所有人都觉得他们始终与众不同！”这个正要离去的怪物转过头来亲切地点了点头并使了个眼色，好像在说：“你选得很对！”

（爱德华·罗兰·希尔）

Chapter 6

Miscellaneous Poems | 杂诗

Music in Camp

预习

Rappahannock 弗吉尼亚州的一条河流。其地理位置在美国内战时期具有重要战略意义

meads 古语，指的是草地

embrasure /ɪmˈbreɪʒər/ 墙壁上因炮火攻击留下的弹孔

iris /ˈaɪrɪs/ 彩虹女神

plaintive /ˈpleɪntɪv/ 哀伤的

sonorous /ˈsɑːnərəs/ 声音响亮而清晰

Two armies covered hill and plain,
Where Rappahannock's waters
Ran deeply crimsoned with the stain
Of battle's recent slaughters.
The summer clouds lay pitched like tents
In meads of heavenly azure,
And each dread gun of the elements.
Slept in its embrasure.
The breeze so softly blew, it made.
No forest leaf to quiver,
And the smoke of the random cannonade
Rolled slowly from the river.
And now, where circling hills looked down
With cannon grimly planted,
Over listless camp and silent town

The golden sunset slanted.
When on the fervid air there came
A strain-now rich, now tender;
The music seemed itself a flame
With day's departing splendor.
A Federal band, which, eve and morn,
Played measures brave and nimble,
Had just struck up, with flute and horn
And lively clash of cymbal.
Down flocked the soldiers to the banks,
Till, margined by its pebbles,
One wooded shore was blue with "Yanks",
And one was gray with "Rebels".
Then all was still, and then the band,
With movement light and tricksy,
Made stream and forest, hill and strand,
Reverberate with "Dixie".
The conscious stream with burnished glow
Went proudly over its pebbles,
But thrilled throughout its deepest flow
With yelling of the Rebels.
Again a pause and then again
The trumpets pealed sonorous,
And "Yankee Doodle", was the strain
To which the shore gave chorus.
The laughing ripple shoreward flew,
To kiss the shining pebbles;
Loud shrieked the swarming Boys in Blue
Defiance to the Rebels.
And yet once more the bugle sang
Above the stormy riot;
No shout upon the evening rang——
There reigned a holy quiet.

The sad, slow stream its noiseless flood
Poured over the glistening pebbles;
All silent now the Yankees stood,
And silent stood the Rebels.
No unresponsive soul had heard
That plaintive note's appealing,
So deeply "Home, Sweet Home" had stirred
The hidden founts of feeling.
Or Blue, or Gray, the soldier sees
As by the wand of fairy,
The cottage beneath the live-oak trees,
The cabin in the prairie.
Or cold, or warm, his native skies
Bend in their beauty over him;
Seen through the tear-mist in his eyes.
His loved ones stand before him.
As fades the iris after rain
In April's tearful weather,
The vision vanished, as the strain
And daylight died together.
But memory, waked by music's art,
Expressed in simplest numbers,
Subdued the sternest Yankee's heart,
Made light the Rebel's slumbers.
And fair the form of music shines,
That bright celestial creature,
Who still, 'mid war's embattled lines,
Gave this one touch of Nature.

(John Reuben Thompson)

译文

军营之歌

两支军队翻越高山，跨过平原，
拉帕汉诺克河的河水
奔流而过，
因战争的杀戮而被染得血红。
夏日的云朵宛如安营扎寨的帐篷，
躺在碧空下的草地上，
每把枪支带来的恐惧感，
沉睡于弹孔中。
微风轻柔，
甚至吹不起林间的树叶，
肆意的炮火掀起阵阵烟雾，
在河流上空盘旋缭绕。
而如今，环山俯瞰大地，
望向地面上的可怖大炮，
透过毫无生机的军营和寂静的城镇。
金色的夕阳斜射下来。
炽热的空气中传来
一阵旋律——时而浑厚，时而轻柔；
这支旋律就像一团火焰，
带着昔日逝去的辉煌。
一个联邦乐团，在黄昏和破晓，
奏响华丽又轻快的乐章，
音乐响起，伴随笛子与号角，
还有热烈的钗钹声。
士兵们迅速集结于海岸上，
溪流中的石头将他们分隔两边，

一边是身着蓝色军装的“杨基佬”，
另一边是灰色军装的“反叛军”。
然后一切仿佛都静止了，唯有那曲调依旧，
每一个乐章轻快又跳跃，
让溪流与森林，丘陵与海滨，
回荡起《迪克西》的阵阵旋律。
溪流闪着明亮的波光
骄傲地越过水中的石块，
但水流深处却散发出
反叛军的呼喊和尖叫。
音乐停下，而后继续，
号角吹出嘹亮的声音，
还有《杨基歌》，与这旋律相应和的
是海岸的齐声歌唱。
欢歌笑语的涟漪向岸边涌来，
亲吻着光滑铿亮的石头；
那一声声尖厉声是群集的蓝装士兵
奋力抵御反叛军。
军号再一次响起，
回荡在激烈战乱的上空；
傍晚不再伴有哭喊，
而是笼罩在可怕的静谧中。
悲伤的小溪缓缓流淌着川流，无声无息，
浇灌在铿亮的石头上；
此刻杨基佬静默站立，
反叛军也静默站立。
敏感的灵魂听到
那悲伤的音符，引人入胜，
《回家，回到甜蜜的家》的旋律深深骚动
在他们的心灵深处。
无论蓝装还是灰衣，士兵们，

像被魔法棒施了魔法一样，
看到了橡树下的房子，
还有草原上的小屋。
无论寒冷，还是温热，家乡的天空，
将美丽置身于他眼前；
透过他满含泪水的眼睛，
他的爱人就站在他的面前。
雨后彩虹慢慢褪去，
在四月的阴雨天中，
视野模糊，直至消失，正如这歌声
与曙光一同逝去。
但记忆，已被音乐唤醒，
用简单的曲调浅吟诉说，
掳获了杨基佬最坚硬的心，
照亮了反叛军的麻木灵魂
音乐之美闪耀夺目，
那是带来光明的美好之物，
它给予作战前线的人们
一抹温柔。

（约翰·鲁本·汤普森）

背景知识

杨基佬，在美国内战时期，代表的是北方联邦军，军装为蓝色。

反叛军，在美国内战时期，代表的是南方联盟集团，军装为灰色。

《迪克西》指的是美国南部诸州从南北战争时期流行至今的战歌。

O Captain! My Captain!

O Captain! My Captain! Our fearful trip is done;
The ship has weathered every rack, the prize we sought is won;
The port is near, the bells I hear, the people all exulting,
While follow eyes the steady keel, the vessel grim and daring:
But O heart! Heart! Heart!
O the bleeding drops of red,
Where on the deck my Captain lies,
Fallen cold and dead!
O Captain! My Captain! rise up and hear the bells;
Rise up——for you the flag is flung——for you the bugle trills;
For you bouquets and ribboned wreaths——for you the shores a-crowding ;
For you they call, the swaying mass, their eager faces turning;
Here Captain! Dear father!
This arm beneath your head;
It is some dream that on the deck,
You've fallen cold and dead.
My Captain does not answer, his lips are pale and still;
My father does not feel my arm, he has no pulse nor will:
The ship is anchored safe and sound, its voyage closed and done;
From fearful trip the victor ship comes in with object won:
Exult, O shores, and ring, O bells!
But I, with mournful tread,
Walk the deck my Captain lies,
Fallen cold and dead.

(Walt Whitman)

译文

啊，船长！我的船长！

啊，船长！我的船长！我们可怕的旅程就要结束；
船只安然渡过了惊涛骇浪，我们载誉而归；
港口临近，钟笛鸣响，人群欢呼，
在众人的目光中，我们的船威严又果敢地前行：
可是，我的心！心啊！心啊！
鲜红的血在流淌，
我的船长躺在甲板上，
那倒下的身躯，冰冷，已经死去！
啊，船长！我的船长！快起来听听这钟声；
快起来——看，旌旗为你飘扬——听，号角为你吹响；
簇簇花束与满是丝带的花圈为你而立，岸上人群为你而来；
攒动的人群呼喊着你，殷切的目光投向你；
在这儿，船长，我亲爱的父亲！
你的头下是我的手臂；
在甲板上，就像在一场梦里
你已经死去，倒下的身躯，已冰冷！
我的船长再也不会回应，嘴唇苍白而平静，
我的父亲感受不到我的臂膀，没有脉搏，没有知觉：
船只平稳靠岸停泊，旅程最终落幕；
历经恐惧，乘胜归来：
欢呼吧，海岸！鸣响吧，钟笛！
可是，我却步履维艰，心情沉重，
漫步在甲板上，我的船长正躺于此，
那倒下的身躯，冰冷，已经死去。

（沃尔特 · 惠特曼）

作者介绍

沃尔特·惠特曼1819年出生于纽约州长岛西山。他有荷兰血统。在孩童时代，他随父母迁往布鲁克林区，在那里的公立学校求学，并学习印刷技术。之后，他在学校教书，做印刷厂学徒，开始写诗。在美国内战时期，他曾作为志愿军护，在华盛顿附近的医院工作了三年。在那之后，他供职于政府部门，任书记员的职位，直到1873年因身体原因不能继续工作。随后，他搬到了新泽西州的卡姆登居住，直到1892年离世。《啊，船长！我的船长！》写于惠特曼听说美国总统林肯遇刺事件之际，此诗是惠特曼代表作之一。

The "Old, Old Song"

When all the world is young, lad,
And all the trees are green;
And every goose a swan, lad,
And every lass a queen,——
Then hey for boot and horse, lad,
And round the world away;
Young blood must have its course, lad,
And every dog has his day.
When all the world is old, lad,
And all the trees are brown;
And all the sport is stale, lad,
And all the wheels run down,——
Creep home, and take your place there,
The spent and maimed among:
God grant you find one face there,
You loved when all was young.

(Charles Kingsley)

译文

古老之歌

当世界尚年轻，伙计，
所有树木都娇翠欲滴；
所有鹅都美若天鹅，伙计，
所有小姑娘都貌似女王，
嘿，她们跳舞骑马，伙计，
周游世界，一骑绝尘；

热血沸腾，青春洋溢，伙计，
人人皆有得意时。
而当世界苍老，伙计啊，
所有树木枯黄；
所有运动无法承受，伙计啊，
所有轮子停止运转，
蹒跚回家，就那么待着吧，
精力枯竭，疾病缠身；
上帝定会让你看到一张面庞，
你满含热爱，因为当时的一切都很年轻。

（查理·金斯莱）

作者介绍

查理·金斯莱是一位英国作家和牧师。他深深地迷恋宗教和科学，对英国工薪阶层状况进行了深入研究，为他们生活状况的提高和改善做了很多工作。查尔斯的作品，正如他的人生一样，题材涉猎广泛。除了宗教类出版物，还包括历史小说，如《希帕蒂亚》《向西去！》《痕迹》《最终》《到西印度》《英雄，希腊童话故事》《怎么样夫人，为什么女士》以及《水孩子》，所选片段正是来自最后一本书。

Liberty and Independence

There was tumult in the city,
In the quaint old Quaker town,
And the streets were rife with people,
Pacing restless up and down;
People gathering at corners,
Where they whispered each to each,
And the sweat stood on their temples,
With the earnestness of speech.
As the black Atlantic currents
Lash the wild Newfoundland shore,
So they beat against the State House,
So they surged against the door;
And the mingling of their voices
Made a harmony profound,
Till the quiet street of Chestnut
Was all turbulent with sound.
"Will they do it?""Dare they do it?"
"Who is speaking?""What's the news?"
"What of Adams?""What of Sherman?"
"Oh, God grant they won't refuse!"
"Make some way, there!""Let me nearer!"
"I am stifling""Stifle, then:
When a nation's life's at hazard,
We've no time to think of men!"
So they beat against the portal,
Man and woman, maid and child;
And the July sun in heaven
On the scene looked down and smiled,
The same sun that saw the Spartan
Shed his patriot blood in vain,

Now beheld the soul of freedom
All unconquered rise again.
Aloft in that high steeple
Sat the bellman, old and gray;
He was weary of the tyrant
And his iron-sceptered sway;
So he sat with one hand ready
On the clapper of the bell,
When his eye should catch the signal
Of the glorious news to tell.
See! See! the dense crowd quivers
Through all its lengthened line,
As the boy beside the portal
Looks forth to give the sign!
With his small hand upward lifted,
Breezes dallying with his hair,
Hark! With deep, clear intonation,
Breaks his young voice on the air.
Hushed the people's swelling murmur,
List the boy's strong joyous cry!
"Ring!" he shouts aloud, "Ring! Grandpa!
Ring! Oh, ring for Liberty!"
And straightway, at the signal,
The old bellman lifts his hand,
Forth he sends the good news, making
Iron music through the land.
How they shouted! What rejoicing!
How the old bell shook the air,
Till the clang of Freedom ruffled
The calmly gliding Delaware!
How the bonfires and the torches
Shone upon the night's repose,
And from the flames, like Phoenix,

Fair Liberty arose!
That old State House bell is silent,
And hushed is now its iron tongue,
But the spirit it awakened
Still is living-ever young.
And while we greet the smiling sunlight
On the fourth of each July,
We'll never forget the bellman,
Who, twists the earth and sky,
Rang out our independence,
Which, please God, shall never die!

(Selected)

译文

自由与独立

城市中充满喧嚣，
在宁静而古老的贵格镇，
街道上人群拥挤来人往，
来去匆匆，步履不停；
街角处人们聚集，
窃窃私语，轻声密谈，
太阳穴爬满了汗珠，
仍继续他们认真的谈话。
就像黑色的大西洋洋流席卷而来
冲刷着荒无人烟的新大陆海岸，
他们猛击着州议会会场，
他们狂奔着涌向大门；
这些声音交汇混杂
构成一首深邃的协奏曲，
安静的栗树街
渐渐被各种声音充斥，演变成骚动。
“他们会行动吗？”“他们敢吗？”
“谁说的？”“有什么新闻？”
“亚当斯怎么样？”“谢尔曼呢？”
“噢，上帝保证他们不会拒绝！”
“让一让！”“让我靠近点！”
“我快窒息了。”“窒息，那么：
当国家的命运危在旦夕，
我们没有时间考虑个人！”
所以他们冲击大门，
有男人和女人，也有女仆和孩子；

七月，天空中艳阳高照
俯视一切，露出微笑，
相同的太阳曾见证斯巴达人
为了国家，徒劳地抛洒热血，
而现在目睹了自由的灵魂
所有未被打倒的人又重新站起。
在那高高的尖塔之上
坐着一位敲钟人，年长，灰白头发；
他厌倦了专制者
按捺不住地摇动着手里的铁杖；
他端坐着，一只手时刻准备着
敲响钟声，
一旦他的目光捕捉到了信号
便会将这一惊人的好消息向全世界宣告。
看！快看！密密的人群人头攒动
排列在长长的延长线上，
大门边上的男孩
张望着准备传达这个信号！
高高举起他的小手，
徐徐微风拂过他的头发，
听！一个低沉、清晰的声音，
他年轻的声音撕裂空气。
人们喧嚣的低吟声渐渐平息，
倾听着男孩强劲且兴奋的哭喊声！
“铃声！”他大声喊道，“铃声！爷爷！铃声！噢，这是自由之声！”
很快，在信号台，
年迈的敲钟人举起他的手，
接着，传达出这个好消息，
大地充满铜铃声，仿佛美妙的音乐。
他们高喊欢呼！多么高兴！
古老的钟声响彻天空，

自由的铿锵声撼动着，
渐渐沸腾的特拉华州！篝火和火炬
照亮了宁静的黑夜，
如凤凰般，浴火重生，
光明的自由冉冉升起！
那座古老的议会会场钟声沉默，
铜铃声现在也安静了下来，
但革命的精神已被唤醒
尽管依旧年幼。
当我们与微笑的晨光相遇
在七月四日那天。
我们将永远铭记敲钟人，
是他，扭转了天地，
敲响了发出了独立的钟声，
上帝啊，独立之魂将世代留存！

（节选）

I Remember, I Remember

I remember, I remember
The house where I was born,
The little window where the sun
Came peeping in at morn.
He never came a wink too soon,
Nor brought too long a day;
But now I often wish the night
Had borne my breath away!
I remember, I remember
The roses, red and white,
The violets, and the lily-cups,
Those flowers made of light!
The lilacs where the robin built,
And where my brother set
The laburnum on his birthday,
The tree is living yet!
I remember, I remember
Where I used to swing,
And thought the air must rush as fresh
To swallows on the wing;
My spirit flew in feathers then,
That is so heavy now.
And summer pools could hardly cool
The fever on my brow!
I remember, I remember
The fir-trees dark and high;
I used to think their slender tops
Were close against the sky.
It was a childish ignorance,
But now it is little joy

To know I'm farther off from Heaven
Than when I was a boy.

译文

我记得，我记得

我记得，我记得，
我出生时的房子，
早晨有阳光从小窗那里，
悄悄地探出脑袋往里张望。
他从不早来片刻，
也不会多留半晌；
但如今我常常希望黑夜，
把我的呼吸带走！
我记得，我记得，
红玫瑰和白玫瑰，
紫罗兰和百合花，
它们是由阳光孕育的花朵！
有知更鸟筑巢的丁香花，
还有我的哥哥在生日那天，
种下的金链花，
现如今依旧生机勃勃！
我记得，我记得，
我常常荡秋千的地方，
当时觉得迎面的风如此凉爽，
燕子的翅膀也一定能感受得到；
那时我的心情如鸿毛般飘荡，
可现在却无比沉重。
夏日的泳池也无法冷却，

我额头上的燥热！
我记得，我记得，
黑黢高耸的杉树；
那时我常想它们细长的树梢，
仿佛要直击云端。
那不过是孩子的天真无知，
但现在我却少有那般的愉悦，
因为我知道比起孩童时代，
我离天堂已经越来越远。

Goodbye

Good-bye, proud world! I'm going home:
Thou art not my friend, and I'm not thine.
Long through thy weary crowds I roam;
A river-ark on the ocean's brine,
Long I've been tossed like the driven foam;
But now, proud world! I'm going home.
Good-bye to Flattery's fawning face;
To Grandeur, with his wise grimace;
To upstart Wealth's averted eye;
To supple Office, low and high;
To crowded halls, to court and street;
To frozen hearts and hasting feet;
To those who go, and those who come:
Good-bye, proud world! I'm going home.
I'm going to my own hearth-stone,
Bosomed in yon green hills alone,
A secret nook in a pleasant land,
Whose groves the frolic fairies planned;
Where arches green, the livelong day,
Echo the blackbird's roundelay,
And vulgar feet have never trod,
A spot that is sacred to thought and God.
Oh, when I am safe in my sylvan home,
I tread on the pride of Greece and Rome;
And when I am stretched beneath the pines,
Where the evening star so holy shines,
I laugh at the lore and the pride of man,
At the sophist schools, and the learned clan,
For what are they all, in their high conceit,
When man in the bush with God may meet?

(Ralph Waldo Emerson)

译文

再见

再见了，高高在上的世界！我要回家：
你不是我的朋友，而我也不是你的。
久久地，漫步于倦怠的人群之中；
像漂浮在海上的一叶扁舟，
不断地，被涌来的浪花摇曳轻荡；
可是，现在，高高在上的世界！我要回家。
再见，奉承者的摇尾乞怜；
再见，权势者的狡黠鬼魅；
再见，富有者的躲闪目光；
再见，大小官员的低眉顺从；
再见，拥挤的礼堂、法庭和街道；
再见，冰冷的心肠，匆忙的步履；
再见，来来往往的人们：
再见，高高在上的世界！我要回家。
我要回我的热炕头，
它在葱郁山峦的环抱之中，独一无二，
是乐土之上，一个隐秘的悠然僻静之所，
小树林是欢快的精灵所造；
拱门青翠，日子悠长，
画眉雀跃，转圈鸣唱，
庸俗的双脚从未踏上这片土地，
这是思想与上帝专用之所。
啊，当我在森林小屋时，安然自得，
就像践踏在希腊与罗马的骄傲之上，
当我慵懒地躺在松树下，
仰望夜晚闪亮夺目的星星时，

我嘲笑人类有限的学识和骄傲自负，
嘲笑诡辩学派和博学者宗派，
当尘世的凡人与上帝相遇之际，
高高在上的他们又算得了什么呢?

（拉尔夫·沃尔多·爱默生）

A Christmas Carol

There's a song in the air!
There's a star in the sky!
There's a mother's deep prayer
And a baby's low cry!
And the star rains its fire while the Beautiful sing,
For the manger of Bethlehem cradles a king.
There's a tumult of joy
Over the wonderful birth,
For the virgin's sweet boy
Is the Lord of the earth.
Ay! the star rains its fire and the Beautiful sing,
For the manger of Bethlehem cradles a king.
In the light of that star
Lie the ages impearled;
And the song from afar
Has swept over the world.
Every hearth is aflame, and the Beautiful sing
In the homes of the nations that Jesus is King.
We rejoice in the light,
And we echo the song
That comes down through the night
From the heavenly throng.
Ay! we shout to the lovely evangel they bring
And we greet in his cradle our Saviour and King.

(Josiah Gilbert Holland)

译文

圣诞颂歌

风中飘着一首歌！
空中闪着一颗星！
一位母亲正深情祈祷
一个宝贝在轻声哭泣！
星星光芒闪耀，应和着美妙的圣诞歌。
在伯利恒的马厩中，诞生了一位王者。
这里洋溢着喜悦，
为了这伟大的诞生，
圣母迎来了可爱的宝贝，
他是世界的救世主。
啊！星星光芒闪耀，应和着美妙的圣诞歌，
在伯利恒的马厩中，诞生了一位王者。
在星星的微光中，
整个时代如珍珠般熠熠生光；
从远方传来的歌声，
响彻世界每个角落。
壁炉中的火焰熊熊燃烧，响起美妙的圣诞歌。
每家每户都知道，这位王者就是耶稣。
我们在微光中欢呼庆祝，
不断唱着这首歌，
这首刺破黑夜的歌，
从天国的神灵间降落。
啊！我们高喊着他们带来的美好福音，
向摇篮中的救世主和王者致意。

（约西亚·吉尔伯特·霍兰）

The New Year

Ring out, O bells, ring silver-sweet over hill and moor and fell!

In mellow echoes, let your chimes their hopeful story tell.

Ring out, ring out, all-jubilant, this joyful glad refrain: "A bright new year, a glad new year, hath come to us again!"

Ah, who can say how much of joy within it there may be stored up for us, who listens now to your sweet melody?

Good-bye, Old Year! Tried, trusty friend, thy tale at last is told.

O New Year, write thou thine for us in lines of brightest gold.

The flowers of spring must bloom at last, when gone the winter's snow,

God grant that after sorrow past, we all some joy may know;

Though tempest-tossed our bark a while on life's rough waves may be,

There comes a day of calm at last, when we the haven see.

Then ring, ring on, O pealing bells! There's music in the sound.

Ring on, ring on, and still ring on, and wake the echoes round,

The while we wish, both for ourselves and all whom we hold dear,

That God may gracious be to us in this the bright new year.

(Selected)

译文

新年

叮铃铃，铃声响，银铃般甜蜜，翻过山巅，越过荒野，跨过田间！

让你的旋律倾诉充满希望的故事，用那圆润的回响。

叮铃铃，叮铃铃，唱起这首喜气洋洋，畅快欢乐的歌曲："光明的新年，喜庆的新年，又来到我们身边！"

啊，数不清多少欢乐蕴藏其中，谁在听这甜蜜的旋律？

再见，旧岁！可靠的朋友，年终之时诉说你的故事。

噢，新年，你用闪耀的金色为我们书写你的所有。当冬雪走过，春之花终将绽放，

上帝答应当悲伤过去，我们就会迎来喜悦；

尽管在人生的惊涛骇浪中，我们的船有时会飘摇不定，

但当港湾出现，一切都将归于平静。

叮铃铃，叮铃铃，铃声齐鸣！声音中跳动着音乐。

叮铃铃，叮铃铃，余音绕梁，掀起阵阵回声，

我们将祝福送给自己及所有我们珍重的人，

上帝会在充满希望的新年赐予我们仁慈与宽厚。

（节选）

《美国语文》译者名录

钱志慧	南京师范大学
帕孜丽娅	暨南大学
尹吴娅琪	中南财经政法大学
侯艺东	南京师范大学
夏婕	南方医科大学
金晓寒	复旦大学
张佳佳	南京林业大学
杜子悦	华中师范大学
高倩	华东师范大学
蒋荟蓉	西南交通大学
赵艺珂	南开大学
苌婧	四川外国语大学
李颖	北京外国语大学

美工

彭慧	华东师范大学